LOOKING FOR
Mr. PRESTON

BOOKS BY JOHN PRESTON

FICTION

Franny, the Queen of Provincetown, 1983, 1995.
Mr. Benson, 1983, 1992.
I Once Had a Master and Other Tales of Erotic Love, 1984. (Short Stories)

"The Mission of Alex Kane."
Volume I: Sweet Dreams, 1984, 1992.
Volume II: Golden Years, 1984, 1992.
Volume III: Deadly Lies, 1985, 1992.
Volume IV: Stolen Moments, 1986, 1993.
Volume V: Secret Dangers, 1986, 1993.
Volume VI: Lethal Secrets, 1987, 1993.

Entertainment for a Master, 1986.
Love of a Master, 1987.
The Heir, 1988, 1992.
In Search of a Master, 1989.
The King, 1992.
Tales From the Dark Lord, 1992. (Short Stories)
The Arena, 1993.
Tales From the Dark Lord II, 1994. (Short Stories)

Edited:
Hot Living: Erotic Stories About Safer Sex, 1985.
Flesh and the Word: An Erotic Anthology, 1992.
Flesh and the Word 2: An Erotic Anthology, 1993.
Flesh and the Word 3: An Erotic Anthology, 1995.

NONFICTION

The Big Gay Book: A Man's Survival Guide for the Nineties, 1991.
Hustling: A Gentleman's Guide to the Fine Art of Homosexual Prostitution, 1993.
My Life as a Pornographer & Other Indecent Acts, 1993.

With Frederick Brandt:
Classified Affairs: The Gay Men's Guide to the Personals, 1984.

With Glenn Swann:
Safe Sex: The Ultimate Erotic Guide, 1987.

Edited:
Personal Dispatches: Writers Confront AIDS, 1989.
Hometowns: Gay Men Write About Where They Belong, 1991.
A Member of the Family: Gay Men Write About Their Families, 1992.

With Joan Nestle:
Sister and Brother: Lesbians and Gay Men Write About Their Lives Together, 1994.

With Michael Lowenthal:
Friends and Lovers: Gay Men Write About the Families They Create, 1995.
Winter's Light: Reflections of a Yankee Queer, 1995.

LOOKING FOR MR. PRESTON

Edited by Laura Antoniou

A portion of the profits from the sale of *Looking For Mr. Preston* will given to the AIDS Project of Southern Maine

ACKNOWLEDGEMENTS:

The original version of "That Place Called Pornography " by Wickie Stamps appeared in *The Guide to the Gay Northeast.*

"Preston" by Andrew Holleran first published in *Christopher Street* magazine, issue #215.

"Ganged" is excerpted from Carol A. Queen's novel-in-progress, *The Leather-Daddy and the Femme.* For the first two chapters, see Pat Califia, ed., *Doing It for Daddy,* Alyson, 1994.

First Richard Kasak Book Edition 1995

First Printing April 1995

ISBN 1-56333-288-4

Cover Design by Kurt Griffith
Back Cover Photo by Miriam Berkeley

Manufactured in the United States of America
Published by Masquerade Books, Inc.
801 Second Avenue
New York, N.Y. 10017

LOOKING FOR MR. PRESTON

FICTION

Introduction

When I first thought of a tribute anthology to John Preston, I was afraid to mention it to my publisher.

I was at a requiem mass in Manhattan, aching from what seemed like weeks of anxiety and expectation, full of a tired kind of grief, awkwardly standing and sitting during the unfamiliar service despite having sprained my ankle the previous day. I barely heard the words spoken, I don't remember if there was music. I kept thinking of the words of the Kaddish, Hebrew mixing with Latin, the aroma of old incense sweet and heavy. But all this wasn't enough to blot out what was really on my mind; how I had wasted the little time I had known this man, and how ridiculous it was for me to feel his absence so passionately.

Yet I did, as did the other people who attended, some of them longtime friends and others who had done nothing more then shake his hand at a book signing. After it was over, the thought of a book to honor him wouldn't leave

1

me, despite the enormous chutzpah of my even thinking of such a thing. I did get up the nerve to mention it to Richard Kasak and immediately followed the proposal with two suggestions for editors, both of whom would have obvious ties to Preston, and would know whom to contact and how to manage the project appropriately.

"Why don't you do it?" he asked immediately.

That same question, asked with the same amount of direct, challenging sincerity was what John Preston had asked me two years before he died. I had already published one or two books with Masquerade when I found out that the Badboy line of books was going to be given a massive push with the rerelease of the classic *Mr. Benson,* a book which I had only been able to find in the lending library at the New York Lesbian and Gay Community Center, the first half of which I had read half-standing in my front hallway, unable to take my eyes off the pages long enough to take off my jacket.

(The second half of the book I read lounging on my living-room couch, laughing out loud.)

In its time, *Mr. Benson* had been a seminal work, a striking piece of entertaining pornography directed at a population hungry for the kind of hypermasculine world of absolutes, where every man was a walking cigarette-poster model and every set of genitals a perfect fit, and every sexual encounter was awash in testosterone-laden bodily fluids. In Mr. Benson's world, there were no negotiations and safewords and seminars on Bondage 101; no agenda meetings, no elections, no leather contests—only beautiful Manhattan penthouses, leather bedspreads, and a community of men whose only purpose in life was to have rough, passionate sex with other men, preferably after suitable sadomasochistic rituals had been completed. Men (and many women, of all sexual orientations) rushed to buy the issues of *Drummer* in which the book first appeared, and early printings sold out. A T-shirt arose, saying LOOKING FOR MR.

BENSON (question mark optional), and helped make cruising that much easier.

I was more than impressed, I was tremendously pleased. Preston's arrival at Masquerade signaled the potential for me to be more than a hack writer in a genre where the most popular author was "anonymous." But even then, I was unsure about exactly where my writing career—if it could ever be a career—would take me, since I had begun it in the genre which polite people call erotica. John Preston, Pat Califia, and Anne Rice were the only writers I knew of who had created substantial works in and out of that genre under their own names. (Although she had used an assortment of noms de plume on her racy material, Rice's identity was, at best, an ill-kept secret in the publishing industry.)

I had no illusions about being coached by Anne Rice about what to do with my literary aspirations. Pat Califia lived in San Francisco, which might as well have been another planet (as I've often suspected.) But here was John Preston, coming to New York to be taken to lunch by his new publisher—how could I turn up an opportunity like that? I had no shame—I begged Kasak to arrange for me to meet him. (I had already seen him read twice before, but had never approached him. Once, at the Lesbian and Gay Community Center, I had stood to tell him that my lesbian friends and I admired his *Master* books very much, and he seemed amused but pleased by the idea.) And just to make sure I would have more than a chance to shake his hand and get an autograph, I dropped by a reading he was doing at the Greenwich Village B. Dalton the night before, running into Reverend Barrett, who was to conduct that requiem mass for him one day, and who shared my enthusiasm for his work. We both had a chance to say hello after the evening was over, and I was ready for the formal meeting in the morning.

It was a brief meeting—no power breakfasts for me at that stage of the game. But I did manage to convey my respects, confirm that the second half of *Mr. Benson* was indeed meant as a grand comedy, and I did manage to get an autograph, despite the fact that such behavior is considered a glaring sign of amateurism. I also complimented him on the first *Flesh and the Word* anthology, which had recently come out. I lamented that there was no similar collection about woman's erotic fiction, especially lesbian porn. Oh, yes, there were several collections which purported to be the "best" of a given year (and there are even more of those titles now). But there was nothing that concentrated on the sheer exuberance of pure porn, raw and powerful sex, with iconographic characters and archetypal imagery. ("You are creating a canon of gay male porn," I told him in a follow-up phone call. He laughed and replied, "Well, that's what we white males do, isn't it?")

"Why don't *you* do it?" he asked easily that morning in Kasak's office.

"Maybe I will," I responded, a touch of bravado that probably came more from the three cups of coffee in me then the intention to do any such thing.

I soon proposed *Leatherwomen* to Richard Kasak, for the Rosebud imprint. It would be the first book published under my real name. I had spoken to Preston once on the phone, asking him about identities and publishing, desperate not to "bother" him, but also hungry for any word of encouragement. He gave me several, and when I told him that I wasn't a good enough judge of literature to create my own canon, but wanted instead to spotlight new and emerging writers, he was downright enthusiastic. "You let me know how you're doing," he said when the call was over.

I didn't take him very seriously. He was, after all, *a big, important writer*. He had better things to do than to spend time chatting with unknown pornographers like me. But I appreciated the time he spent being so gracious, and I went about trying to gather the stories for that anthology.

Several times during that process, I felt like calling him, mostly because I never thought it would be so difficult to do. Pat Califia had just announced that she was collecting for *The Second Coming,* the long-awaited sequel to *Coming to Power,* and it seemed like every other women I contacted had sent her best stories off to Pat and her coeditor, Robin Sweeney. There were many things stacked against me, the greatest being my relative obscurity. I had to battle with a recurring rumor that I didn't exist, spread with much glee through the disinformation superhighway. So, in desperation, as my deadline approached, I actually wrote several stories under a variety of pseudonyms and used them to fill out the collection.

John Preston, in his only phone call to me, laughed and identified almost every one. "Was it my style?" I asked, petrified that I was found out so quickly. "Am I that obvious?"

"No," he replied. "It's that I'm an editor. I can see these things. Why don't you publish your work under your own name?"

I didn't know; I couldn't tell him. I did tell him about the novels I had just contracted to write, under my pen name of Sara Adamson, and he laughed again. "You're just planning to do what Anne did," he teased. "Someday they'll be rereleased with your real name, and sell twice as much."

"From your mouth to God's ears," I said. I congratulated him on his series of mainstream successes with his new anthologies, one winner after another. How did he do it, I asked, how did he break out of the porn genre to become such a literary leader? "Just keep writing," he told me. "If you're good, editors will know. They'll know you can deliver, and you'll do whatever you want. And you'll have readers who will read only your porn, and readers who will read only your mainstream stuff, and you'll have the crossover readers who will buy anything with your name on it." (He was, of course, correct, even though many of the mainstream periodicals that published obituaries about him did tend to ignore or downplay the success of his own erotic tales.) Once again, he told me to keep him informed—thanked me for a party I had helped arrange at my favorite New York SM club (Paddles)—and once again I thought how gracious he was to spend a few minutes talking to me.

Stupidity was not bred into me—I struggled to achieve it.

It was at the debut party for the rerelease of *Mr. Benson* that Preston and I spoke the most. I had already produced a charity entertainment at the location previously, and knew that the owner would allow me to do another one to honor this famous pornographer. And so, with the help from some grand gentlemen and their bondage sculptures, and several New York–area titleholders and personal friends in leather jockstraps, we had a literary event at a club that was better known for its bondage wheel and the late-night fevered dancing of hundreds of men. Preston seemed to have a great time (he wrote about how that party had been a delightful contrast to his more sedate literary meetings that same week) and he fulfilled an earlier promise to introduce me to V. K. McCarty. When I found him later on, both of us at least one sheet to the wind, I mourned my lack of contacts in the publishing industry, even the tiny queer corner of it.

"Don't worry," he commanded me, gripping my arm. "Next year, you come to OutWrite, and I'll introduce you to everyone. All the big shots. All the editors, all the writers you want. I owe you that for this *fabulous* affair." Typically, he pronounced *fabulous* the way any proper queen would, and we both laughed.

He also promised, after swearing me to secrecy, to show me his basic work on a proposed series of science-fiction fantasy books based on a world where women were superior and held men in bondage, a mirror image of the notorious *Gor* books by John Norman, which he had found hilarious. "There are lots more submissive straight men then dominant ones," he said repeating what was only common knowledge. "Why not write about that aspect? It'll make millions! I'll let you read it—you can tell me if it's worthwhile."

He asked me that night where to go in New York for a good time among men who would appreciate someone who liked to spank young men until they cried. At the time, a bar called The Altar was considered a hot spot, so I suggested it. Later on, I was to find out that he had been refused entrance—a déjà vu experience that had already become legendary—because he was not wearing the proper clothing.

I couldn't make it to the last OutWrite that John appeared at. My career as a writer was hampered by my sudden layoff from my day job, leaving me without the stability to even hop up to Boston and try to find someone to crash with for the weekend. I called him afterward, and he said, "Next year, next year."

Of course, there was no "next year." That winter, rumors of his fading health came to me from all kinds of sources. I kept thinking about calling, writing. (It didn't occur to me to send a fax, for two reasons. One—I didn't have a fax machine. Two—I hadn't found out what a faxing maven he was.)

Besides, I still didn't want to bother him.

What a colossal waste, in 20-20 hindsight. As I started working on this collection, I had no idea how many young writers he had encouraged, chatted with, even mentored. I had no idea that he had such a passionate interest in the next generation of pornographers and their literary siblings in other genres, male and female. Again, I have no illusions. I would hardly have become one of his "mentettes." But during the months I have worked on this manuscript, my telephone conversations and brief letter and fax exchanges with the men and women whose lives Preston touched have indeed plugged me into the very network I felt I lacked when I stood next to him at the bar. By working on this book, I have managed to help Preston keep one of his promises to me: I have been introduced to some of the best and the brightest.

And I have gotten other things as well. Over and over again, I've heard people say, "Writing this has helped me deal with my sense of loss"—another cliché, but in this case one so basically true that you can't shrug it off. There has been a stir among the people who knew him as they contacted each other and encouraged each other to contribute. And there has been a revelation of such loss that words cannot be put on paper; several people called me to say that it was just too difficult, too painful to even to consider. In a group of people who write because they are driven, that is a profound statement in itself.

The book is divided into two sections, nonfiction essays and interviews, and fiction. In the first part are the personal remembrances, interviews and brunches, ABA conferences and OutWrites, from the glorious nights at The Mineshaft to the advent of the fax age. Certain themes are repeated, as they must be in any collection of stories about one man. There are also the poignancy of lost moments, the bitterness of survivor guilt, and the simple sense of loss that recur in essay after essay. Be patient. I've alternated longer and shorter pieces, and situated the more biographical ones toward the first part of the section.

The second part is as eclectic as Preston's own body of works, from Agnes Bushell's portrayal of John as a character in a novel to the sexually charged pornographic celebration of *Mr. Benson* as J/O material and inspiration in Carol Queen's tribute. No collection honoring John Preston would be complete without some hypermasculine leather-sex in it; what is unique here is that every SM-tinged piece of porn in this anthology is written by a woman. I like to think that John would have liked that—found it hilarious, too, but liked it nonetheless.

There is only one thing to add before I open the doors to this gathering of memories and tributes.

John Preston made his mark not only by being a prolific and talented writer and editor, but also by building and maintaining a growing network of others in the publishing world and actively encouraging younger writers in their early careers. In an interview, Felice Picano tells Preston that other writers don't seem to be pursuing this same kind of active nurturing, at least not to the extent that John had. Preston seemed surprised by this; apparently it was only natural for him to seek out the newer writers, and to help them. (Although he also acknowledges that he finds the presence of hot young male bodies to be personally inspiring on a different level!)

Reading the many obituaries that appeared following his death, you have to wonder whose life Preston didn't manage to touch in some way. Like Monteagudo, whose deceptively simple piece heads this collection, dozens of editors and writers had more to discuss than the fact that Preston had written quite a bit. Somehow they felt a connection to him that was strong enough to provide something tangible: inspiration, encouragement.

Perhaps what we find when we look for Mr. Preston is that sense of the vitality of the future, through the younger and emerging writers. Now I know why he was so enthusiastic when I decided my anthologies would go in that direction—he knew that no writer or editor should stand alone with only his or her forward course to engage them. The legacy of his works will last as long as the printed word does. But the legacy of his example has the potential to carry itself through generations of writers to come.

Laura Antoniou
September 1994

VISIONS OF PRESTON

Jesse Monteagudo

Though AIDS has affected every profession, it has been particularly devastating to the arts. AIDS has killed more talented people than any historical event since the Holocaust. Even if we limit ourselves to nominees of the Lambda Literary Award the names and numbers are staggering: Reinaldo Arenas, Allen Barnett, Robert Chesley, Melvin Dixon, Robert Ferro, Herve Guibert, Richard Hall, Mike Hippler, Bo Huston, Jay B. Laws, Peter McGellee, Assoto Saint, Randy Shilts, George Stambolian, T. R. Witomski, David Wojnarowicz, Roy Wood...

One of the brightest literary lights to be taken from us by AIDS was a personal and artistic favorite of mine. One of our most prolific gay writers, John Preston has written or edited a total of twenty-six gay-themed books, not to mention a series of "straight" adventure novels written under a pseudonym. In 1983–1984 alone Preston put out the book version of his SM cult classic *Mr. Benson* (which originally appeared in *Drummer*); the novel *Franny, the Queen of Provincetown; I Once Had a Master,* (the first of the *Master* series); and *Sweet Dreams,* the first of six *Mission of Alex Kane*s. This literary output impressed me, then the book critic for Miami's *Weekly News,* and inspired me to anoint Preston the "Author of the Year" for 1983–84. I wrote him a letter to that effect and he replied graciously, thanking me and supplying me with a photo and personal facts for my article.

My "Author of the Year" article was the start of a literary relationship of sorts between John Preston and me. I continued to send Preston clips of my reviews, and he returned the favor by sending me copies of his books, notices, and his always-delightful Christmas cards. It was about this time that Preston learned he was HIV+, which led to a temporary halt in his prolific writing schedule. Happily for literature, Preston resumed his writing career as editor of *Hot Living* (1985), a safe-sex fiction anthology, and *Personal Dispatches: Writers Confront AIDS* (1989).

The publication of *Personal Dispatches* led to Preston's first appearance at the Miami Book Fair International, as the moderator of a panel of the same name that featured *Dispatches* contributors Larry Duplechan, Andrew Holleran, Paul Monette, and Edmund White. Preston's participation in the AIDS literary panel gave me the opportunity to meet my idol face to face for the first time. From the audience, Preston cut a formidable figure; while in person I found him to be both stern and serious, jovial and friendly, a literary lion at ease among his subjects. Though Preston's health declined steadily during his final years, his spirits were sustained by his prodigious writing, his speaking engagements, and his involvement with a series of young, literary protégés. A native of Medford, Massachusetts, Preston chose to live out his final decade in Portland, Maine, where he was active in the local gay and AIDS communities. Preston's community consciousness is evident in *The Big Gay Book* (1991), a still-useful, in-depth resource for gay men everywhere that truly lived up to its name. Another of John Preston's literary projects at that time was the anthology *Hometowns: Gay Men Write About Where They Belong* (1991). John encouraged my offer to contribute to *Hometowns,* which allowed me to discover another facet of his complex personality. As an anthology editor Preston was the consummate professional, quick to point out the weak points in his contributors' work while at the same time sensitive enough not to hurt their feelings when doing so. Preston's work as an anthologist provided many gay writers with the opportunity to express themselves, and launched many literary careers.

The publication of *Hometowns* led to John Preston's second appearance as moderator of a panel at the Miami Book Fair. This time I had the honor to be a panelist, along with Andrew Holleran, Christopher Bram, Steven Saylor and Bob Summer. For me, the highlight of that weekend was not the panel itself but the opportunity to socialize with John and the other panelists, not to mention the hangers-on who came by to shine in the reflection of his light. Accompanied by a nineteen-year-old "protégé" (no doubt a literary perk), John dominated that weekend's cocktail-party and dinner conversations as masterfully as he did the panel, always allowing the rest of us to say our piece and have our moments of glory. I was not to see Preston again until May 1993, when he returned to Miami to receive a well-deserved Lambda Literary Award for the anthology *A Member of the Family: Gay Men Write About Their Families.*

A self-styled "pornographer," Preston was proud of his erotic fiction. For John Preston "and for many other gay men [myself included], pornographic writings were how we learned the parameters of our sexual life. We could have more than a simple ejaculation with a nameless partner, if we wanted. Pornography was how we developed our fantasies, both sexual and emotional." Much of "the dark lord's" gayrotic fiction was the product of his final years, when he defied the sexual negativity of AIDS with his own sex-positive message: *The Heir* (1986); *The King* (1992); *Tales From the Dark Lord* (1992); and *The Arena* (1993). Preston also established a canon of male erotic fiction with the two *Flesh and the Word* anthologies he edited in 1992 and 1993.

In *My Life as a Pornographer and Other Indecent Acts,* a collection of Preston's best nonfiction work, Preston made "an attempt to show just why I think [pornography] is important, why it's worth looking at, and why…it's very funny." In the title essay, which was adapted from a lecture he delivered at Harvard University (April 15, 1993), Preston wrote: "Pornography has made me be honest, about myself and some of the most intimate details of my life and my fantasies.… Once I had exposed my own sexual fantasies, my most intimate desires, I feared little else about self-exposure as a writer." As I was then first trying my hand as a gayrotic fiction writer, I learned much from John Preston's honesty, his example, and his encouragement.

The last time I saw John Preston was during Columbus Day Weekend 1993, at the OutWrite Conference in Boston, where Preston was one of the keynote speakers and I was one of the panelists in a workshop on book reviewing and criticism. Though clearly affected by his illness, John was in high spirits, affectionate in a reserved New England sort of way, and still concerned about the future of gay writers and gay writings. Though I had already missed the deadline for *Friends and Lovers,* his next anthology, he encouraged me to submit an essay. The posthumous publication of *Friends and Lovers,* edited by Michael Lowenthal (one of Preston's most brilliant protégés), will be, like the present volume, a living memorial to our most influential gay writer and editor.

On Saturday night of the OutWrite Conference Weekend many of us went to Boston's Ramrod, a men's Levi's-leather bar, for a book-signing party held in conjunction with Preston's *Flesh and the Word 2.* Joined by *Flesh and the Word* contributors Michael Bronski, Michael Lowenthal and Scott O'Hara (among others), John signed autographs and worked the crowd like a seasoned politician. I was impressed but not surprised to see hard-core leathermen and bears flock around Preston, shaking his hand, buying copies of his book and telling him how his writings have changed their lives. These men, the much-maligned "clones" (whom Preston praised and defended in his controversial essay, "Good-bye, Sally Gearhart"), were this writer's preferred audience; "gay everymen" who might not be "political" in the strict sense of the word but who act out the goals of gay liberation in their daily lives and who have stood by one another through the most devastating epidemic of our times. Preston's passing left a gap in their lives, just as it did in mine. His work will endure as long as there are gay men willing to say yes to our selves and to our sexuality.

LAMBDA LITERARY AWARDS SPEECH
27 MAY 1994, LOS ANGELES
Michael Denneny

John Preston was a man of many accomplishments. He helped to establish and then became the director of the first gay community center in this country, in Minneapolis in 1971. He was editor of the *Advocate* in 1975. Already a legendary topman in SM circles by the mid-seventies, the publication of *Mr. Benson* serially in *Drummer* magazine established him as our leading pornographer, along with his good friends Sam Steward and Steven Saylor. Under a pseudonym, he was the author of dozens of mass-market male adventure novels, as well as the creator of a gay-male adventure series, *The Mission of Alex Kane,* for Sasha Alyson. He became a frequent essayist as well as our leading anthologist, while remaining a political activist. The ad card we're putting into the new edition of *Franny, the Queen of Provincetown,* will list some thirty books that John either wrote under his own name or edited.

John Preston was a man of many talents, but the rarest

and most valuable of these was his natural gift for friend-ship. John had more friends than most of us can even imagine. And he was wise enough to know that friendships, like gardens, need nurturing; in endless letters, phone calls, and faxes, he constantly tended to his friends.

My own friendship with John went back seventeen years. It started over drinks one evening after work when John was interviewing me—for the *Advocate,* I think—and I was so amused when I found out that this legendary topman had a master's degree in sexology (academic credentials, right?) that I started interviewing *him.* We talked until the restau-rant closed, and that evening began what in retrospect seems to me a seventeen-year-long conversation. At one point we had on tape over fourteen hours of our conversa-tions and arguments over SM—we were planning some kind of joint project on the subject—but the high point of our early friendship was surely the night we were both thrown out of The Mineshaft. Deep into a discussion of SM that by then had been going on for weeks if not months, we got distracted from the original purpose of the evening, which was sex, and kept pointing out to each other various tableaux that strengthened some point one of us had been making. Unfortunately, we were oblivious to the fact that we were ruining the atmosphere for everyone else there, those who had not forgotten that the point of the evening was not intellectual clarity. The management was forbear-ing—after all, this was the author of *Mr. Benson*—but finally they had had it and told us in no uncertain terms that our behavior was totally inappropriate and rude. Since we were standing between the area where the slings were set up on one side and a bathtub where people were enjoying water sports on the other, this struck me as hilar-ious, a reaction no doubt buoyed by whatever chemicals we were on that night. For a moment, John's eyes flashed with fury at this lèse-majesté. Then he broke into a grin. We both apologized and, giggling, took ourselves to the street where we started talking about rudeness and the surprisingly elaborate code of politeness that held sway at the trucks and why no one had written about it. I think we wandered through Greenwich Village till dawn talking, always talking.

For John, friendship manifested itself mainly in conversation, a way of sharing the world with others by talking about it. Conversation was important to him because it was how John came to know the shape of the world and to find his place in it. The series of anthologies he began with *Personal Dispatches* resembles nothing so much as one huge conversation about our place in the world and the people with whom we share it: our natural families and the families we create out of the fabric of friendship. Even his column about publishing in the *Lambda Book Report* was a way of talking to people he didn't know, young writers just setting out whom he wanted to help. For, by the time he came to write this column, John had achieved literary success by anybody's definition, and he felt the pressing need to give something back to the community.

The gay and lesbian population did finally have something like a literary community, and John had contributed mightily to this. I think he never forgot his hurt at the standoffishness of New York's gay literati when I first introduced him around. He thought they looked down at the fact that he was a pornographer; I think they were intimidated by the fact that he was a famous hustler and topman who was also a writer. In any event, he was determined never to act that way toward younger writers. He even proposed in his column the idea that every established gay or lesbian author should take on two or three younger writers in an explicit mentor role, advising them not only about their work but explaining the intricacies of publishing and helping them to get their work into print. John was constantly networking, and the networking was a significant contribution to the emergence of a literary community of our own.

In retrospect, it strikes me as ironic that this man who,

in the seventies, had an almost legendary reputation as a literary and erotic outlaw—and that in a community itself virtually outlawed—that this man's central theme, in both his life and his writings, was community. Virtually all of John's books, from *Franny, the Queen of Provincetown* to the forthcoming *Friends and Lovers* are, fundamentally, about community. He was one of the few people I have known for whom the need for community was an immediate and tangible reality. He spent years moving from city to city until he realized that at heart he was a New Englander and he settled in Portland, to be near his roots and his family. What was important about Portland was that there he could know by name the people who worked in the post office, there he was accepted by the guys at the barbershop, there he knew the governor as well as the members of the leather fraternity, there he felt truly at home.

And it was in Portland that John slowly—and much to his own amusement—came to the realization that he, this man of many masks and personas, was in essence a New England bachelor, a "curmudgeonly New England bachelor" in his own words. In one of the phone conversations we had during this time, I told him that he had finally become the person he always wanted to be, and that pleased him immensely. And it was true.

Surrounded by young men who valued their connection with him as intensely as he valued his connection with the late Sam Steward—young men he took to calling his nephews—the transition was complete: the bad boy of gay porn had become the good uncle of the gay community, a trusted and respected elder whose help and guidance was sought eagerly and given generously. John had achieved a singular status within the gay community, and his passing will be felt from Portland, Maine, to Portland, Oregon.

In the last conversation I had with John, a few days before his death, after we settled the final details for the revision of *Franny* he wanted published, I told him I was having trouble believing that we might never again have such a conversation. I told him his friendship had been one of the great pleasures and honors of my life and had sustained me through many rocky times in the last decade or so. And I thanked him for seventeen years of the best conversation I have had.

I know that thousands upon thousands of gay people across this land feel the same loss I do, for we are all diminished. John was one of our leaders, one of our heroes, one of our storytellers; but, above all, he was one of our best friends.

A PLAYER AND
A PARTICIPANT
Sasha Alyson

I met John Preston in about 1980, during a conference at Boston University. My career as a publisher was then only a year old. Hard as this may be to believe today, John had written many stories and articles, but had not yet written a single book.

Or, more precisely, no book of his had been *published*. He did happen to have a short manuscript, titled *Franny, the Queen of Provincetown*. With most people, this story would take one of two predictable paths from that point. He would give me the manuscript and I would either publish it (and thus begin an ongoing relationship), or I would reject it (and we'd lose touch until there was a new manuscript to consider).

Not so with John. Rather than approach me to publish *Franny*, he first asked whether he could interview me for a gay magazine. Following a long and enjoyable interview, he wrote an article that would have provided some much-needed publicity for my struggling new company—except that the magazine changed editors, and the piece never appeared.

From some people, I would have assumed that the interview had just been a ploy, a way to butter me up before presenting me with a manuscript. And certainly John Preston would go to great lengths to see his work published. But the gesture was no ploy. John was as genuinely eager to support a nascent gay publisher as he was to benefit from it.

That enthusiasm showed another side a few years later, as we got our first glimpses of the AIDS epidemic that was descending upon us.

As 1982 wore into 1983 and 1984, as safe sex came to be considered smart rather than evidence of paranoia, gay writers were slow to respond. Few of the manuscripts coming across my desk in those years even acknowledged the existence of AIDS; fewer still explored the erotic possibilities of safer sex. A remarkably large number of gay novelists set their books back in the 1970s, or ahead in a post-AIDS world, as an excuse for ignoring a subject that was increasingly on everyone's mind.

To this day, I don't entirely understand why. Many were patently in denial. Some thought it would be hard to make safer sex sound erotic. For still others, political correctness got in the way. Sex was good, and anything that equated sex with death simply could not be accommodated in their worldview.

John Preston was among the first to insist that gay literature should reflect the realities of AIDS. (Paul Reed, author of the aptly named novel *Facing It,* deserves mention as another.) When I suggested an anthology of safer-sex erotica, John instantly supported the idea and offered to act as editor for free, so that all the royalties could go toward fighting AIDS. A few years later, he donated many hours of behind-the-scenes labor and good advice when I coordinated the free industry-sponsored book, *You Can Do Something About AIDS.*

As his anthologies became regular fixtures on the gay best-seller lists, John's lifetime of giving his talents to the gay community were repaid. He could have coasted on his successes and cut back on the time spent on activism. Instead, he stayed involved in gay, AIDS, and literary worlds, and took particular pride in his role of mentor to several upcoming writers.

If we are looking for Mr. Preston, I think that was his essence. He received many rewards, both psychic and tangible, from his work, and he gave back a great deal more. He was a player and a participant in our community, and he did it all with passion. No one could ask to leave a greater legacy.

INTERVIEW WITH JOHN PRESTON

Felice Picano

Two sides of author John Preston seemed to coalesce finally in the keynote address he gave (in place of Tony Kushner, who canceled) at OutWrite '93 in Boston, where he read a moving autobiographical essay about being a young man in Boston with the wrong accent, the wrong credentials. In short: the alienated outsider. We'd known another John Preston. Anyone who's been in a gay bookstore lately has seen those inexpensive paperbacks with their black-and-white cover photos of hot young men: a new line called Badboy Books. Several of their best-selling titles are by—who else?—John Preston! Of all the writers during the late seventies in the newly emerging and evolving gay literature, few presented a more distinct image than Preston, with his SM erotic fiction: *Mr. Benson* and *I Once Had a Master.*

At the same time, in newspapers and magazines, literary quarterlies and anthologies, Preston was presenting another image: the politically astute, probing essayist. When *My Life*

as a Pornographer was announced by Richard Kasak Books—
its title piece, a talk Preston had given at Harvard University
—I asked for an early look at the book and found it to be as
varied, accomplished, finally as solid a collection of essays
as any addressed to the gay reader. With his earlier works in
print, and the second volume of his collection *Flesh and the
Word* now out from Dutton, this seemed as good a time as
any to speak with Preston and find out whether he really
was becoming as venerable as it appeared. Yes, it turned
out. And, gratifyingly, no.

FELICE PICANO: Because you write such personal—if ultimately also more widely relevant—essays, that seem designed to evoke personal feelings from your readers, I'm going to—gently, I hope—turn the tables and ask relatively personal questions about you and your work. At OutWrite '93, in the keynote address you gave in place of Tony Kushner (who canceled), you read a moving piece about being a young man in Boston with the wrong accent, the wrong credentials. In short, an outsider. How has being an outsider aided or hindered you as a writer in the newly emerging and evolving gay literature?

JOHN PRESTON: It hung with me a long time. It was a major impediment to writing itself. By 1975 I'd become editor of the *Advocate*...

FP: You must have been awfully young for a job like that.

JP: I was. I was hired to take over the *Advocate* when Al Goodstein bought the magazine. Do you remember him? He was this out gay entrepreneur, and he would only have an equally out editor. When he hired me, I was the only out gay editor in New York.

FP: So there you were already an editor...

JP: An editor. I certainly worked with words. But I'd already received a very strong message that a person like me should *not* be a writer.

FP: A person like how?

JP: I was a big galumphing kid, a farm boy, with the wrong accent. I was pretty much told that someone like myself could never become an English major and have the privilege of working with words.

FP: Let me get this straight: you felt that someone else owned the words?

JP: Yes. But there's a massive contradiction here. I'd grown up in rural New England and the history books were written about New England, so they were written about me and my family and place. They were written for me. I was a part of history and certainly I belonged. I'm the firstborn son of a rural New England family. My father was from the urban poor. My father's family was desperately striving. My mother's family only a little less so. So, naturally, there's always been this feeling of terrific insecurity. And at the same time, because of where we were, of entitlement. When I went to college in the Midwest, the entitlement of being a New Englander was given back to me.

FP: And no one in the Midwest knew you had the wrong accent?

JP: I worked to change that anyway. In college I worked to change myself from this kid who'd been such an outsider.

FP: So the passion you felt at being an outsider must have fueled your work?

JP: Eventually. Being the outsider combined with my sexuality meant that I had a very specific audience. One that was *not* perceived as being something I was barred from. Therefore, when *Drummer* and a few other magazines like it began being published, they were not barred to me.

FP: Whereas other, more literary ones like *Christopher Street* were?

JP: That's what I thought. So there I was editing the preeminent gay magazine in the country, and I wouldn't write for it. I started as a porn writer, and I started to feel comfortable with that. I'm always writing to a particular audience. I'm having an intimate conversation with this audience; if someone else can hear what we're saying, that's fine.

FP: So to an extent pornography become the place you fled to, hid in?

JP: Pornography was a place where I did not expect the judgment of the academy, which said I could not be an English major. While I was growing up, there was no world outside of Boston and the academy.

FP: So you created "Preston the Outsider"? But wouldn't you almost have had to create him if he hadn't already existed?

JP: All that dates really from my moving to Maine. Before that I was feeling my way. I'd been living in California and didn't fit in. I was in New York very briefly and didn't want to stay. I was always lonely outside of New England.... I had no intentions of being a writer. I just started writing *Mr. Benson* in *Drummer* in 1978. That got the whole thing going. By the way, I never really liked the piece. The late George Whitmore was one of the few people who understood that *Mr. Benson* was a comedy. And people didn't understand that. They thought it was real. They saw an archetype where I saw a cartoon.

FP: I still have my "Looking for Mr. Benson" T-shirt. It obviously had an effect.

JP: Partly that's because of the porn that was being published. Most of the writing was terrible and not very inventive. I was writing about real fantasies, and I was writing about locales that my readers knew. And about feelings that they knew on some level. I didn't have a lot of intent when I wrote *Mr. Benson.* But what happened was that in some way I caught that moment in time. This was 1978. You remember in the Castro and in Chelsea, how the leather scene was just getting going, the boys out on the corners at night, the backroom clubs.… And when you have audience response like I did with *Mr. Benson,* it sort of slaps you in the face and you think, "Well, what are you going to do now?"

FP: Isn't there an inherently self-destructive element to pornography? Its function is to make you horny enough to come—that's the only true guarantee of its success. Then what? It's disposable, no? What else can it do?

JP: If porn is not striking, then yes, it is disposable. But readers tell me how often they return to it. So the repetition, the turning back to it, has meaning. It also teaches a lot, in terms of giving someone a means to reflect on what's going on sexually. We're not at all finished with our sexuality. Porn gives us new ways to reflect on what life is like. What stimuli do we respond to? And there's a question of story. A lot of gay men are not stunned at all by the sexual explicitness. They aren't responding so much to the transgressive nature of porn, but to the stories it tells. Because the stories are already familiar.

FP: It's like having a terrifically hot sexual encounter and masturbating as you remember it.… In the essay "The Theater of Sexual Initiation," you write about the "ritualization" involved in many of the "theatrics" developed at The Mineshaft and similar places in the seventies. Theatrics as an initiation into manhood. How does that ritual, that initiation work, really?

JP: I'm not sure what you're asking. That essay was written for a theater anthology and what I was doing was showing how a place like The Mineshaft could be considered theater. I wanted to take the reader through it, as the reader would go into any other theater space, and show the function of each area and its relationship.

FP: That works. But even though you say it's a metaphor, anyone who's been in a sex club like The Mineshaft knows very well that something beyond "playing" is also happening there, and you're by no means the first person to talk of it's being a place where boys became men.... Is humiliation always a part of the initiation into manhood? Is pain—the endurance of physical pain—important in achieving manhood?

JP: Neither is needed. But exposure is part of what is going on. Exposure in many different ways. For example, being at a bathhouse is being naked—exposed—in front of other men. Performing public sex is the same thing. It's exposure. Yourself as outlaw.

FP: In another essay, "What Happened," you write of how the leather and SM scene has become so softened. Is that because it has become commercialized, commodified? Can it be changed back to what it used to be?

JP: As more and more men join these organizations—and lots of them *are* joining—it's become more and clear to me that if they were straight men, they'd belong to the Rotary Club. They're really more intent on being part of a group, and that has very little to do with sex. It's more about being part of a men's group. And when they try to turn it into a civil rights cause, which they are trying to do...I really think this cannot bear the weight. Then they go around demanding that others accept them. I mean, are they listening to themselves? You have to ask if Middle America is ready to embrace the idea of SM clubs all over the country?

FP: But even within the movement, something is happening....

JP: There's this odd and irresistible impulse to turn SM into a science. They now have slave schools, and then—separately—they have top schools, and the slave and top schools get together for a test. Sort of a final examination. The wonder and banality of SM is how it is so easily codified. But there's a level of intent beyond that which can ever be codified. And now there's all this business of who initiates and trains whom. Lately more and more it's the bottom who's doing the training. It seems to me that top should be the mentor and the initiator. That was my experience. To have an SM scene run by a bunch of pushy bottoms seems very bizarre to me.

FP: When I was young and gay, I saw myself as a danger to society. I was proud of that. Now everyone gay seems to want to want to adopt babies and live in the suburbs and shop at K Mart and be like everyone else. What's going on?

JP: I believe people of our generation sort of created it. By defining the goals of the gay movement and by saying that gay people should have as many options as others have. That people should not be barred from anything for any reason: certainly not for being a lesbian or a gay man. That's what all this business about gays in the military is about. On the other hand, you really can't expect a mass of people to become artists and revolutionaries.… But there is clearly some sort of revolutionary arch in who we are, and that's become re-manifested in the Queer movement. Which I truly have come to love even though at first I was really suspicious of it. I mean ACT UP and Queer Nation and all that.

FP: Which is generational. It's like not those gays directly after us, but another generation later.

JP: Right. The next group of gays took our lesson of being out and gay and turned it into wanting to be accepted.

Now, there's all the people who just assume they're going to get acceptance. I'm surprised by how much of what I'm doing is facilitated by people now in their twenties. Bill Mann, for instance, of *The Hartford Metro Line.* The first two gay books he read were mine. He came out reading my books. The big thing he wanted to do when he became a publisher was to find John Preston and publish him. These supertalented people in their twenties assume they're going to have the ability and space to use their talents, and to reward those who came before them.

FP: You speak fondly of and have a number of younger colleagues—of protégés, even—unlike many gay writers of our time. Why is that? Because of the sexual element of your work?

JP: You mean others don't?

FP: I don't. Holleran doesn't. I don't think Maupin or Monette do.

JP: I think Edmund White does. They are folks he met when he was teaching at Brown in Providence.... It's not because of the sexual element I don't really think, although some of these kids are...I could just rip their clothes off. There's a certain young male sensibility—although there are women as well—they're the people who can follow me from porn into the more serious writing I do, without any problem at all. People my age are much more surprised that I can publish in literary journals as well as do all this porn. And I love young guys. They're on their absolute best behavior with me. Their lovers and friends go nuts. One lover turned to me and said, "I hope you know this isn't a real person you're seeing."

FP: You speak of Sam Steward fondly, and other writers— George Whitmore—turned me onto the Phil Andros stories.

But I always found something missing from them. Something that kept them from being memorable. Do you know what I'm talking about?

JP: Sam Steward was more important for me because of his lifestyles and the way he integrated them in being a writer. Moving with such ease between the Gertrude Stein set in Paris and being a tattoo artist in California, then a porn writer and activist. A few other writers influenced me because of the way they structured their books. Marguerite Yourcenar for example, whom I never met, taught me that you can write a novel and at the end tell the reader what he or she just read. I remember saying, "Look what this woman did." And I did it too.

FP: You speak often of the late T. R. Witomski, whom I never met, and whose manuscripts of porn I read, admired, and turned down for publication at GPNY. I admit that his great anger at me and his published bitterness against many people—including me—kept me from ever getting to know him or his work more closely. What is Witomski's real contribution?

JP: Who knows what any one of our generation's contribution has been? But T. R. Witomski was an extraordinarily difficult person. Very smart. Jesuit education. But just filled with... He would say the most insulting things to me. After a while, I was the only one left who'd even talk to him. He amused me terrifically. I didn't take what he said at all seriously. A very difficult man.

FP: In the essay "How Dare You Even Think about It?" You bring up—but don't really expatiate upon—the situation of HIV-positive people—even AIDS-symptomatic people having sex. But you don't go any further. Will you now?

JP: The outrage is telling HIV-positive and -symptomatic people *not* to have sex. The stealing of your sexuality... When I first got my diagnosis, I saw that happening to me, and saw that it was something I collaborated in.

FP: How did your book *My Life as a Pornographer* come about?

JP: The process of the book was amazing. Richard Kasak read the Harvard lecture—[ed. note: the title piece of the anthology] and said he wanted to publish it. He'd put it out with any other two hundred pages I gave him. What I loved about the Harvard lecture was that this professor said I was the personification of Umberto Eco's literary theories. I didn't know who Eco was or what his theories were about. I perceived that what Kasak wanted was to fill out the book with similar stuff. So I gathered other pieces, the Sally Gearhart essay published in *Christopher Street* in 1983, the piece on Sam Steward, and a few others. I sat down and read what I had—about half of the current book—and it was pretty good. So I consciously set out to make a book of it. The four portraits had been for a book that had not panned out. The whiplash of self-image. How I write my pornography. And some other lighter pieces.

FP: Two of my favorites are the lighter ones. Humor is always difficult, but "Underwear as Pornography" is very smart and funny, and your final piece, "A Modest Proposal for the Support of Pornography" is a hoot.

JP: I wrote that because I wasn't getting any sex.

FP: You've got two books coming out, *Flesh and the Word— Volume 2* and *My Life as a Pornographer*...

JP: And I'm doing a third volume in the *Flesh and the Word* series. I've got a fabulous dirty story about Harvard.

I got this really good, hot story, and when I reached the end, I found that the author had footnoted it! Oh, I thought, I've got to go back and get out the MLA manual and check the footnoting to see if the attributions are done correctly.

FP: To what do you ascribe the success of the first volume?

JP: Superb writing is being done in areas that are never validated elsewhere. These are works that fully deserve to be brought to a wider audience, but won't be because of the subject matter or handling. There are pieces in both books that were sent in literally mimeographed. Some stories, especially Steven Saylor's works, deserve a truly wider audience. I guess the first book sold because it was delivering erotic writing into places where people felt okay about buying them. Waterstone's Bookstore in Boston's Back Bay, rather than at the local adult bookstore or even the local gay bookshop. You realize that it was mentioned in both *USA Today* and the *Times*. I'm proud that it's bringing new writers too. In the second volume are five people for whom this is their first work ever in print.... And I now consider this series my annuity.

FP: How do you wish to be known? What particular works do you want to be known for? And how?

JP: A bunch of stuff is happening right now. And there's a huge discrepancy between who I am and who I think I am. I think of my fiction as well-crafted entertainment that will not last. If I have a special skill, it's in essays. I have another book of essays coming out in 1995 from University Presses of New England, titled *Winter's Light.* I'm finding that I really like the essay form. No book editor ever pointed me in that direction. I would do it on my own, without encouragement. But in the past couple of years I discovered that I've got various outlets for it.

The *Boston Phoenix* will take longish pieces. So more and more I want to be the boy Molly Ivins. I'm also becoming more of a curmudgeon, so I want to tell people off more. I'm stunned. But this is my form.

PRIDE AND PREJUDICE:
REMEMBERING JOHN PRESTON
Laurence Senelick

The last time I saw John Preston, at lunch on a pier over-looking his beloved Portland, he was glowing with pride. This pride had two sources. One was a handsome Hungarian vizsla (pointer), his constant companion. Vlad the Impaler, as he was named, was a gift from Anne Rice after Preston nearly died of pneumonia in May 1991, and served as an urging to action and life. His other source of pride was another kind of invitation: to speak at Harvard to the Harvard Gay and Lesbian Caucus. For him, this was the consummation devoutly to be wished, the establishment's validation of his long career as an activist and writer. His chosen subject, "My Life as a Pornographer," flung a leather gauntlet at academic values. Even as his body wasted, his reputation was taking on a healthy glow.

Pride also infused his announcement that his latest works were being published by the most reputable of firms, Penguin, Dell, and now the University Press of New England, which would issue his autobiography. Meanwhile, his early erotica was being reissued by a more Grub Street but equally effective publisher, Badboy Books. The slippage between these two worlds amused Preston no end.

Our first meeting had been at a similar overlapping of different worlds. Its causes could not have been yuppier. In 1981, my lover, Michael McDowell, and I were fleeing from an extensive house renovation. Royalties from his horror novels had enabled us to put in a new kitchen, and the demolition was noisy and unabating. We decided to take up the offer of his editor at Avon Books, Susan Moldow, to sublet for two weeks the cabin in Maine she had been leasing. When we arrived, we found not only Susan, packed and ready to go, but her houseguest, Felice Picano. Over mounds of fried clams, Felice insisted that we must phone John Preston, who was eager to meet us and who had recently moved to Portland, half an hour's drive from our oceanside retreat.

Friendly though Preston sounded over the phone, his fearsome reputation preceded him. At this time, he was known as the Master of Masters, whose sadomasochistic feuilleton, *Mr. Benson,* had been the making of *Drummer,* the newest and farthest out of the gay magazines sold openly at newsstands. Those who had known him in San Francisco as the first editor of the *Advocate* or in New York as part of the homosexual glitterati were rattled by his recent sequestration in Maine. Self-exile from the pleasures of the Village was unthinkable! Had he gone round the bend, his friends wondered, to immerse himself in living out even-wilder fantasies?

Well, yes and no. We found that Preston was living in a massive triplex warehouse near the waterfront. Portland was one of the New England towns so economically depressed that it had never demolished its old city and replaced it with that hideous modern architecture. Consequently, it was filled with stately Grant-era Gothic buildings, which it now had the sense to refurbish as a draw for the tourist trade. Though stark, Preston's habitation was located in a rapidly gentrifying area. The living quarters were spacious, but furnished vaguely and messily, with an emphasis on equipment for writing and photography. Virtually every gay publication was represented by stacks of back issues. Stone stairs led to a loft decked out with plastic sheets, harnesses, and chains attached to wooden beams—all the paraphernalia of SM indoor sport.

The household genius of this walk-up dungeon was Preston's lover of the period, Jason, a liquid-eyed young man in a dog collar who, long before the fashion, had been pierced in all the likely and unlikely places. Like most serious masochists, Jason was the driving factor in the sexual equation, making the demands which his "Master" had perforce to carry out. Outside the torture chamber, he was charming and personable, but far more dogmatic than Preston himself.

There was nothing forbidding at all about Preston; rather, like Noël Coward's white elephants, he came across as "very, very sweet." Physically, however, Preston answered to all expectations. He was the model from which cookie-cutter clones were struck. Tall, rangy rather than well-built, he affected the lumberjack shirts, blue jeans, and work boots which were becoming a uniform but which, in the Maine setting, simply seemed local purchase from L. L. Bean. His head was large, rather elliptical in shape. balding and close-cropped, its lower third shadowed by a guardsman's mustache. His eyes were his best feature: gray corneas circled with sharp black outlines, piercing and full of intelligence. They were surmounted with circumflex eyebrows that gave him a somewhat Mephistophelian look. But the effect of those compelling eyes was literally undercut by hideous teeth, discolored and snaggled, which bespoke his impover-

ished childhood and chain-smoking. As to his sexual equipment, he was to reply to a question from an admirer, "Let's
just say that that is not one of my insecurities." (His mother,
the town clerk of Medfield, Massachusetts, once got a letter
from a clerk in Boston Right-of-Way with the P.S. "I would
like to thank you personally for having refused, thirty-eight
years ago, to have your son John circumcised.")

Our friendship was sealed quickly, not least because of
Preston's seriousness about writing. He and Michael were
the fractional percentage of writers who lived exclusively
off their creations, without recourse to academic jobs,
computer programming or other subsidies. They had
neither pretensions nor false modesty about their work,
which they considered important even though the genres
in which they worked were despised. Eventually, under the
name "Mike McCray," they collaborated on a series of
action novels in the Black Beret and Michael Sheriff series.
The publisher swore them to secrecy about their identities,
because it would have been fatal if the readers of these
violent fantasies about ultramacho renegade marines were
to learn that they had been penned by two men, one
known for his gay porno and the other for his gay detective
novels. Even so, they left coded messages for the initiate,
and the relationship between the protagonist and his surrogate son was so obviously a "daddy–slave boy" one that
only an obtuse hetero could ignore it.

For Preston, who adored the daddy role, such ciphers
would prove insufficient, and he would later write the Alex
Kane series, indulging every wish fulfillment and quirk of
poetic justice. It was trash, but trash with political purpose:
in his eyes, it empowered the gay reader. He never apologized for what others might consider hackwork.

In fact, a major reason for Preston's leaving new York
had been his detestation of the incestuous literary scene
there. The Violet Quill and its members struck him as
precious and self-serving. He agreed quickly to the comparison when I cited Mark Twain's description of the Sandwich

Islanders, who "make a living by taking in one another's washing." So far as Preston was concerned, a writer needed to address himself to the widest possible audience through journalism, popular fiction and, indeed, pornography, in order to make a serious cultural impact. He detested elitism of any kind, even the elitism of talent if it were frittered away on self-regarding esoterica. Certainly he had the most copious fan mail of anyone I have ever met, and had early on rented a large post-office box to accommodate the inundation of letters not just from those who wanted to be beaten up by "Mr. Benson," but by those who had been liberated by his prose.

All politics is local, Tip O'Neill was fond of saying. For Preston, Portland was more than a refuge from the ingrown literary community of Manhattan. It became his "hometown," where his championing of gay rights made him a major celebrity. When a young queer in Bangor was pushed off a bridge and drowned, or antigay legislation was in the offing, Preston was a rallying point for protest. He campaigned against the persecutions that were making Ogunquit, long a gay haven, homophobic. His appearances at readings or bars were a cynosure for young men and women just gathering the courage to come out.

One of his many unfinished projects was a book of interviews with "the Gay Men of Maine," oral histories of small-town individuals. In a letter, he described one interview he had taken "that had me in tears when it was over":

[B— G—] the guy in Lewiston who had endured 36 years of being the town faggot. Essentially, taking the verbal abuse from men who would later come to his apartment for blowjobs was the only way he had ever known of being gay. He thought it was okay and even fell in love with one man who used to abuse him verbally, but who ended up on his bed for six years as a regular. But this past winter [1986] the abuse turned very ugly. He was terribly harassed by a gang of teenagers. He went and got a gun. One night they tried to break into his apartment when he was there. He ended up shooting and killing one of them. The result has been horrible. He was judged by a grand jury to have committed justifiable homicide. The leader of the gang was the only other one to go to trial and he got a $35 fine. The kids eventually came back after him and he gave up. He moved out of town and lives under an assumed name, trying to convince his neighbors that he's not gay, never wanting to go through what, he thinks, is the result of being gay again. I wept when he left. I have seldom felt so powerless in my life.

In an impoverished, underpopulated, rural state, whose homosexual citizenry was widely dispersed and isolated, Preston waved a kind of banner under which to close ranks. He insisted that his colleagues leave the metropolis and act as role models in other backward parts of the nation. Gay youth, he explained, needed good gay uncles and aunts. (He resisted my suggestion that they be called "fairy godmothers and godfathers.") Under his influence, country boys moved to Portland, "the big city," bought houses, staked out lovers, and declared themselves wicked and immoral while glowing in the penumbra of his following. The PNEBs, he called them—Perfect New England Boys. For he preserved a sense of humor about all this. He once remarked, "I know all these construction workers in Maine—and what they want to do is get into retail women's clothing. In New York I know all these men in retail women's clothing, and they all want to be construction workers. I've been trying to work out an exchange program, with buses going back and forth."

For a number of years we remained very close. Preston would submit to us first drafts of his more ambitious works and never quailed before the harshest criticism, whether of his style, grammar, or spelling. When soliciting advice in literary matters, he was more a slave than a master. I was particularly brutal about his first-person narrative *Franny,* supposedly told by a Provincetown drag queen; he hadn't seemed to get under the skin of the character. He took the abuse like a lamb and rewrote the book, achieving considerable popularity with it. At his readings in Boston, the room was invariably packed, with "lying down and groveling room only." On these occasions, Michael and I were often his hosts, though appalled by his heavy smoking and drinking. He could easily work his way through a quart of scotch or brandy in the course of an evening, while protesting that in Portland he drank only milk.

His stay might be a halfway station to a book signing or a club opening in New York, for he was still a vivid presence in publishers' offices and burgeoning sex clubs. Negotiating a contract was as great a source of arousal for him as shoving a boot in a groin. One of his closest friends on these jaunts and on weekend trips to our house was "Mam'zelle Victoire," aka V. K. aka Victoria McCarty, New York's leading dominatrix and editor of *Penthouse Variations*. Statuesque, her clear-cut features crowned by a Gibson Girl aureole of red hair, V. K. was a Victorian at heart; she would attend dinner parties in full nineteenth-century dress for deportment before changing into her leather gear for a descent into local back rooms. Once a year she would check into an Anglican convent the way a gourmand might visit a spa, to take the excess weight off her conscience before plunging back into the fleshpots.

Over the course of the '80s, things began to change for Preston. Jason, who had never acclimated to Portland, moved back to San Francisco to be in the thick of things. Barely a year later, he hanged himself accidentally in one of his masturbatory exercises. As Preston's first lover had committed suicide after their parting, this death confirmed his fear of a developing pattern. Preston never had an official lover after that; instead, a succession of good-looking young men, usually college students, imbibed lessons in discipline from him for a few years at a time. A mutual admiration sprang up between him and Anne Rice, and he was among the first to praise her erotica, published under the pseudonym A. N. Roquelaure. At his urging, I read it;

but I never cared much for the overornate prose, the unspecific fairy-tale background, or, for that matter, the emphasis on pain. One man's goad is another man's turnoff. But Rice inspired Preston with the idea that pornography was more than just a quick buck or mock fuck, that it had its own literary credentials, and deserved a format more lasting than the pulpy pages and smeared type of "adult" publishers. Under her influence, he returned to porn, which he had earlier regarded as potboilers, and crafted more careful pieces.

This ran up against the increasing feminist and fundamentalist attacks on pornography. Antisexers he called its proponents, those who could not distinguish between fantasy and reality and who would put barbed wire around the territory where the imagination would range. Preston projected an anthology with the working title "In Defense of the Erotic Imagination" to combat their moves with reasoned argument, legal analysis, personal experience, and educational stratagems. Alas, it was never realized. Instead, he proselytized for pornography all the more actively through his own writings and lectures.

AIDS was another turning point. In 1983 Preston was dismissing it vituperatively as a tiresome conversation piece and joked that it was probably transmitted at brunch. For years he listened to the rumors and reports with impatience, as an unwelcome brake on the activity that defined his life. When he was himself diagnosed as HIV-positive in 1987, he had a perfectly idiosyncratic response. With a handsome hunk as his demonstration model, he went on a lecture tour to explain how safe sex could be just as exciting and satisfactory as the dangerous kind.

Preston did not reveal his status to me until 1989, when we shared news of the death of a mutual friend and collaborator, Philip Blackwell, the African-American playwright. Preston recalled the letter in which Phil had announced his diagnosis.

I've read that letter so often now, from so many people—the one about being brave and taking command of his care in a "real" partnership with his doctor and on and on. I hear those words over and over again, and I can't respond anymore. Not that I think everyone is doomed—I'm actually on the positive side of that debate—but because the recitation is so shallow and unconvincing. I'm much better when people are facing death straight on and want to talk about that, not that they're creating self-fulfilling prophesies—I'm very aware of that trap and stop that one from going very far—but I have a much easier time when someone wants to talk about what's been done and what won't be done. If that makes any sense. The "I'm going to be the warrior who wins this battle" gets very tired when it's said on the battlefield where so many have already fallen. There is, somehow, a balance between hope and reality, and it's so seldom achieved or even striven for anymore.

Preston tried to strike that balance, but bad reactions to AZT kept him fluctuating between terror and overcompensation in work. He was rarely sick, but hated to have his writing schedules altered by changes in his T-cell count. His sex life remained active if sporadic, but erotica as a surrogate and a sexual aid became even more crucial. As at his back he would "seem to hear Time's wingèd chariot hurrying near," the always-prolific Preston appeared at countless conferences, signed endless book contracts, and spawned several volumes a year, from the encyclopedic *Big Gay Book* to his anthologies *Flesh and the Word* to his series on gay men and their families and hometowns. All this was accomplished single-handedly, without the aid of secretaries or amanuenses. There was much more in store, including a gay male anthology to be called "The Family Jewels," a handbook on hustling, and his only-partially-completed memoirs. He exulted at having entered the mainstream.

This exultation was, in part, personal justification. Preston both boasted of and was ashamed of his proletarian background, his failure to go to grad school, the spottiness of his general education. He considered himself a self-made gay icon. This is why he so idolized Samuel Steward, tattoo artist, essayist and creator of the Phil Andros stories. Preston regretted that he never had Steward's elegance of expression or breadth of allusion. Money ironed out the problems he had with what he called his "psychotic family"; when his *Advocate* expense account allowed him to take his parents out to dinner at Locke-Ober or his royalties enabled him to pay his father's nursing-home bills, all was well. Still, he enjoyed the working-class male bonding of his weekend returns to the domestic bosom, and he tried to cultivate a close relation with his younger brother, a binge-prone marine. Preston liked to plant this nugget in desultory conversation, if only to hear his listener gasp, "You have a brother who's a marine?" Reality, that tease, was rubbing up against fantasy again.

Geographic distance made for personal distance. I saw John only when I could go to Portland for an antique-paper show, or he would come down to Boston for an OutWrite conference. Inveterate letter-writers, we kept up our correspondence, lavish in advice or questions. Typical of his queries for some project or other: Who said, "War insults nature by forcing the old to bury their young"? What do you know about temple prostitution? Can you lend me your copy of the 1683 *Whore's Rhetorick* as a model for my hustler's handbook? I answered as best I could. His last letter was typical: reflections on the receptions of his latest book, plans for future publications, jokes about a recent lecturer who "actually managed to make masturbation—by which he is evidently obsessed—boring," and praise for his dog, which "takes up most of my spare time and emotions, and does better with both than have most human males."

It was over the radio that I heard that John Preston had died. This surprised me for two reasons. First, his illness never seemed to impede the torrent of his activities, and so I never thought of him as near death. And then there was the fact that his death might be considered newsworthy enough for a national broadcast. In the course of a decade, he had moved from the margins to the very heart of our debates on the way we live now. Preston had every right to be proud.

PRESTON!

Larry Townsend

West Hollywood, CA

Being one of the most prolific writers in our genre (not that I turn 'em out that fast, simply that I've been at it for a long time), I seldom have trouble getting started on a new piece. But for many days after being asked to compose a few words for a book memorializing John Preston, I sat staring at a blank computer screen, unable to put my myriad thoughts into any kind of order, hesitant to describe the private moments we had shared, because some often really weren't anyone else's business—others (in my mind) unlikely to be of interest to other people. Then I talked to Laura, our editor, and to V. K., another close friend of Preston's, and each of them said to tell it like it was and share whatever I could of a relationship that was going to be very different from most others because Preston and I had been friends since "way back when."

Although we did not see each other very often in recent years—we lived at opposite ends of the country—I always had the sense of my friend's advice or support being no farther away than the phone or fax machine. In fact, checking over my Preston file, I find a stack of his faxes, the older ones fading—appropriately, I guess. (I always addressed my electronic notes to him as "PRESTON!" He liked that, probably because the "!" had some wonderful significance.) My own notes, of course, are originals—still clear, pristine copy. Survivors. And that's the toughest part, isn't it—the grief or guilt of the survivor?

I first met Preston when David Goodstein hired him to edit the *Advocate,* back in the mid-70s, pre-AIDS, in the midst of that exciting period when the cause of gay rights was becoming visible, but—as yet—not quite respectable. Our relationship, our relative status, was very different from what it would later become. Preston had yet to write the many stories, articles, books that would bring him fame and infamy, whereas I already had *The Leatherman's Handbook,* plus some fifteen other published titles to my credit. Then, in the succeeding years, as we drifted apart, he went on to gain his well-deserved status among the East Coast establishment of gay literati, while I allowed a successful mail-order/small-press publishing endeavor to absorb my time and energies—publishing mostly other people's work, to the exclusion of my own.

In connection with this publishing enterprise, I had my first conflict with the *Advocate* people—at the same time, my first conflab with Preston where I heeded his sage advice. A pair of low-level Mafia crooks (one in New York, one in Philadelphia) had gotten together and blatantly ripped off my first eight books—simply republished them with different (green) covers and undercut my price. I was, of course, very upset! I came to Palo Alto to see David Goodstein and ask his help. I wanted him to curtail the advertising for the two companies which had stolen my books.

Now, I have to explain that my relationship with David

was already a bit strained, because he had talked me into joining the Whitman-Radclyffe Foundation board of directors, and committing myself to its support within the community. Then, without warning, he bought the *Advocate* and resigned as president of the W-R board, leaving all of us holding the empty bag he had promised to fund until we were able to get a proper cadre of contributors. ("Us" being Jim Foster, Evelyn Hooker, a couple of big-name shrinks, and several other movement people in addition to myself…)

David listened to my sad tale and then flabbergasted me by asking, "How do I know they were really your books, and not theirs first?"

"Because I'm telling you they're mine, and because we've supposedly been friends for the last five or six years," I told him.

Well, that wasn't good enough, and David refused to help, although he did suggest that I might discuss it with "his editor." Now really steaming, I sat down with Preston, who sympathized with me and wanted to help, but—like everyone else who worked for "The Emperor"—he knew better than to question the great man's decision. Instead, he helped me plan my "Don't be ripped off" ad campaign, which actually netted me a very large number of new mail-order customers. However, my dispute with Goodstein resulted in the *Advocate*'s canceling the column I had been doing for them, since well before David's acquisition of the magazine. As a result of this situation, I had only minimal contact with anyone in Preston's office for quite some time.

Thus, several years passed without our seeing one another. Preston had left the *Advocate,* and had done a lot of writing for *Drummer,* including the *Mr. Benson* and *Master* stories. Eventually, Preston started making trips to the West Coast to promote his "nonleather mainline" books. Since this was before his more affluent period, when his publisher(s) began to pay his way, he used to stay with Fred and me, and we would do our best to entertain our friend, the visiting celebrity—already the Lion of Literature. (Or so we teased him.) He was now the feted celebrity author, with a string of younger sycophants dogging his trail, begging to sit at the feet of greatness. We laughed about this, remembering the time when money was scarce and fame seemed so elusive. But, we both agreed, there were few old men who could command the obedient compliance of so many willing youngsters, as we could.

Then we discussed the critics—and all the wonderful punishments we might inflict upon them. He even made suggestions for some improvements in my dungeon when and if the day should arrive. But, of course, it never could. These were the fantasies of two inspired, commingled imaginations. But how I would have enjoyed working with him to exact a proper degree of pain and anguish from a couple of our favorite targets—twits who had presumed to deprecate our efforts without understanding the significance of half the things they criticized! Then, too, we commiserated with each other that neither of us would ever win an award for our most favorite works—stories that were too vulgar for the elegant literati who controlled the award-giving process. We should establish our own "Gay Academy Awards," we decided, with the man's Oscar being a large upright penis, then shuddered to imagine what the female equivalent would have to be.

It was during an early trip to the West Coast that Preston told me he had AIDS. I don't think he had gone public with the news, because he was concerned about the effect it would have on his career if his condition became common knowledge. What would it do to his credibility as an advocate of safe sex? Then we discussed the irony of the situation. His was one of the early voices of caution; he had practiced these defensive measures himself, and here he was positive, anyway. It didn't seem fair, and it wasn't. How many other guys were out doing whatever felt good and surviving, while a man of sane and cautious resolve was stricken?

"Make it a positive quality," I advised him. "You've got it; you can't back off and start over. Better to use it as a positive standard, a battle cry—to flaunt it yourself, rather than have your detractors whispering behind your back. There are so many other valuable people afflicted, you will simply become one of a distinguished company." We were sitting on my terrace, in the hills overlooking West Holly-wood; and when I finished my fatherly advice we were both silent for a long time. I wasn't the first to discuss this with him, I was sure, but I felt he was seeking some consensus.

Finally he looked up, shaking his head as he responded to my suggestions. "In the company of the condemned," he said bitterly. But having said this, he seemed to brighten. Although we discussed his health, its ups and downs, several times over the succeeding years, I never sensed this bitterness again—not until the very end. Instead, his HIV status seemed to propel him forward, as if he were aware that his time was limited and he wanted to finished as many things as he could. (Although he once told me, laughingly, that he was really working so hard because he needed the money. I empathized with him; it was a condition with which all writers must contend. But it's surely a sweeter pie when one's product becomes desirable enough that publishers are actually asking when a specific piece is going to be finished.)

If I were to describe my overall relationship with Preston, I would have to say that it was an uncomplicated friendship, characterized by an almost cynical awareness of the foibles of which we had each been guilty, and the knowledge that each was far more vulnerable to human frailties than our respective (but somewhat overlapping) audiences would allow us to admit—except to each other, and to very few others. It was this catalog of shared secrets that helped bind us together in a long-standing friendship that has now been shattered so cruelly.

I had known for some time that Preston's health was declining, of course, but the imminence of doom was brought home most strikingly when I learned that he had donated his library to the archives at Brown University. It was the first time that I wanted to question him, but couldn't frame the words. How do you ask a man if he is nearing death? How do you offer comfort or encouragement when there isn't any hope? (It's a dilemma we all have faced over the last decade, isn't it? It's not unique to Preston and me; it's something we should now have learned to live with. Yet each time it happens, the pain and frustrations are fresh and sharp, and nothing makes it easier.) There was little I could do or say. I could only think about the man, and worry, and wish things might be different.

They say that it is most difficult for young people to accept death because it is generally a quality so foreign to their lives. But I think it's even worse for those of us in later life. There is a finality to the loss of a friend, and the sure knowledge that the long history of shared intimacies can never be replaced. I greatly regret not being able to say a proper "good-bye." But this is also a common problem, especially when we are separated by a long distance from someone about to be taken by this disease that has decimated the ranks of our best and most talented. Preston! was certainly one of these. I count myself fortunate to be one of the few to know him as the man, a personality above and beyond the legend. He was my friend, and I'll miss him.

MR. PRESTON
AT THE ABA
Bob Summer

My memories of John Preston—or Mr. Preston, as I always jokingly greeted him, whether by phone, letter or in person—are bound inextricably with those of the American Booksellers Association's convention, that annual high point of the year for the book industry and an event he used as a setting for *Entertainment for a Master.* As bookmen, to use an old-fashioned term for men professionally involved in books, attending the ABA was not only a virtual must for us, but also provided a venue for our yearly get-togethers since we lived in widely separated parts of the country.

Indeed, it was at the ABA where I both met Mr. Preston and saw him for the last time, the former in New Orleans and the latter in his beloved Miami Beach. Just over a dozen or so years evolved between those two occasions, but I'll begin setting up my remembrance by recounting the night we were introduced by Sasha Alyson at a restaurant in the French Quarter on the eve of the New Orleans

ABA. I had seen an announcement of the latest of John's (even then) numerous books, and of course, I knew who he was, since like hordes of gay men, I had greedily lapped up the spellbinding delights of his *Mr. Benson, I Once Had a Master and Other Erotic Tales,* and *Franny, the Queen of Provincetown,* along with four of the *Mission of Alex Kane* books. From his books and underground reputation, I had expected John to be wearing leather, even in New Orleans' early-summer sultriness. Instead, he was wearing a polo shirt and chinos, the yuppie uniform then fashionable. But he *did* have the most commandingly piercing ice-blue eyes I've ever seen, and I remember being initially taken aback by the steeliness of his gaze until he relaxed his mustachioed handsomeness into an engagingly shy smile and extended his hand to me. With the formalities of introduction out of the way, I relaxed also when I discovered that we shared a love for dishy stories about books and writers. It was as though our friendship was sealed that night, and shortly after he returned home to Portland, Maine, and I to Macon, Georgia, we began exchanging frequent letters in that pre-fax and -E-mail era. And in one of the first letters he wrote, I recall, something pretty close to "this could be dangerous—two gay men in small cities keeping in touch by writing."

But I'm getting ahead of myself. As fate would have it, Sergeant Glenn Swann, John's *Safe Sex* coauthor, was also in New Orleans with his john (a Club Baths mogul, if memory serves me correctly), and John had an invitation to a private party they were giving later that night at the guest house in the Quarter where they were staying. But it was an after-hours party, and John asked me to meet him there after we had gone on to the intervening ABA parties on our separate rounds. At the time, Sergeant Swann, an ex-marine, was the heartthrob of gay America for the strip shows he would open by appearing in his military dress uniform. And he *was* absolutely gorgeous, with a powerfully masculine body to die for, just the ticket to send a macho-starved gay man into cardiac arrest. I don't remember the parties I went to after leaving the restaurant, but I do remember how horny I was from the prospect John had opened for me. I mean, meeting Mr. Preston and Sergeant Swann all in one night—how much excitement can a boy take?

I found out, but not in the way I was expecting. Actually, John and I never got it on together; we simply weren't sexually attracted to each other. And the orgy I had anticipated at the after-hours party failed to materialize. Oh, I did meet Sergeant Swann, and I still have a picture of me hugging him that was snapped there, and his private strip show for six or so invited ABA-goers *was* something to see. But the performance was so controlled that it was a sexual turnoff. After we were greeted, plied with some second-rate whiskey and photographed individually with Sergeant Swann (who was wearing his Marine gym togs), he left the room. And so did Mr. Preston, who told me he had seen the show numerous times, and would leave me to enjoy it while he headed on to another previous engagement.

Soon the john, a paunchy and sleazy sort, dimmed the lights in the rather tacky suite, flipped on a record of military marches, and Sergeant Hunk reentered. He was wearing only his uniform's tunic and cap plus a dangerous-looking military sword— no, not his cock, but an actual steel sword. The guests, mostly older booksellers and publishing personnel, were seated around the room, darkened except for a spotlight the john was shining on his protégé. As he made his surprisingly subdued entrance, I felt the hand of the guy sitting next to me, the only young man present. (He turned out to be a macho poster model himself.) We looked at each other, he smiled, and he returned his gaze to Sergeant Swann strutting around the room swinging his ceremonial sword ominously in time to the marches' beat.

I looked at the poster man next to me, he looked back, and we leaned into each other and kissed. But suddenly, I was distracted by a moist jerking sound; I turned my head to behold Sergeant Swann with his tunic open to reveal his rippling ridge of abs and a fully engorged *huge* cock. Before I could bob my mouth around it, he backed away to continue his strutting. Well, I figured, he wasn't a striptease artist for nothing. Out of the corner of my eye, I saw some of the other men busy jerking off, even if everyone (except for the model beside me) seemed to be in his own little space. The john was having his own little fantasy, too, writhing on the floor while looking at Sergeant Swann and beating off what the semidarkness revealed to be a little stub of a cock. He was moaning and casting some slavish dirty-talk pleas in his stud's direction.

Maybe he got what he wanted, too, because Sergeant Swann strutted over and kicked the john without missing a stroke. I don't know how he got out of his tunic, but he did, and flung it to the john, who let out whimpers of gratitude. The whimpers grew louder as the evening's putative object of desire marched over to kick the john again. Then, while caressing his shapely pecs with the hand that wasn't stroking his cock, Sergeant Swann stomped over to the guy to whom he had given his sword. I couldn't quite see what happened next, but from the slurping sounds, I could guess.

What's going on here? I asked myself. I guess my seatmate was wondering the same thing because I heard him whisper, "Let's get out of here," as he pulled me up and, after stepping over the spent body of the weeping john, out the door. He was staying at a hotel nearby, and we made a beeline there to wash away the tepid spectacle with some private erotic amusement of our own. But to give Sergeant Swann his due, watching him *had* made us horny, even if the gathering was not what both of us hoped it would be. I spotted some military uniforms hanging around the model's room and feared momentarily that I was in the hands of another guy with a uniform fetish. No, he reassured me, they were only for his posters and the ABA clients he was booked to entertain in New Orleans. Sergeant Swann may have become a gay celebrity and safe-sex role model when the onset of AIDS was increasingly forcing us to reexamine the ways we got off with each other, but this guy was the real thing: a topman to make his bottom buddy see God.

The night—or, more exactly, the morning—was still young after he drove me to heaven and, while we were showering, we decided to head out for a nightcap at Café Lafitte in Exile, one of the oldest and most famous gay bars in America. While the crowd outside the Bourbon Street landmark was dense, it parted miraculously for my stud-god with me in tow, yet another indication that in gaydom, beauty certainly has its privileges.

After we stopped at the bar upstairs and walked out onto the balcony above the street, whom did we spot but Mr. Preston, at the center of a circle of young men who seemed to be holding onto his every word. We stood back and listened to him for a while, but he saw us and motioned us to join the group.

"How did it go?" he asked.

"Great!" I exclaimed before realizing he was asking about the Sergeant Swann denouement. "Oh, that. Well…"

But before I could add anything else, one of the young men interrupted, and asked if John was really John Preston. Was he the real Mr. Benson, another wanted to know. The most comely of the acolytes wondered why he wasn't dressed in leather. John inquired bemusedly if the beauty was looking for a leatherman for a daddy. But the joshing interplay between the two took a more serious turn when the young man blushed boyishly and, after a timid pause, pulled his clenched fists together and extended them in quiet supplication. John gave me a what-else-can-I-do look, and then took command of what he was being offered. In a few minutes, we watched over the balcony as they exited the bar and turned up Bourbon Street toward John's hotel. We cheered them on, but neither looked back.

That was the last I saw of John in New Orleans, and I never quizzed him abut what the Lafitte in Exile scene had led to. But occasionally John did tell me about the calls he received from young men who had read his books and were curious about SM, and once he kept me on edge for several weeks with intimations of sexy phone conversations he was having with a self-identified Navy Seal. (Ultimately, they came to nothing when the guy failed to show up for a designated tryst.)

Then, when we shared adjoining rooms in a gay-friendly bed-and-breakfast inn during a Washington ABA, we stayed up far into the night exchanging praises of the lovelies we had paired with earlier that evening—he with a "wonderfully charming young man" discovered in a leather bar, and me with the model I had coupled with in New Orleans, where his posters had been such an ABA hit that he had returned to nurture his increasingly lucrative business with specialty retailers.

After only a few hours of sleep, we roused ourselves with a pot of hot coffee and headed over to the convention center and picked up our ABA press credentials. The opening of the ABA—so many new books to see, so much palpable excitement in the air! It's always a high in and of itself, and we capped the heady experience with lunch at the Occidental, a downtown Washington restaurant that's a traditional favorite of political movers and shakers.

When we were seated and had perused the menu, John asked if I knew who the good looking youngish man at the corner table was. I had recognized him right away and pointed out that he was Bill Clinton, the governor of Arkansas, who, according to friends in Little Rock, had presidential ambitions, despite a reputation for womanizing. "Well, he certainly looks presidential," John said, "After the drab Reagan-Bush crowd, we could use some excitement in the White House."

(But Clinton's election to the presidency was years ahead, and we had no glimmering that this southern charmer would eventually break our hearts by abandoning his campaign pledge to end the military's gay ban, caving in to the cruel and probably unconstitutional "don't ask, don't tell" hoax.)

It was during that ABA when John and I went to Deacon Maccubbin's apartment to hear the plans he was finalizing to launch the *Lambda Book Report* at Lambda Rising, the bookstore he had founded and still headed. We liked what we heard, especially since we had talked from time to time about the need for a comprehensive review medium for gay and lesbian books. John signed on to write a regular column on matters relating to book publishing, and I later joined as a contributing editor. Our participation in *LBR* provided another bond for our friendship, and at intervals we would call each other and dish about editors there, writers who were negotiating or had signed contracts for larger or (more usually) smaller advances, and even books we disagreed on. And since I was a correspondent for *Publishers Weekly,* we would sometimes trade industry tips. As a book columnist, John had keen insights and an impressive array of sources, and through the *LBR* columns he wrote until shortly before he died he made a real contribution to the gay and lesbian publishing community.

When the *LBR* was off and running, Deacon inaugurated the Lambda Literary Awards, the annual winners of which would be announced at a gala banquet held on the evening before each ABA. From then on, the presentation of the Lammies became an essential event on our ABA schedules, since John was often a nominee and I covered them for *PW*'s ABA newsletter, *Show Daily.*

Those were some of our best times together, and over drinks after the awards had been handed out we would review the evening—grousing about this or that winner, commenting on how great (or terrible) someone looked, and of course, pointing out the cute guys we had spotted. Bitchy digs came from me; while John relished gossip, he was rarely mean-spirited. As he got older, he cast himself increasingly as a middle-aged New England curmudgeon, but he never convinced me of that. During the relatively long span of our friendship, I saw him only once give way to what I considered real sarcasm, and that, perhaps predictably, was over Bruce Bawer's *A Place at the Table,* which had been published several months before John died.

In candor, I must admit I was stung by his response to my *LBR* review of Bawer's heatedly debated book. While I thought I had been evenhanded about a book I knew was going to be controversial and even condemned as a conservative tract (or what passes for a conservative tract in this politically muddled era), John construed my review as a defense of Bawer's commentary on and analysis of both the gay "subculture" and the gay "mainstream." Sadly, his final illness and swift decline prevented us from talking over our differing interpretations of the book's content. Nevertheless, I choose to believe that had he been healthy, our mutual generosity with each other would have opened a way to finding a common ground for understanding.

But again I'm getting distracted. Back to the Lammies, since it's impossible to disentangle them from my store of memories of John at the ABA. It was at the reception preceding the Lambda Awards banquet on the eve of the New York ABA where John gave me the happy news that *Hometowns* (in which I was proud to be included with an essay on growing up in Oak Ridge, Tennessee), had been chosen to be a Book-of-the-Month-Club selection. But somehow the anthology was passed over for a Lammy the following year, even though John found some consolation in at least receiving a nomination for it. At the Las Vegas ABA, he confided to me his chagrin that *Personal Dispatches,* which was nominated for a Lammy in two different categories, didn't receive "one fucking thing."

Still, what John perceived as a failure in the validation of his peers was, in actuality, no more than a small dip in his writing career. "A book is a book," I reminded him, "and book awards are book awards. Merit in the first is not automatically recognized with the second." In any case, the curve of his career continued rising, and by the time of the Miami Beach ABA, its ascendancy was nearing its apogee.

The recognition he garnered there couldn't have happened in a more appropriate place. Other ABA-goers may have been turned off by the second-class (or worse) hotel accommodations, vast distances between sessions and party sites, the area's high crime rate, and the week's blowing rain, but not John. Just being in Miami, whether he was there on vacation or attending the Miami Book Fair International, always served as an invigorating tonic for him. Geographically and professionally, he was in his element. He spoke on a gay and lesbian publishing panel organized by the Publishing Triangle, went to some of the best parties, and finally was awarded a Lammy for *A Member of the Family*. (*Flesh and the Word* had also received a nomination that year.)

Again I was the busy reporter; but after I had gathered comments from other winners on hand for my *Show Daily* report on the Lammies, I joined John and a small party downstairs in the hotel's bar. He was beaming, and yes, he looked terrific in the dapper outfit he told me he had bought during his "ABA shopping." Indeed, that night he radiated the charm of a man who has found his rightful place in the world. And when I congratulated him on his Lammy, he exclaimed, "It's about time I got one!"

The Miami Beach ABA was the last time I saw John. He died the next spring, just over a month before the Los Angeles ABA, thus, for me, casting a pall over the annual convention. But others felt a deep loss, too; and when Michael Denneny completed his eloquent tribute to John at the Lammies, the banquet hall's capacity audience of over 350 of my late friend's fellow writers, publishing and bookseller associates, and readers—the community to which he had devoted his life—rose in a standing ovation, a tribute of their own to a departed comrade.

But I didn't see any tears. Even in my sadness, I stoically kept the dry-eyed objectivity of a reporter. Until, that is, I got back to my hotel room to write my report in order to make an early-morning deadline. When I began threading my notes together, the delayed impact of the evening's emotion broke down my resolve, and my tear ducts opened. Oh, God, I thought, not now, you sappy queer. Cry on your own time; you've got a job to do. And somehow, even through the tears I had to keep brushing away to see the laptop's keyboard and screen, I got the piece composed and ready for the printer with a few hours left for sleep before it was due. When the front-page story ran, John got an ABA headline. I think he would have been pleased.

PRESTON

Andrew Holleran

Preston.

That's how he signed his letters: not John, or John Preston—just "Preston." It went, somehow with the author of *Mr. Benson*—his famous fictional slavemaster with the apartment on lower Fifth Avenue—though I don't think John ever wanted to be confused with that. He was just as fond of another character he created—*Franny, the Queen of Province-town*—and was writing her a sequel when he died.

His letters are scattered through my house in brown grocery bags filled with people's correspondence I plan to throw out and can't. John's letters were particularly good—a pen pal's dream—crisply written, entertaining, always filled with dish. I suspect Preston was proud of his amazing connectedness; he wrote a column on publishing for the *Lambda Book Report,* but that contained only a fraction of what he knew—the personal, unprintable dish culled from lunches with editors and scenes in hotel rooms (John's favorite venue). It was a challenge to tell him something about a gay writer or gay publishing story that he didn't know already, in much more detail. After editing the *Advocate,* living in San Francisco, Los Angeles, and New York, he left Manhattan for Portland, Maine, about a decade ago, to create what amounted to—with a fax machine, a word processor, and his incredible energy—a one-man publishing house from which he turned out some of his thirty books.

Preston loved publishing—both the writing and the marketing, the prose and the publicity. Lunch with an editor was one version of his idea of heaven. "There are serious reasons why we authors want to be lunched," he wrote to *Publishers Weekly* in a mock vein in 1990, after an article appeared suggesting that publishers save money on author's lunches and spend it on advertising instead. "We are, we know deep down inside, just the suppliers of product to many publishing people. But an editor—that instrument of the real powers that be—is able to convince us otherwise over stylishly cooked meals in loud Manhattan restaurants." John loved every cup of tea, every scone at the Stanhope, every *crème brûlée* at the Ritz. Some writers shrink from playing the role; not John. The man who was once a hustler himself, who supplied stories to *Advocate Men* on occasion, and was republishing his early porn novels for Badboy Books, creating the *Flesh and the Word* series, and working on a memoir called *My Life as a Pornographer,* was not only "respectable," but coming into his own—since one of Preston's outstanding qualities was his lack of shame about his sexual identity. Not only was he the openly gay author who wrote unapologetically about sex, he was an openly gay man with AIDS, who helped AIDS organizations in Maine and spoke and wrote frequently on these subjects. By 1990, it had all sort of snowballed, and the author of *Mr. Benson* was now a requested authority on coming out, safe sex, homophobia, invited to speak on college campuses—a role he saw in all its ironies. A 1990 letter said:

I'm having sexual flights over a speaking engagement I'm doing at the University of Maine next week. I had once met the kid who's organized everything. I thought he was cute, cuter than most gay-lib organizers, but he seemed a bit baggy somehow, not dressed for sex, with unruly hair. He didn't strike me as much. He's obviously in the depths of hero worship—having read another of my books every time I talk to him. In conversation last week he let drop that he's on the swim team. My image of him totally changed at that moment, and I could see him only as a nineteen-year-old with shaved legs in a Speedo.

Then it came out that there's a big gay-rights thing going on—a kid in ROTC came out and challenged their antigay policy on campus. He's going to speak with me now—this is all part of National Coming-Out Day—and I just saw his picture in uniform. Oh, my dear...

I'm going to spend two days on a university campus with these two young things. One of the things I'm going to do, in addition to speaking on the one night, is meet with the athletic coaching staff. Seems a swimmer came out and got harassed, and so they want to deal with homophobia in the field house—with me. How times change.

Indeed: "I actually had to realize that Sex God Ernie is even more attractive than I thought," he wrote after an AIDS fund-raiser in a neighbor's apartment, "—you know, the kind of guy who has perfect skin, a wonderful smile, so forth. Alas, I'm pretty sure I'm just too old for him. All those guys are taking to me like an uncle. It's a good thing I'm into that."

On aging in general, he was quite helpful:

You were in *such* a mess when you wrote last. It is the time of age for us to be questioning all our decisions—has this been worth it? Why didn't I set out to social climb? Etc., etc. I don't mean to discredit your angst, but it just seems, well, appropriate for this time in life. As is a faint hope in hair-loss creams. Dear, I hardly have any hair left! I'm a fine one to ask. But you assumed correctly when you went from my judgments about dying to conjecture that I wouldn't be supportive about hair restoratives. Do it gracefully, age gracefully! I'll let you know how it's done as soon as I figure it out myself.

It seemed to me he had—happy in his work, with a new puppy, his incredible network of friends, his book projects (anthologies like *Personal Dispatches: Writers Confront AIDS*; *The Big Gay Book*; *Hometowns: Gay Men Write About Where They Belong*), the reissue of *Mr. Benson* and his earlier porn novels by Badboy Books, and the young men whose friendship, whose presence, was an important part of his domestic happiness, and the domestic happiness itself: "Raw, harsh weather. It's the kind of day to stay in the house and read and respond to letters while a football game plays in the background. The only real warmth is turning my chair around to the set to see the naked tummies of all those muscular young men. Sometimes I am so easily pleased."

On What Really Pleased Him:

New York. It was quite amazing. I flew in on Thursday just in time for the Knopf party. Arrived with Anne Rice, Robert, and other pseudo-luminaries at the New York Public Library, the entrance redone with canopies and all, lights flashing into the sky, à la Hollywood openings. Everyone in the publishing world was there. The heads of all the companies, all the famous editors. There were very few writers, but those who were in attendance!!! I stopped processing when I realized that with Anne Rice on my arm, Toni

Morrison, John Updike, and Eudora Welty were all within five feet of me. I couldn't handle anything more than that.

On What Really, Really Pleased Him:

Robert and I left and we went to our hotel, the Stanhope. We'd only been there for tea before—the best tea in New York, if you didn't know—but Anne Rice said it was also the best hotel room in the city, if a little pricey. It was very pricey. The room, for two nights, cost the equivalent of two months' rent for my apartment, by the time we had a few little things from room service. But it was spectacular. Really. The Ritz in Naples is going to have a hard time matching all of this.

On How at His Age He Was Still Able to Get a Paramour to Pay for All of It:

Well, I pretty much demand it, I'm afraid, all part of the Chinese courtesan role. 'You mean you want me to stay at a Holiday Inn?' I can say that line with a certain caustic sound that demolishes him. I also so much enjoy extravagance that I don't have to pay for that I gush with honest appreciation when it's given. I think it's all training, to tell the truth…. I only raise an eyebrow and ask, 'Why are we staying someplace like that when there's a Ritz in town?'

Except Ralph Lauren Underwear:

Saturday R. and I went to walking and shopping. Went to the new Bergdorf Goodman for Men. You must have heard about it. Too much for words. You know that I collect underwear from various places

I've been. I went to pick up a pair here until R. saw
the price tag: $70. *For a single pair of knock-off Jockey
shorts?!?!* Can you believe it? I'm too much a New
Englander for all of that kind of thing.

Which was very true. "I have never been able to read
Firbank," he wrote in another letter. "I don't get him, at all. I
think I'm too working-class New England, and too happy
with that, to get into his preciousness. I have especially never
understood how and why he's so important to so many
other gay men, especially writers. Enlighten me!"

"Tennessee (such lovely exposed stomachs) and Notre
Dame are battling it out in the background. I have to go
and watch more carefully."

Occasionally, the fabled past that preceded the Chinese
courtesan, the past he left behind to return to New England—
the past that gave rise, perhaps, to *Mr. Benson*—was referred
to; but very seldom:

When I left New York ten years ago, I had a strange
relationship with two German youths. Very attractive, one an artist, the other an intellectual. They
were best friends. I slept with one of them regularly
and then, just as I was leaving for Maine, had a
remarkable SM experience with the other, which
caused some distress, because of their friendship.
Then, after I'd left, I published some pictures of them
in *Mandate,* and the bastards sued the magazine,
which came after me for the money! It was a remarkable example of bad communication and sharp
tempers. We wrote cross letters to one another, and
then dropped all communication. Suddenly, out of
the blue, I have a letter from Amsterdam from one of
them, saying he'd be visiting the other, who still lives
in Manhattan, Thanksgiving weekend. We'll have a
reunion! I don't want to see my old boyfriend, but I'd
love to tie up his friend again!

But even this was not the original Preston, I realized; I got a glimpse of that only once, when I asked him in a letter about the best sex he'd ever had: "My most memorable sexual experience—need I tell how memorable that must have been, given the competition?—was on Race Point Beach in Provincetown," he wrote back.

It was windy, brilliantly clear, wonderfully Cape Cod. I was with a basketball player from St. Joseph's College here in Maine, I was just out of college myself. We got naked and used our heavy coats for blankets, mine on the sand, his over us, and it was utterly majestic. I knew at the time, and told myself so, that this was major. It was one of those times that's so beautiful one knows it's going to be a companion in one's old age, even as it's happening. His body was one of the most wonderful I've ever had, hard, sharply defined belly, long, sleek legs, a butt more firm that most other men's biceps, all of those pornographic images pertain. *All of them!* I've never repeated that, really, the few blowjobs I've given/gotten on a dark beach after a bar closed seemed so sleazy in comparison. There was no comparison.

A scene that finds its philosophy in a sentence in another letter, prompted by some problem I'd asked his advice on: "Life is short and you should be taking advantage of its gifts when they occur."

That's what John did, actually—took advantage of its gifts when they occurred. They included good hotels, dinners, Miami Beach, publishing and all its gossip, book tours, a youth who interviewed him and then asked if he could kneel in front of him and jerk off—permission was granted—friendship, family, work, travel, the Miami Book Fair, the ABA, his dog Vlad the Impaler, football players' stomachs, the vacuum cleaner, BarcaLounger, the laptop computer a wealthy friend gave him, his protégés, the red silk boxer shorts he sent one of them, working-class New England men, the egg he ate after coming out of a thirty-six-hour sleep his doctors did not think he would waken from, the cigarette he smoked with a friend the last day of his life, his creation of Preston, his career. He once said to me, during a discussion of outing, that his dream was of a day when being homosexual wouldn't make any difference—that is, would be a neutral fact. He worked a great deal toward making this true. He was very clear about his values, and could give you his analysis of any moral dilemma. And yet, though a New Englander—if that cliché has any validity—he was less puritanical than anyone I knew. His last book, the result of a lecture he delivered at Harvard, was *My Life as a Pornographer*; I sent him clippings that mentioned it even as he lay dying in Portland. Nobody more than John would have enjoyed his posthumous mentions: his obituary in *Time* magazine, the longer one in the *New York Times,* or the space Anne Rice bought in that paper for her own words on what he had accomplished. It seems especially odd that this piece in *Christopher Street* will not be something he can read, or that never again will a letter, or a big manila envelope, be in the mailbox with that magical return address: Box 5314, Portland, Maine 04101.

SEX FOR JOHN

Joan Nestle

In the back of a new index to gay and lesbian literature, there is a listing of writers under the subject of pornography. Out of the over 200 writers indexed, only five of us made this list: Pat Califia, b.1954; Andrea Dworkin, b.1954; Joan Nestle, b.1940; John Preston, b.1945; and Algernon Swinburne, 1837–1909. Indexes, like life, make strange bedfellows.

This writing about the queer body, this revealing of open thighs and scratched backs, this wet, hard use of language is not always an easy thing to do. This mapping of where hands push in, of where mouths suck out, this capturing of sex sound, of murmurs and moans, of shouts and cries, of yes and more and now and now and please don't stop is not always welcomed in this world. And because the heart follows the mouth and the hand, when I am on knees before my lover, cupping her ass with my spread fingers, pushing her forward into my mouth, my breasts swelling with the weight of all her wonder, I am always surprised by the depth of anger awaiting the public description. But something pushes at me to keep finding words for the bend of the back, the thrust of the fist, the woman's cock in a woman's mouth, the taste of the cunt, the breast covered with the wetness of want, legs spread so far apart that countries could enter.

And so I wrote of these things, as a fem woman, as a woman who has lain on her back and pushed at her lover's hand for more, who has helped buckle the leather straps of her lover's harness so desire could shape the air. John read my words. From long distances over years, he kept a lookout for the assaults; postcards would arrive after some public battle, just a sentence from one pornographer to another. "Be strong, my friend," he said. Later, when we spent more time together, I learned as he spoke in his raspy, tired voice that he, too, was always saying "thank you, thank you" to the middle-aged salesman who had taken a young man to his hotel room one night, and after the stroking and sucking, as their bodies cooled down, had demanded from him the promise: Never betray your own voice, your own working-class New England cock-loving voice.

It is not easy to open the body to words, to make a life of sex writing. Comrades are needed, friends who understand both the bravado and the yearning, friends who know that even if all your skill is poured into the portrait of the ass raised for entry, you will never be called a writer. Preston, as he signed his letters, stood so tall, to me he was so gallant. He knew that a woman writing about sex was different from a man, but he always wanted more, more challenges to the silences imposed on the body.

My dear pornographer, we had planned so much together, collaborations of erotic wanderings anchored fiercely in clear, direct, visible language. Now you have traveled ahead, your words of comfort pieces of a treasure. When once again the body calls for its own language, for its own image of desire, I will write sex for John.

JOHN PRESTON, UNDERWEAR, AND OTHER LEGACIES

Michael Lowenthal

"*I* am wearing a black *slip* while I'm writing this."

That's how John Preston begins his essay "Underwear as Pornography." He describes the French-style "bikini brief" that cupped his groin as he typed the line, and the circumstances of his introduction to that style of apparel by his literary mentor Sam Steward, a.k.a. Phil Andros, the gay porn pioneer. Preston wears the *slip* in tribute to Steward, he writes, because Steward was "the first to alert me to the erotic possibilities of men's underwear."

These were things that were of utmost importance to John: underwear, pornography, literature, mentoring. And so, then, let me begin again with my own homage.

I am wearing black Calvin Klein boxer briefs while I'm writing this.

I am wearing them in tribute to John Preston, who was the first to alert me to the erotic possibilities of men's underwear—and so much more about a writer's life.

These boxer briefs are one of the two-dozen pairs of designer underwear that arrived in a large UPS package on my porch about a year ago. John describes the occasion from his point of view at the end of the underwear essay: "Michael sent me a first-person story where the narrator was wearing Sears briefs. I was *appalled* that this suggested that he himself was wearing the same thing. I confronted him with my concerns. They were true." That week John made the rounds of the malls and factory outlets in southern Maine, shopping until he had assembled a smorgasbord of stylish underwear to send me. He writes with professorial assurance, "introducing [Michael] to the wonders of underwear as a pornographic instrument is one of the most important things I could do for him."

When I received the package of underwear from John, I knew he would eventually be writing about it. John wrote about *everything*. The tired cliché—"his writing was his life, and his life was his writing"—is in fact an accurate description of John, more in a logistical sense than a philosophical one. You could never be sure if John did something for its own sake and then happened to write about it, or if he contrived an event or encounter specifically *in order* to write about it.

I have a hunch that the underwear ploy conformed to the latter situation. John saw a great ending to his essay, and to be able to write about it in a nonfiction book, he had to actually go out and spend the couple of hundred dollars on jockstraps and bikinis and briefs.

I had never spent more than six dollars on a package of four Jockey shorts, so I was horrified by the expense of the present. "It's all a tax write-off," John reassured me, his standard line whenever he took me to restaurants more expensive than he could afford, when our daily phone conversations ran past an hour, when he sent me silk shirts for my birthday. (Never mind that when you don't pay taxes, it's hard to deduct anything against them. But that's another story.)

John felt justified in writing off any expense related to our relationship because we were more than just friends. I was his project, his self-conscious literary endeavor.

This all started one day when John called me at the office. We had been friends for a while, talking frequently on the phone, exchanging occasional letters. John had accepted an essay of mine for one of his anthologies and had read some of my stories. We had met in person two or three times at conferences and gay-pride events.

After the usual chatter, his voice turned more serious, hesitant. He told me he'd like to propose an idea. He hoped I didn't think it was silly. "What is it, John?" I asked. "I'd like to be your mentor," he said finally. "And you'd be my protégé"—as if these roles were as clear-cut and conventional as agent and author, or doctor and patient. John continued, "It would be my job to give you as much attention as you need, to read anything you send me, to help you make contacts in the publishing world. Do you think you'd be interested?"

Interested?! I could barely keep from screaming and sprinting down the hall. It was any young writer's dream come true. Looking back, I am amazed how tentative John was. This avowed egomaniac, this man who took himself and his writing more seriously than any other I've known, seemed suddenly to be a shy, nervous schoolboy. It was one of the only moments in the time I knew John, including during his final weeks, when I saw him emotionally vulnerable.

I signed on to the project immediately. There would be three of us, John told me. The others were Michael Rowe in Toronto and Owen Keehnen in Chicago. We were three young writers whom he admired, each of us needing a different kind of guidance.

The only warning John gave me was that he would probably write about us and about the experience. This was an important experiment for him, and he wanted to be able to reflect on the results in print.

"No problem," I said, picturing my name in lights. "Heck, I might even write about you."

John did write about me a few times, usually identifying me as "Michael Lowenthal, a promising young writer." There's the "Underwear as Pornography" piece, brief mentions in a few other essays and interviews, a *Lambda Book Report* column about the mentoring project. I will admit that every time I saw my name in print I felt giddy, honored. Each time he mentioned me as a "writer," I believed more and more that maybe I was one. There's nothing like having somebody else take you seriously to make you feel the same way about yourself.

I wrote about John only once while he was alive. It was an article about an AIDS "simulation" I participated in at the local medical school, and I contrasted the experience of pretending to be sick with the stark reality of John's actual illness. Somehow it seemed inappropriate to mention him; I worried that I was exploiting his sickness. I named him only as "my friend John," and only those who know me knew who I was referring to.

When the article came out, John complimented me on the piece and then asked, with a mixture of playfulness and honest hurt in his voice, why I hadn't named him outright. I think he worried that I hadn't absorbed the lessons he was trying so desperately to instill in me before he died. Among the ones relevant in this particular case: (1) never hesitate to drop the biggest name you can in any given situation; (2) every mention in print (even if it's about your impending death from AIDS) is free publicity; (3) always acknowledge your friends.

I still have my own mixed feelings about the article. As a piece of personal essay writing, I'm confident that it's crafted thoughtfully. I think the references to John are what really make the piece. But the essay is tinged with sadness, with all the feelings of powerlessness and desperation I felt as John became more and more ill. In the essay, I wrote that since his HIV diagnosis six years earlier, John had "been holding up pretty well. But in recent weeks he had been feeling fatigued, he'd been running fevers, his cough had worsened." In October, when I wrote those words, they were entirely accurate. John was just a bit under the weather. He and his doctor thought it might just be a flu. The essay's last line is "My friend John sat in his apartment, waiting for the doctor to call."

In early January, on the day I finished revising the article for publication, John called me. He had just been to Boston to see his doctor. His first words were, "Well, honey. This is it." His T-cell count had plummeted to sixty-eight. His six-foot-plus frame was down to 159 pounds. He knew this was the beginning of the end.

By mid-February, when the article finally appeared in print, John's counts had dropped even lower. He had been diagnosed with M.A.I., an incurable opportunistic infection. He'd had two blood transfusions. He was so weak that even with the new laptop computer he'd acquired, with the hope of writing in bed or on the couch, he couldn't even type a business letter.

The day after the article hit the newsstands, John was admitted to Maine Medical Center. He would stay in the hospital for three weeks, during which time he would, among other things, have a feeding tube cut into his abdomen and be diagnosed with a malignant lymphoma in his stomach. A month and a half later, and he was dead.

John died four weeks ago yesterday. Yesterday I received a check in payment for my article because it is being reprinted this summer in another magazine. It's strange but perhaps appropriate that while John's remains are in a pewter urn on his friend Tom's mantel, in the essay he will forever be "waiting for the doctor to call."

More than anybody I know, John believed in the power of words and books to grant immortality. In his last few weeks he was consumed with arranging for his books-in-process to be completed, and for a new edition of *Franny, the Queen of Provincetown* to be contracted. One of his final lucid days was spent with a woman from the special collections department of the Brown University library, discussing in detail the archiving of his papers and correspondence. As he was dying, he asked that the cover mock-up for his forthcoming anthology *Sister and Brother* be framed and placed where he could see it from his bed.

John was too proud to ask me to write about him, or even to discuss this possibility beyond his single comment when my article appeared. But I know that he wanted me to. As much as it was a way of creating material for himself, John's mentoring project was a means of giving us protégés material. He knew that we would be able to spin endless yarns about "when the literary giant John Preston became my mentor." Formalizing his relationships with three young writers was like taking out an insurance policy for his memory.

In the days immediately after his death, a number of magazines and newspapers asked me to write about John. I declined, using the excuse that the experience was still too close, too painful for me to get down on paper. There was a good deal of truth to that, but I was also terrified of examining just how much influence John has had on me. How did a nice Jewish boy suddenly become a part-time pornographer? Has John given me an inflated sense of my writing that I don't deserve? Does my participation in this "old-boy network" make people resent me?

Whatever misgivings I might have, I know that John's friendship has had an inescapable and permanent effect on my writing and on my life. Every time I sit at the computer, I hear his encouraging voice.

I suppose I owe John the tribute of writing about him, but it doesn't feel like a burdensome debt. I want to pay tribute to him and to his example. I look forward to years of telling people about our friendship.

As I prepared to write this, the first of what I'm sure will be many stories about John, I knew instantly that I had to don a pair of the underwear he gave me. I went upstairs, showered and shaved, and then tugged on the snug cotton briefs. Not that I actually find the underwear conducive to writing, despite John's confidence that I would. (The underwear has come in very handy this past year, spicing up many nights with my lover Chris, but it has not had an appreciable effect on my literary output.)

No, I put on the Calvin Klein boxer briefs because I knew it would make a good opening for this essay. I knew I could use them to create a literary moment. And if John Preston taught me any lesson, it's that everything—*everything* must be done with the writing in mind.

WHY YOU SHOULD NEVER WRITE LETTERS

Scott O'Hara

Dear Scott:

Howard Cruse passed on your address to me. As you can see by the enclosed, I'm putting together the 1988 Gay Engagement Calendar. Howard correctly assumed I'd be interested in including people involved in what I'll call "vernacular" entertainment…

And that was my first contact with Preston. Yes the calendar eventually happened (in 1989); of the half-dozen other collaborations we talked about, most came to fruition. Mostly, though, we wrote letters, sent faxes, and played an elaborate game of hide and seek all around the country. "I'm going to Seattle for Living in Leather—will you be there?" "Nope—but I'll be in Miami the following week for ABA…" "How about Mr. Drummer…?" "The Black Party in NYC?" and so forth. And my occasional departures from the country just forced him, as he put it, to "find someone else to harass."

Dear Spunky:

Thanks for the postcard. I just discovered something I found amusing: You and my parents were both in Australia at the same time. I'm not quite sure how I would have arranged a meeting, but it could have been interesting…. Those weren't nude beaches you went to, were they? I mean, you didn't compromise your tan-line did you? There is nothing quite so horrible as this drive toward naturism in your California gay world. Depriving all of us tops of those big white targets is utterly deviant behavior….

And then a month later:

Dear Spunky:

You deserve severe punishment for not calling the old man with your phone number when he asked you to.

(I love being able to give out lines like that.)

I've done something which I hope is all right. Forum *magazine had gotten a hold of me to help them compile a "Best and Worst of Sex" piece. One thing they needed was a titlist for the "Best Male Stripper." You won. No one else in the world has to know it was by default. They had to have a picture right away. I've given them one of the self-portraits that you'd sent for the calendar. I hope that's okay. If it's not, call me* immediately.

You know, you may end up owing me a great deal, Spunk. We'll have to think about the more interesting ways you could show your appreciation.

True. I ended up owing that man much of my eventual career. And, considering that I spent a total of only about ten hours with him, over the seven years of our acquaintance, he had a remarkable effect on me and my writing. You might even call him "a manipulative old bastard"—if you were sufficiently sacrilegious.

July 10th, '87: on the train from San Francisco to Seattle, I wrote a letter proposing that Preston write a script for a serious, well produced, well-acted porno flick—starring (but modestly) Scott O'Hara. I ended my letter by teasing him:

"I've been out at Land's End quite a bit lately, and of course I always forget to take my suit—I really need to be punished, I suspect, for disobeying your express desires— but hey, red is probably even better than white, what?

disrespectfully,

Scott."

Dear Spunky:

You have the nerve to tell me you're not wearing a bathing suit while you sun and then turn around and ask me if I'd write a screenplay for you?

That goes beyond gall!

And no, red ass isn't as good as a white one unless I've made it red!

(You know, this game of baiting the sadist has gotten many a boy into trouble; you should watch your step in this little dance you're trying to pull off. You know the old adage: Watch out what you ask for; your request might be fulfilled.)

Three days later:

Dear Spunky:

God, am I pissed at you!

So, what happened...

The day I wrote you that last letter expressing some interest in the idea of a porn film script, I got another letter from my Hollywood friend. Enclosed was a copy of his latest feature-film screenplay. So I sat down and read his script. I'd never actually studied one before, though I'd seen them. "Oh," I thought to myself, "this is how they do it."...

Two days later I have a complete 60-page shooting script for a 90-minute fuck film. I mean complete. *Up to and including camera angles....*

Why am I pissed then? Because the last thing in the world I should have done with the last two days is write a porn script. I have a fucking book *due in August, and I haven't even begun it! All I need, to miss another deadline.*

The next year was spent in negotiations: trying to find a director, trying to find stars. The screenplay—called *The Network*—was a serious SM tale, as you might expect, and couldn't be cast with your usual porn-puppies—even if we'd been able to find some who could act. Of course, John had written a large part of the screenplay to accommodate my expressed desire to have my tits repierced on film (though he conceded that the piercing "could be changed to you getting beaten, but it would have to be a really, really *hot* beating [chortle, chortle]). What a sweetie. Who's the manipulator here, who the puppet? Dunno. I thought we worked well together. He even talked about doing that piercing himself…but then got cold feet. He spent beaucoup pages explaining to me that he was doing "respectable" lecturing at universities around the country, and couldn't be seen onscreen in a porn flick—it would *ruin* his credibility. It was one subject that would reliably get a rise out of him. I don't think he liked being "in the closet" even to that small degree.

I realize that I sign my letters "Preston," but wonder what your use of that name—without even so much as a passing "Mr." on the envelope—is supposed to signify? Is this creeping disrespect? A futile attempt to become a peer? An invitation to a sadistic response? You boys certainly do keep me on my toes…

Just took a look at your photos in Angles *again. You know, you're really going to have to work on that tummy if you're going to be in* my *movie.*

" 'Dear John—'
And that is precisely what the singular surname was designed to avoid. As well as indicating, perhaps, to receptive readers, that I don't much care what your fantasy of me is. If your fantasy has a perfect stomach, your decrepit old imagination may have to come up with a new fantasy

object. My stomach has never abused me; I'm not about
to start abusing it."

Oh, well—what family doesn't have its ups and downs?

It's a real pity, really, that he never got around to making
my butt red personally. No I don't enjoy being beaten; I've
been with men who enjoyed spanking/whipping/caning,
and I've endured it, and I've never found the pleasure in it
that others do. Nor do I find it entertaining when the
performers in a Falcon film engage in a little spanking as
part of a "rape" scene. They're so obviously acting, it isn't
even funny—much less erotic. But watching two men who I
know for a fact both get turned on by spanking? Even if
they're not cute and hunky like Falcon models? Now, *that*
gets me hot. Takes my breath away. And I would've turned
up my butt for John any day because I believe that his libido
was such that my essential disinterest in being spanked
would have been pure aphrodisiac to him; and because,
despite my deliberate disrespect, I venerated his every vowel.
The consonants were good, too.

How quickly I can go through seven years of correspondence: barely an afternoon's reading. His letters, as you
might expect, are among the best I've ever gotten, and of
course he spurred me to create some extraordinary prose
myself. In July 1990, in my first letter after moving to
Wisconsin, I told him that I was insisting on "an environ-
ment more conducive to my long-term survival… I continue
to maintain that I am not sick, that the purple blotches here
and there are *friendly* purple blotches, that I am as well as I
have ever been. Because that's the way I feel, and because I
abhor the popular trend toward prostration on the altar of
Medicine…"

Dear Scott:

*But of course, darling, you never told me you ever had any
purple spots, either friendly or otherwise. But then have I ever
told you that I have all kinds of viruses in my mouth, my own*

little symptoms from HIV that are, I suppose, in the prison of medical jargon, my tickets to full-bloom AIDS? Such are the times we live in…. Enough of all this bliss. Write more about your Wisconsin aerie and the life you're constructing for yourself. I don't need porn to entertain myself, and there need not be any erotic adventures. I like only honesty and inspection—ongoing values, aren't they?

My love…

About this time John started the *Flesh and the Word* series: anthologies of serious porn stories, published by a serious press. Did I have any recommendations? Yes, actually: Barry Lowe, Lance Lester, and Leigh Rutledge all ended up in Volume One, and I also submitted one of my essays—"Thinking Off"—while I was at it. To my amazement he accepted it. Whaddya know—my first appearance in hardcover. Yes, I did end up owing him quite a lot.

A year later, he proposed an anthology about the relationships between lesbians and gay men. Did I have any experience along those lines? Oh, dear (I wrote back): yes, of course, but are you ready? I queried him about just how PC he wanted submissions to be:

Dear Scott:

No, I didn't know that you had a lesbian sister who committed suicide and that you then married her lover. Dear, I think there's a book in there. You should write it….

And then four months later:

Are you going to be at OutWrite in Boston next month? We're going to have a party for Flesh and the Word *and I have to find more boys willing to pass hors d'oeuvres while wearing Jockey shorts.*

Yes, I went. How could I pass up an invitation like that? Tom and I were the only ones in Jockey shorts, however; I tried to get the other "boy" present (who had photographed John for the dust jacket of one of his other books) to strip down, to no avail.

The following October, I was attending OutWrite as a publisher/editor (and, ironically, John's publisher/editor—we'd run a Great Editorial of his in the Spring issue of *Steam*); *Flesh and the Word 2* had just hit the stands, and the release was at The Ramrod. There was a camera crew, taping interviews with the writers in attendance; fortunately, there was also a buffet, since the schedule of events that day had left me without a free minute to have breakfast, lunch, or dinner. I hobbled back to the hotel around midnight, and of course it wasn't until considerably later that the spanking demos got underway. Spontaneously, I'm told. Guess I missed my best chance to be Entertainment for the Master.

One of my next projects will be a how-to-get published book for gay boys and girls...I get so professorial and paternal and give out so much advice, often unsolicited, I might as well find a way to earn some money from it.

Of the thousands of words that we exchanged in seven years (there's a lengthy novel in that correspondence, if only there were more conflict!), the most memorable to me is what he said when I was golly-gee-whizzing him about his expressed admiration for "Thinking Off": *You really shouldn't be so uptight about your writing. Where most people fuck up is trying to hard to* create *a style, and loosing sight of the content.* It amused me no end that, even while giving that famous paternal, pithy advice, he could still indulge in a casual typo.

WALKING WITH THE GHOST OF JOHN PRESTON

Michael Rowe

On the day after John Preston's memorial service at St. Luke's Cathedral in Portland, Maine, I took a walk down Congress Street through the driving rain and tried to bring him back to life for a few hours by seeing his adopted hometown as he might have seen it if he had been walking with me. The last time I saw him was in October 1993, at the OutWrite gay and lesbian writers' conference in Boston, perhaps John's last blazing moment of pure star power before his illness finally foreclosed on his writing and his life. More than once in the months after he became unable to communicate, I wondered how much this last dazzling turn in the public eye had cost him. He had pneumonia that weekend, but you wouldn't have necessarily guessed how ill he really was.

I photographed John with Joan Nestle on Boston Common that weekend, for the dust jacket of *Sister and Brother*. The night before our session, after the launch party for *Flesh and the Word 2,* John went on a bit of a spree. The next morning, ironically, the puffiness that accompanies a night of drinking actually worked to our advantage, filling out his face for the photograph in way that was most attractive. My last mental image of him is the one I saw through the lens of my Nikon, wreathed in gold and yellow. Behind him, a brilliant autumn sky. The undisputed star of the OutWrite conference, the gray eminence receiving his adoring public as he sipped his cocktail in the lobby of the Park Plaza Hotel.

The image was at odds with the one I was trying to conjure, John walking with me through these wet Portland streets, on this slate-gray morning in the rain.

The day of the service had been as flawless as an L. L. Bean catalog cover. The sky was as clear and blue as ice, the warm ocean breeze drifting across Casco Bay carried a lick of salt. Through the eyes of a visitor from Canada, the town appeared to gleam with white-clapboard red-bricked perfection. From the window of my suite at the Holiday Inn on Spring Street, Portland looked the way John described it in *Hometowns*: "the archetypical Yankee city."

John had always been so proud of his New England roots. It seemed as though he had orchestrated the entire scene for the people who had come to say good night: the Episcopal service for the dead, the incense, the high drama of ritual, the elegant reception following the service, and all that brilliant white sunlight pouring luxuriously through the floor-to-ceiling windows of the restaurant like liquid platinum.

And then, the next day, after his friends had gone home, it was as though he flipped the switch to "off," and the rain came. Oh, John. I see your hand in all of this. This is *so you.*

I met John in March 1992, at the first OutWrite conference I attended. I noted the event in my diary, although nothing on earth would make me forget anything as awful as that first handshake. I had been an avid reader of John Preston's work since I first encountered *I Once Had a*

Master in the old Glad Day bookstore in Toronto. The elegance of the prose spoke to my mind, and the razor-edged sexual imagery left me light-headed. I never missed a John Preston book publication. I would try to push his work on my friends, tell them, "You have to read this guy!" but something about the content would distress them, and they would hand the books back to me unread, watching me strangely for weeks afterward.

I approached him shyly at the preconference cocktail part. I chain-eat when I'm nervous, the same way other, slimmer people chain-smoke. I ate a piece of cheese on a cracker, and swallowed it before I went to speak with the Great Man.

"Mr. Preston," I said. "It's such a pleasure to meet you. I'm a big fan of your work—"

At that exact moment, a renegade sliver of Brie, lodged undetected between my cheek and my gums, suddenly disengaged itself and slid out of my mouth and down the side of my face.

If the chandelier had chosen that instant to come crashing down from the center of the ceiling and crush me beneath its weight, sparks flying, people screaming, I could have made a good death of it. The thing with the cheese might have been forgotten by my hero, and my friends might have mourned the dazzling literary career that ended before it began, the moment the chandelier fell.

No such luck.

"Thank you very much," said John Preston, eyeing the cheese, my Brooks Brothers blazer, and my rep tie with equal distaste. His eyes had already glazed over. I died in that moment. I prayed he would forget me, and he did. Immediately.

That summer, after eight years as a magazine journalist, and on the cusp of turning thirty, I went to Harvard Summer School to take a summer program in creative writing. I needed to be away from my partner Brian and our home in Milton, Ontario, while I cleared my head and decided if "being a writer" was what I really wanted to do. I moved into Adams House with my word processor, bought a telephone, and went to a barber in Cambridge who gave me a military haircut. I spent my days writing and doing course work, my evenings exploring the bookstores and pubs of Cambridge, and my nights at The Ramrod. On the weekends, I visited friends on Martha's Vineyard and in Amesbury. I grew very tanned.

Before I left Milton, I had convinced Dayne Ogilvie, the editor of *Xtra!,* Toronto's gay and lesbian magazine, to assign me a profile of John Preston. My intention was to travel from Boston to his home in Maine and interview him in his natural habitat—beard him in his lair, as it were. Mercifully, when we spoke on the phone, he didn't remember me at all (not that I did anything to remind him).

John met me on the steps of his apartment, and we went inside and talked for a while before going to lunch, which he subsequently insisted on paying for. Back at his apartment, we consumed two or three bottles of wine and talked through three cassette tapes about *everything*. I missed my bus, and we went out for dinner. I left Portland on the last bus to Boston, loaded down with paperback copies of his work, which had just been rereleased by Badboy (a fact that delighted him), and his address.

"Can I write to you?" I had asked him.

"If you don't," he said, "I'll be very angry."

I shivered, not entirely from fear. But I smiled all the way back to Cambridge, and the books kept me up late. The interview, which I count as one of the best I've ever done, made me indisputably sure of one thing: I *did* want to be a writer.

The following weekend, I won a wrestling contest at The Ramrod. I wrote him and told him of my victory, feeling quite gladiatorial.

"I *adored* the image of you wrestling at The Ramrod,"

he drawled in his letter, which I received almost immediately. "And you won! Such a good boy."

This began a correspondence with him which continued after I left Cambridge and returned home to Milton. We exchanged letters regularly. His attention made me feel, somehow, important. His letters were a warm arm around my shoulder when, on my birthday, I was sucker-punched by a handwritten rejection letter of untrammeled nastiness from the *Harvard Review*. ("Those people exist to publish their friends because no one else will publish them," John told me.)

It was a relationship that no one else understood, no matter how much I tried to explain it. I don't think I understood it myself. All I knew was that there was something about John which addressed something in me that only he was able to touch. Whatever it was, I stretched toward it as a plant stretches toward the sun after the rain.

I learned how to listen for the variegated timbres and cadences of his speech whenever I read his nonfiction. Another voice altogether took over in his fiction, so I read and reread his essays and introductions. When he was slow to respond to my letters, I wrote to him and called him on it. John once said that an SM top could tie up an SM bottom and leave him tied up for an hour. The bottom would be fantasizing the entire time. The top would be reading the *New York Times*. John was, by his own admission, all top. He wrote back that although he was known for his "long letters," he had just been "teasing" me by not writing. "The SM impulse is so strong in some people," he said by way of explanation. "Young people are such fun to tease."

John loved the idea of "young people."

"You young people have no idea about what life was like back then," he scolded in our interview. Or, on another occasion, when letters I had promised him failed to materialize, he sighed, "Young people are so unpredictable." But he loved saying it; and, at thirty, I wasn't going to look the proverbial gift horse in the mouth.

In November he sent me galleys of *The Arena* and said that he was including me in the "admittedly long" list of dedicatees. For a week following that letter, I was impossible to be with.

On December 15, he telephoned me at home in Milton and asked me formally if he could "adopt" me as his literary protégé, along with two other young American writers, Michael Lowenthal and Owen Keehnen. His purpose, he said, was to introduce us (as part of a new generation of gay writers) to the world of book publishing. He wanted to guide my career and protect me while I developed the talents he saw in my work. I was—quite literally—speechless. When I recovered, I accepted. It was any writer's dream. For me, because it was John Preston, it became more than that.

Over the next few months, he read work I sent him, calling one story "a very good writing-class story" (which was as mean as John ever got). He mentioned the three of us in an interview in the *Gay and Lesbian Times of Maine*. He wrote about us in his "Preston On Publishing" column in the *Lambda Book Report*.

Together we worked on my essay for *Friends and Lovers*. The essay I was writing dealt with one of my deepest and most combustible relationships—the one I have with my friend Barney, my first lover (for lack of a better word), whom I had known in boarding school, and who has remained one of the three men I call my brothers. John patiently helped me excise the excess emotion from the essay, showing me where anger and love overtook rationality, both in the essay and in real life. (In fact, Barney and his various exploits became so much a part of the mythology of our conversations and letters that at one point John suggested that I write "The Tales of Barney" as my contribution to *Flesh and the Word 3*.)

And he gave us a fat-free education on the reality of writing and publishing, the likes of which we never would have received in CREA 101, or in the pages of *Writer's Digest*.

John loved the idea of being a "gay uncle," and he passed that sense of family down to me through his letters and telephone calls. I began to think of Owen Keehnen, in Chicago, and Michael Lowenthal, in New Hampshire, as cousins, of a sort. Although I thought nothing of it at the time, John mentioned in one letter how different the needs of his three protégés were turning out to be. Aside from the fact that Michael Lowenthal was a gifted short-story writer, and Owen and I were journalists, I came to suspect that the differences ran deeper than that.

Owen and Michael will doubtless write their own stories of what John meant to them. For my part, John became as much of a life-mentor to me as a writing-mentor. By the time he and I finally met, I had been a working journalist for nearly a decade, and I had won accolades for my work. What John gave me, in our relationship, was a context in which to merge my identities as a gay man and as a writer, moving past purely objective journalism and into issue-oriented gay journalism and creative nonfiction. But, deeper than that, we explored the issues of maleness: what it meant to be a man—and a gay man—in these uncertain decades.

John's celebration of his own advancing years opened a window on the dignity and power inherent in age. He relished his position as an elder. As part of a generation of gay men raised with the lurking fear that an inevitable loss of taut muscle tone and smooth skin heralded the loss of something far more significant than mere beauty, John's delight in his "curmudgeon" status intimated to me that the second half of a man's life could be more powerful— and indeed more erotic—than the first half. No topic was ever off-limits during our exchanges. Once, for instance, in response to questions that I had about SM and masculinity, he wrote and impressed upon me how important his sense of male identity was to him, and sent me a copy of his essay, "The Theater of Sexual Initiation," which would be subsequently republished in *My Life as a Pornographer.*

Censorship was anathema to John, and he suggested, only half in jest I'm sure, that when he went to testify on behalf of Vancouver's Little Sister's bookstore (from which several of his books had been seized by Canada Customs, the free world's spiritual heirs to the Nazi book-burners) some buddies and I should flank him in full leather.

My Canadian-ness was a source of endless mirth to John. He listened for me to say "eh?" or "oot and aboot" (out and about). But I was craftier than that.

"Can't I be a Yankee too, Uncle John?" I asked him plaintively one evening.

"No," he said crisply. "You have to be born that way." He paused, then said, not unkindly, "Well, maybe we can get someone to adopt you."

As the child of a Canadian father and an American-born mother, John's intensely Yankee identity spoke to some atavistic yearning in me for an American identity of my own, any trace of which had been completely sublimated by my proper British-inflected Canadian upbringing. (The joke about the cultural duality of American-Canadian children really *does* have a ring of truth to it: we can be loud and obnoxious one minute, and shocked and appalled by our own rudeness the next.) I admired John's islophilic New England sense of himself and his place in the world. I saw it in his prose, and in his letters to me. I admired his work ethic, and his ability to project a self-effacing nonchalance when, in fact, he loved attention. Most of all, though, I was spellbound by his unfailing generosity with time and advice when it must have been taxing for him to extend it. Quaint as it might sound, John Preston was a gentleman to his fingertips. If I've learned anything at all from him, I hope it's that.

I cannot honestly say that I was looking for a father figure in John Preston. But I can say that his views on older men initiating younger ones into their society struck a chord in me that was profound and primal.

Our communication began to slow down almost imperceptibly in mid–1993. At first, I assumed that he was just busy with his writing, and the duration of our phone calls was a measure of how much work he had to do. He wasn't as quick to respond to my letters, and when he did, they were short—no less witty and dry than they ever had been—but shorter. He was loath to indulge in self-pity, and when he brushed off his illness, I clutched his nonchalance and held on to it as though it were a life preserver. The thought of losing him (which I knew, intellectually, would happen far sooner than I was ready to have it happen) was more than I could bear. Every once in a while, he would scold me sharply for not working harder with my fiction writing. Instead of taking this as well-intentioned chivvying, I became paralyzed by the fear of ultimately disappointing him. Ironically, his assurances of his good health and state of mind exacerbated the problem: had he been healthy and happy (and I wanted him to be, so he had to be), the only valid reason for his silence could have been his displeasure.

When John asked me to photograph him with Joan Nestle at OutWrite 93, I took it as a grace note. When I saw him at the preconference cocktail party, I was relieved to see that he was looking well. He had a terrible cough, but he had lovely color. He introduced me to Michael Lowenthal, who was younger than I'd imagined. Michael had a beautiful smile and a warm manner that I took to immediately.

John gave the opening plenary address that first night. He spoke of his history, his writing, and the meaning of legacy. His legacy. Of taking his place in the time-honored pantheon of New England "bachelor uncles." My throat was full, listening to him. Selfishly, or perhaps because John prized his ability to speak directly to his audience, I took his words, and held them tightly. His voice was ravaged and raw by the end of the speech, but he finished it to a standing ovation. He had come home, and he knew it.

I saw little of him that weekend. His time was precious, and many people had a claim on it. On Sunday, after we had taken the photographs, and the OutWrite conference dispersed with the same odd sadness that marks the end of summer camp, we drove my friend Ron Oliver to the airport so that he could catch his flight home to Los Angeles.

John could barely talk. A less-obsessive personality than mine might have guessed that he was very ill; but he didn't *look* ill, and he insisted he *wasn't* ill, so I believed him, and suffered under his silence. I was convinced that my inability to produce the writing he demanded of me had been the final blow to our mentorship. Tonight, writing this, I am appalled by my myopia, but it seemed far less clear back then.

John's letters began to dwindle further, both in length and in frequency. By this time, he was blunt about how sick he actually was, and the dread of losing him, which I had been holding at bay, finally broke free. I was furious at myself when Joan Nestle told me that he had had pneumonia at OutWrite. The shame I felt for my fear of his displeasure overwhelmed me, and I had no place to hide. He had been trying to stay alive, trying to communicate with his people one last time. *Idiot!* I raged at myself. *Self-centered idiot! "Lovely color" indeed! Where the hell were your eyes?*

He managed a short note thanking me for the photos ("I think they're fab!") of him and Joan.

Then, in early 1994, the communication ceased altogether. I telephoned Michael Lowenthal in New Hampshire and asked him to keep me abreast of John's condition. I continued to write to John on a regular basis in the same way that you hold the hand of a dying person and whisper softly to them, on the off-chance that can they hear you. I wrote letters about practically nothing, relating the minutiae of my life, telling him things that I normally wouldn't even note in my journal. I knew what the silence meant, but I wrote anyway. I became obsessed with adding my voice and my love to the good love of friends which surrounded him around the clock.

Sensing my desperation, I think, Michael Lowenthal called and wrote to me about John on a regular basis, moving beyond his own grief to inject into my silence and darkness a note of such grace and pure human kindness that I was, and still am, humbled by it.

In March 1994, New England was paralyzed by a blinding snowstorm of historic proportions. I was staying with my big sister, Nancy Bowers, and her husband Jay, at their house in the woods of western Massachusetts. Wild turkeys flock at the edge of the forest near the house, and deer come into the yard early in the morning. The forest trails wind for miles, through the woods and into New Hampshire. Their house in Warwick is my ultimate refuge. I go there when I need to think, or heal.

The night of the storm, I fell asleep listening to the wind whipping fistfuls of snow at my window and tormenting the branches of the trees outside the house. I dreamed that John and I were driving along Duval Street, in Key West. He was tanned and strong, and he handled the wheel of the car as though he hadn't a care in the world.

"If only it could be different," I said to the dream-John. He reached over with his other arm, and squeezed my knee. Beneath the rosy-bronze skin, his forearm was well-muscled.

"It *is* different," said the dream-John, smiling at me. His famous ice-green eyes, the source of so much conjecture and anecdote, were warm and sparkling with life and humor.

I woke from that dream feeling the first peace I had felt in months.

On the morning John died, Michael called me at home and told me that it was over. I tried to tell the people around me what a light had gone out of the world, out of our literature, but they didn't really understand, even the ones who wanted to. I built a fire in the fireplace, pulled the shades, made myself a cup of tea, and read his essay on Portland from *Hometowns*. But for some reason, I couldn't hear his voice in the words this time.

I met Owen Keehnen for the first time, at the memorial service. We shared a room at the Holiday Inn. After the service and the reception following, John's friend Robert Riger generously chartered a boat for an evening tour of Casco Bay. We boarded the boat: Owen, me, Michael, Will Leber, Tom Hagerty, Tom's friend Mark, and Royal Fraser, a young ex-varsity swimmer who had become a good friend of John's, and wanted to become a writer himself.

The sun went down, and a cool wind came up across the water. The seascape took on the green-gray-blue tones for which Maine is justly famous. More than one of us remarked that the mood seemed festive. There was none of the funereal gloom that accompanies so many such occasions. More than one of us noted that John would have loved this: a boatload of young gay men experiencing the beauty of Portland at twilight from the water, thinking of him.

Robert took photographs inside the boat.

"Let's have one with just the protégés," said Robert, and we all leaned in, touching, and smiled while the flash exploded. I felt the strength in all those bodies, the life of them, and was warmed by it.

"The grieving mentettes," someone teased, and we all cracked up. The flash exploded again, recording, I hope, that laugh. The sunset faded from the sky, and the lights of Portland ran together in the black water of the harbor like paint. The boat docked, and we went dancing.

The next day, the rain came, and I started to walk. I walked the length of the town, running my fingers along the rough brick of the buildings as I passed them, hungry for texture. I sipped a cup of Red Zinger tea at a bookstore café, under a wall display of hardcover editions of *Flesh and the Word.* It was the same bookstore where, two years earlier, I sat and nervously assembled my notes for our interview, checking and rechecking the batteries in my tape recorder to make sure they were working. I had come full circle. In an hour, I would ride to Boston with Michael Lowenthal and Will Leber, and I would not likely ever set foot in Portland, Maine, again.

I walked with the ghost of John Preston because I carry him with me everywhere. But I didn't see him that morning, and I didn't hear him speak to me.

In June, I was in the Glad Day Bookstore on Yonge Street in Toronto. As is my custom, I checked both the *P* section and the Gay Men's Anthology section. I visit those sections at Glad Day the way other people—those people who are lucky enough to have them—visit loved ones' graves. In the *P* section was *Tales From the Dark Lord 2,* which I had not seen previously. Eagerly, I flipped to the back of the book, and found our 1992 interview. I would read it when I got home, I told myself.

In the Gay Men's Anthology section, I found a copy of *Personal Dispatches: Writers Confront AIDS,* the only book of John's that I had not read, and, in fact, had avoided studiously. I reached for it and opened the book to the introduction. The voice that filled my head was one I knew well, one I despaired of ever hearing again. Through streaming eyes, I read, and I listened.

"Two years ago," said the ghost of John Preston, "in 1986, a young bodybuilder came and asked whether he could pose for me. I had had some success as a physique photographer years ago when I lived in Manhattan...."

Good night, Dark Lord. Sleep well, Uncle John.

THAT PLACE CALLED PORNOGRAPHY

Wickie Stamps

John Preston attributed his evolution as a gay man to the reading of porn. He was also a storyteller who loved to tell hot, sweaty stories filled with dangerous men and dark desires. "Ed White might have the crowd from the *New York Review of Books,* but I was the star of *Drummer,*" John asserted in his last book, *My Life as a Pornographer.* He was right. Published as a book in 1983, *Mr. Benson* went on to cult status in the gay men's SM scene. Even *Penthouse* recognized this book as one of the ten best SM works ever published.

Despite a writing career that took him into the mainstream, Book-of-the-Month publishing, John always believed that his work as a pornographer—the label John chose for himself—not only kept him honest but was the "most important part of my whole career."

Most successful writers take their careers too seriously, but Preston always maintained a tongue-in-cheek attitude toward his success. When invited to speak at Harvard, John made sure to get his lecture published beforehand in the notorious gay-porn mag *Inches*. It was the first Harvard lecture to be given that honor, he told the audience.

John showed the same insouciance on book tours. He told me that he and writer Dennis Cooper had decided that the big mainstream publishing houses, where both were now published, needed education on how to work with gay-porn writers. According to John, he and Dennis thought the big houses could start by giving them line items for the hustlers he and Dennis would need on their respective tours. "We could call it research," John joked as he and I stood on the Massachusetts State House steps at a National Writers Union (NWU) demonstration in Boston. It was in one of John's NWU workshops that I also heard him say, "Don't be a writer unless you have to be!"

As an author committed to "seducing" his readers, John always gauged the success or failure of his public book readings by whether any of his fans offered him sex afterward. If no offers were forthcoming, John would distract himself from his disappointment by going home and writing even raunchier porn. In "A Modest Proposal for the Support of the Arts," published in *Steam,* John suggested that if gay men really wanted to support their pornographers, they should have more sex—especially with John! That "research" thing again.

The last time I saw John was on a snowy night in Cambridge, Massachusetts. He was one of several writers attending a party thrown by fellow writer and friend Michael Bronski. When I walked into the party, he was sitting on Michael's bed talking with Dorothy Allison, in whose honor the party was being held. John, along with Dorothy, was engaged in his first love: storytelling. As always, he was dressed in an L. L. Bean turtleneck and loafers, a fact that always shocked and perturbed his leathermen fans. In his hand was a glass of bourbon. John was always wearing a turtleneck. And he was almost always drinking.

That particular night ended in a cocktail lounge in Harvard Square. John downed another five or six bourbons and I listened as he and Dorothy talked bout being queer and being writers. He then went on to tell a story about a hot, steamy night many years ago in New Orleans when he had stumbled into a bar full of black drag queens and stayed until dawn. Then he listened to my story about my friendship with an aging drag queen that he encouraged me to write. John always had a cadre of fledgling writers he supported. "All you have to do is tell your stories," he said to me as Dorothy listened and nodded her head. A year later, I took his advice. I wrote my story and, with his guidance, shaped it until it was accepted in his and Joan Nestle's anthology about relationships among gay men and lesbians.

John Preston was also very fond of quoting his friend and fellow writer Anne Rice, who says, "Pornography is a place where one visits, not where one lives."

I, who after six years still consider myself a fledgling writer, feel very lucky to have met John Preston—a man who had to be a writer. And as one who frequents the world of pornography, I am deeply grateful that, during one of my adventures, I met another frequenter to the world of porn—John Preston.

RESEARCHING FOR MR. PRESTON
Rev. Dr. E. M. Barrett

I'd always enjoyed the skill of John Preston the writer, but it was John Preston the man who captured my heart. I enjoy keeping people's preconceptions off balance, and to see the high priest of leathermen walk into a reading attired nattily in a poplin suit, Brooks Brothers shirt and tie, and penny loafers gave me a real kick. And then there was the last time I saw him, painfully thin and hoarse, but accepting the plaudits of his pierced and Levi's-clad disciples in a pair of beautiful cashmere slacks.

But the thing I think I liked most about John, besides his carelessness about stereotypes and his disconcertingly incisive literary portrayals of people he loved, was the way he got me to think and to dig up all kinds of data for him. As a priest and a medievalist, I'm used to being asked all sorts of questions about religion and history, but John could come up with some real goodies. It began innocently enough at a book party, when his tuxedoed form materialized at my elbow and asked casually, "What do you know about temple prostitution in the ancient Mediterranean world?" Coughing to cover how close I'd come to choking on my seltzer, I replied, "Not much, but give me a couple of days, and I'll fax you what I can find out. How much detail do you want?" Those first two-and-a-half pages led to more research, some of it in my own area of expertise, some of it, like the temple prostitutes, a bit off the beaten track. If John sprang questions on me at odd times, I know there were times I told him more than he ever wanted to know about a subject. As our acquaintance ripened, I'm sure he knew he'd be hip deep in data when he asked for information about Irish monasticism in general and Iona in particular. That one got him a long letter about how Irish monks were different from those on the Continent, and a full description of the island and its monastery. Hints he'd given me about a potential story plot led me to include some stuff about how the monks might have carried on some remnants of pagan traditions, and so it went.

Each report of mine would be answered by one of his famous postcards, each picture suited to the subject I had looked up, though I suspect he sent me his most decorous selections in deference to my cloth. The ancient world was acknowledged by a classically posed bowman on a Greek helmet. The Irish monks got a lovely young man immersed in a book, and another one got a famous muscleman of the late-nineteenth century. After an inquiry of his that led to a report on the eight major and minor Sabbats of the pagan year and their appropriate ceremonies, I tickled his fancy by sending cards to wish him happy Samhain or Solstice, knowing that he liked the fact that so many of the festivals were said to be good times for polymorphous sex-magic.

I miss John a lot. I wish I could have told him how much his friendship meant to me and how grateful I was for the chance to stretch my brains on his wildly assorted questions when my work life seemed to be anything but intellectually challenging. I wish, in fact, that I could have told him how much I loved him, but that would have embarrassed us both. He's probably shaking his head in exasperation that I said a requiem mass for the repose of his soul, but I think his respect for ritual would have been broad-minded enough to allow me that—for myself and for his friends in New York, even though he wanted no memorial service for himself. Good night, my dear. *In Paradisum deducant te angeli.* Into Paradise may the angels lead you, and may you know the joy you gave to those who knew and loved you as a writer and as a man.

THE WELL
Owen Keehnen

Looking upon the nude shaven forms below my aching triceps, I think of him, the man with the flesh-papered den. His walls were hung with strips of chiseled chests, marble asses, muscled arms and legs and phalli in all states of full and semiarousal. Never as deep as what they inspired, the images opened flat, glossy, fleshless. They were the overseers of desire, sentinels to the heaven within and an infinite sexual imagination funneling downward, escaping like water down a drain; perhaps the center grille of the YMCA open showers....

Tile lines lead to two muscled forms curled in steam and spray, a clenching fist of flesh, stereotypically falling into itself in shape and sound. Sperm flew and landed as points upon a grid until it, too, was washed into the whorl of the downward circle. Moans became their own accompaniment, climbing and falling as echoes, rolling through the trees as wind, rising as steam upon his page.

The rhythm of sound and fantasy rounded den corners and bowed den walls. Sex was a revelation to change the contours of all. Torches brightened the den, illuminating the shadowed core where there now stood a well of lichen lined stone. He advanced without fear or hesitation. Moss cushioned his palms as he craned to see inside. There was a slight blast of coolness. Round and at the bottom was his reflection, but beneath the surface he glimpsed a swaying similar to seaweed or fins, but still unlike anything he had ever before seen. It was the water itself which hinted at more. Looking farther into the pool, he saw another side of himself, and another world where he ruled as The Dark Lord.

An empire stretched beyond the slicked sides of the adults-only looking glass, like a world upside down or on the end of a tube. It opened into an expanse of viaducts, truck cabs, taxicabs, warehouses, outhouses, bunkhouses, jails, barracks, dungeons, deserts, tearooms, alleys, fire escapes, forests, Ferris wheels, and even bedrooms. It was a tableau tarped in pleasure, an earth-toned, flesh-toned land-scape oiled in sweat, blood, urine, and sperm…a kaleidoscope of skin. Rapture and ecstasy ruled here. Their varied cries, moans, and fucktalk howled through the streets and nonstreets, sweeping as winds through that place.

All knew the measured approach of his boots and the leathered lean look of The Dark Lord. Packed in black he stood solid, legs firm and apart and veed to a luring bulge. The sanctity of the sensations and the vision awed him. Peaks and fields of fantasy were mounted, reaped, and rendered mostly with a sexy smile. He savored the sharing as a holy transference. His eyes sparked cyclones, autumnal leafed fantasies rising and whirling, quickening like kettled contents over a flame, over and upon itself till speed found a voice.

The Dark Lord was partial to chivalrous deeds and noble codes. Gallantry suited him, so his art adopted that tone.

He rode to resurrect sex as a life force and drive, to place it both in a back room and a tabernacle. He knew it must be saved from sinner stigmas, embarrassment, indifference.

His quest was a trail of ink, a feathered pen teasing an unfurling cock, making nipples reach, assholes wink. He captured it all; bound balls and titclamps, dildos and whips, pumps and plugs, chains and razors. His pen injected blood and lust and under his control the images swelled. Sweat and life filled the words and they rose from the contours of flesh, higher, moving across the imagination. Below, borders oozed like oils, slipping over and into one another, becoming one, sexual alchemy.

As he knelt at the well, he knew there was also a world behind him. He had ambitious goals there as well. He was an idealist with deeply pragmatic roots, a Master who knew the value of serving. He saw power in our numbers, in unity, many, and community. The belief was seated deep and released in one form or another, in every hydrant of his commentary smoke. It moved through his pen as well, pillowing upon the pages of his varied anthologies, his fiction, his duties and titles and family.

Rivers of writers ran through his lands as well, below hanging bows like my now-aching arms. They varied in size, speed, and flow, but were all of the element. It was a cosmos exploded from a common source, a luminescent connection of fireworks at mid-burst. Most were threaded through letter, phone, and fax into a massive web of his weaving, a net not to trap but to hold, connect, stand complete. He took great joy in its construction and maintenance. It still hangs, perhaps stronger, lines aware of joinings and origins.

His sense of community greened and grew, intertwining as vines through his life and mind, flourishing as tradition, as heritage. Branches hooking into stone as tendrils wound around the quill over his heart, on his chest, in his skin, reaching and firming with a hungry grip. The pen was the core of it all, the hollows of the funnel, tool of tools, dick to make him drool the most....

Musing at a new position, boom man on a porn set. The Dark Lord would approve. The two-beat titillated laugh is almost audible, an amused exhalation to follow. His brows would peak as a fluffer rolls a rubber on The Star. Accommodating. Do fluffers ever get carried away? Therein lies a tale. A star in need of discipline, another. The crew participating, another.

Seeing stories, scenarios, fantasies, and fetishes everywhere is easier after knowing and reading him. The force of his language and the breadth of his erotic imagination urge the reader to look in the well. Reflections of cool water curl scales from eyes, a vision is transferred, and so it goes, eternal.

Sweat centers, forming a river down the ravine of the top's perfect spine...natural as dew, pure as water from a well. It collects in the back basin, then rolls over the compressing ass stones, the rapids of another river entirely. It will still be a while before either one comes. I consider my aching triceps, create another scenario, and think of him some more.

MY SHORT, HAPPY LIFE WITH JOHN PRESTON

Martin Palmer

"No. He wasn't wondering if he could do it; he was wondering if he wanted to do it. Mr. Benson never questions his own abilities."

—*Mr. Benson*

This was John Preston.

In January 1990 I first heard from John. "[Andrew Holleran] told me about a marvelous story you'd written to him in a letter, I believe it was, about a Thanksgiving with a group of gay friends in Alaska. It sounded quite perfect for what I'm trying to accomplish and I wonder if you'd like to write it up? The whole point of the book is to capture those kinds of moments in gay life…"

This was the beginning of *Hometowns,* his anthology of gay places, and the beginning of my tutorials with a superb editor and an unusual friend. It was characteristic of John's lively intelligence and wide curiosity that he looked everywhere for material and that he was willing to take chances on an unknown in finding, in putting together, and in shaping his vision of the variety of the gay experience in this country today. To him, all of our stories were worth knowing.

Those of us who had created our own extended families with the love and interdependence and trust that may have superseded what we had known in our biological families were validated. Those of us who were still coping actually or in memory with bad experiences were validated, too, and could tell it like it was and is. He opened doors, as he always had. This is what he said in his letter:

When a writer chooses to examine his birthplace as his hometown, as opposed to where he currently lives, that examination must begin with a clear statement of where the writer is now.... At least half the book will be about the chosen hometowns that gay men have created for themselves.

At that time, I had lived in Anchorage, Alaska, for twenty-two years. During that time, I had formed and helped nurture a family with intense bonds. The nucleus of our family was Jim and Guy, both younger than I, who had been together since meeting in San Francisco in 1972. As time passed, we saw that our bonds were often expressed, along with many other ways, in the basic communion of sharing meals, from a simple "Come on over for supper," to gathering all of us for holidays, birthdays, and occasions we fashioned simply because we loved each other and enjoyed being together. And one of the traditions we created was our elaborate Thanksgiving celebration at the cabin up in the woods in the depths of an Alaskan November. It lit the darkness and warmed our spirits. This is what I wanted to share.

As an editor, John knew exactly what he wanted. "This book should have a very strong sense of place," he wrote. "That is the real key. And, just typing this out, a focus structure seems to be forming. You are *all* immigrants in Anchorage. One of the rich elements of gay life is to create a community among diverse types. Here, in a place without a great deal of history, or at least with its history constantly changing, you gay immigrants are coming together and forming your own hometown."

Precisely. The genesis of this book must have come from his own strong sense of place, of belonging, as he expressed it in his piece on Medfield, Massachusetts. "One of the first questions that a gay man has to answer," he wrote, "revolves around the issue: Where do I belong? What comfort, protection, support and nurture should there be?" After his many voyages, John gave me the impression in this piece that Medfield was "…an Eden that still has its appeal" (though from the convenient distance of Portland, Maine). His attention to detail for each writer was painstaking. That was his way, even though there were twenty-eight contributors besides his own piece on Medfield.

After I finished the essay for *Hometowns,* John asked me to contribute to his next collection about families, and I decided to write about my father. He was one of the strongest influences in my life, an icon for me. For this reason, and because his memory dominated everything in my childhood and adolescence, it was difficult for me to focus on a beginning. I grew up in a household with many figures: relatives, friends, helpers, nannies, my father's patients, each with a story. John's comment as an editor on my initial efforts was typically dry: "You have the great strengths, and weakness, of the southern writer. I say that in all humor and goodwill. I smile and chuckle while I read your stories. They're what bring you and your affection for your father to life. But your southern storytelling also seems an invitation to ramble off on tangents. (It wasn't by accident that Allan Gurganus's last novel was so very long.)"

When *Hometowns* was published, John arranged a reading in San Francisco at A Different Light Bookstore in which he participated. It was a Preston-efficient occasion. We were lined up like paratroopers, ready to peel off and bail out when we were called to the microphone under the stern eye of our commander. It was fun because John's support got the troops through without a hitch, and he was there for all of us, introducing us expertly and carefully. We had no choice but to follow through and to do our best. We made Mr. Benson proud of his squad. I always enjoyed his readings and spending time with him afterward.

"I'm back up and running crazily after that bit of time with bad health," John wrote in a 1991 letter. This was unusual because he never mentioned his health or discussed matters that personal. A friend had written me that he had developed pneumonia after an exhausting lecture tour through the South, and I feared the worst. In a later postcard, he assured me that it was not pneumocystis; but, all the same, I felt uneasy.

I hadn't known until then that John had AIDS. That summer, also, Guy told me that he and Jim were infected with HIV. The news was painful. First I suppressed it; then I tried to parcel it out among other problems, to break it up into something manageable. This proved impossible. There was no way to get past it, around, beneath, or over it. It blocked everything. Sometimes as I walked downtown to pick up laundry or when I filled my cart in the supermarket with that week's groceries, the tears welled up; there was no escape. Jim and Guy would be uncomfortable with my tears; so would John Preston. I felt mute, frustrated, blocking my feelings and my urgent questions: When? How long? How can they live with HIV? What do they draw on? How do they face the ordinary day? What am *I* to do? I never found the courage to ask them, and I regret it.

John Preston is connected inextricably with Jim and Guy because writing about them in John's book let me say how I felt about our lives as I re-created it for readers. In the summer of 1991 he wrote me, "I had a meeting with the editors of the Book-of-the-Month Club. You probably know by now that they've taken *Hometowns*. The editor who made the decision was particularly rapturous about your essay; I thought you'd like to know that. He described it as every gay man's dream, to be with a group of gay friends in the wilderness, sharing a holiday." John was pleased when the *Anchorage Daily News* published my essay in full in its Sunday supplement, *We Alaskans,* that fall. There were many comments about the essay, all of them favorable. A local bookstore held a signing sale for *Hometowns*; several dozen copies were sold.

That October I got a note from John enclosing a copy of an article in the *Maine Sunday Telegram* from Portland. There he was, holding Vlad, his vizsla pup (vizslas have strong masculine features, like John), John looking straight at the camera with a what-the-hell-are-you-doing-here expression (John himself wrote that his eyes had been described as "demonic"). The title of the article was "A Gay Writer's Survival Guide: John Preston of Portland went into a tail-spin when he learned he had the AIDS virus. He came out of it, and now he's a leading author of gay literature." John wrote, "I came home to find the enclosed in the local Sunday newspaper, the best publicity that came out of the whole grueling trip! Note the handsome dog. Note the little male nude photographs in the background! I can't wait to see what the letters to the editor say about them!"

But my newspaper episode got me into deep trouble with my family. Without asking Jim's and Guy's permission, I gave the paper several photographs we'd taken at the cabin; the editor wanted to illustrate my piece. Earlier, Guy had been hit by a lung infection right after their return from a long trip. AIDS crept up on both; Guy was already inhaling pentamidine to prevent pneumocystis, and their doctor had started Jim on AZT, a fact he kept private. Anxious, strained, fighting all this, they found the photographs, the exposure, too much to take. I was summarily banished as punishment, a painful result of my tactlessness and their present state. John thought their reaction was "extreme," but he had never had trouble coming out himself.

During our family years, we had had our quarrels and differences from time to time; we were able to have them because of the strength of our affections. But this was the severest of all. My remorse was acute, and our friends were distressed. Finally, I pointed out that at my age and in their condition none of us had time—literally—to continue the estrangement. Forgiveness was unconditional, and we closed ranks again. Time—precious time. All of us were losing. There wasn't a day to waste. John Preston, too, was on my mind. I was haunted by a sense of remanence, a term used by dowsers to describe finding the memory of something that has vanished and left no trace of itself.

John was the guide then as he remained for the next essays. I asked him questions about everything concerned with putting books together. He was patient. I sent him a story I had written that had AIDS as one of the themes. He wrote back that the treatment was wrong; no one would react that way. My premise wouldn't fly. Reluctantly, I accepted his judgment; he was the experienced writer and editor. (I still think he was wrong, but I haven't sent the story out again.) I am a sometime poet with a few publications. He replied briskly, "There's no hope for an agent for poetry. There's no $ to be made. Can't help, sorry." I was too inexperienced not to trust him in both.

It wasn't until I went to the second OutWrite Conference in San Francisco that I met John. A handsome man with a raptor's alert features, he was New England personified for me: brisk, unsentimental, direct, a little scary; intelligent. About himself he wrote:

I had determined to do this coming-out business in a big way. I was not going to just enter into a social world of other gay men. I was going to take the political and organizational skills I'd learned in the civil-rights movements and other social-change organizations and give them to my own kind. Within a year, I became one of the cofounders of the gay community center in the Twin Cities. I was on television; I gave newspaper interviews; I wrote polemics.... When I was asked why I worked so hard at gay liberation, I said I did it so there would be more healthy men to love, and I meant it.

When I read in the *Advocate* that Michael Denneny of St. Martin's Press called John a "curmudgeonly New England bachelor whose life was one huge conversation among gay men and lesbians," I smiled at the accuracy of the sketch.

By that time I had almost completed my essay for John's next project, *A Member of the Family,* which came out in 1992. For that project, I wrote to John to recommend a strong essay by a friend, Brian Kilpatrick, whom I had met at the second OutWrite Conference. John, always open to recommendations, agreed that it was a fine essay and included it in the book. At that second conference, one of the keynote speakers was Edward Albee, who started his talk by reminding us that he was speaking as a white, middle-aged playwright who happened to be gay. John was amused at the immediate flurry of catcalls from the large contingent who didn't like these specifications, and who seemed determined for a while to prevent Albee's finishing his speech. He noted that the first OutWrite Conference the year before was such a novelty, such a surprise, bringing 1,200 gay and lesbian writers together when maybe 200 had been expected, that it had been a love feast. Now politics were setting in, as he had predicted.

In March 1992 the third OutWrite Conference took place, this time in Boston. John was active in several of the seminars and discussions. The evening that the conference opened, he was at the cocktail party, active and unchanged as far as I could tell. I liked to be around him on such an occasion; he always introduced his writers around, letting us meet other writers, sparking the conversation. In the discussions and seminars, he was brisk and informative, humorous and pointed. Wherever he talked, the room was full, and his treatment of everything from getting an agent to how to write pornography was stimulating. At that conference he sent out invitations to a cocktail party he held in his suite at the elegant old Copley Plaza Hotel. It was crowded. The food and drink were what one could expect from John Preston, and so were the three gorgeous bartenders he had imported (he said) from Maine. I remember particularly the body builder in the carefully ripped B.U.M. T-shirt with his little baseball cap on backward in such a setting. A sly cliché, it was *echt*-Preston.

Later that year John, with Joan Nestle, launched the project to be called *Sister and Brother,* in which gay men and lesbians write about gays of the other sex who have made a difference in their lives, and they asked me for a contribution. At the same time, John was completing his erotic anthology, *Flesh and the Word 2,* as well as gathering material for *Flesh and the Word 3.* I began an essay about a close lesbian friend who was in my class at medical school and finished an erotic tale to submit for *Flesh and the Word.* The erotic piece was fun and no problem. I wrestled with the essay on my lesbian friend for several months, and John wrestled with me. His comment about my medical school on one draft was succinct: "Sexist! Racist! Snobs!"

Meanwhile, in the family, Guy had returned from the Barcelona Olympics with a chronic intestinal problem that grew into a generalized mycobacterium avium infection. He lost over twenty pounds, looked emaciated, felt terrible, but kept going. He loathed hospitals and hated being sick. Around Christmas of that year we thought he was going to die. He didn't, but he didn't recover, either. Jim was stable; such is AIDS. We prepared for the worst. I heard nothing about John's health. After he told me about his bout with pneumonia, he never mentioned it again, and I didn't ask. I think that for him it was irrelevant.

The fourth OutWrite Conference took place in Boston in October 1993. That was the last time I saw John Preston. He was at the opening reception and was as active as ever at the various sessions. On the third night he gave a party at The Ramrod, a local leather bar, for the guys who contributed to *Flesh and the Word*. There was Mr. Benson himself in full leather surrounded by a chain of sexy men, also in full leather, some of them half-nude. At the microphone, John introduced them individually to a rapt house, after which we could besiege them for autographs in our copies of the book. The party was a success. The only thing about John that was different was his voice: he was severely hoarse, painfully so. I thought he simply had a bad cold; in any case, he never deigned to mention it.

A poignant part of these conferences as the years passed was saying good-bye to the participants who knew they probably would not make it to the next one. I know of no other public gathering where we've had to do this. Each person has his own style. David Fineberg remarked at one conference that his T-cell count was now lower than his IQ. Melvin Dixon was particularly eloquent in his speech at the closing session in 1992, before he died. "Call my name" became a refrain as he commanded us to remember him. Bo Huston of San Francisco told us good-bye when he chaired one of the writing panels. Walta Borawski, the poet, movingly acknowledged his frailty in one of the poetry sessions. The list goes on; and every time we meet, more are gone.

Because Tony Kushner had some last-minute fixing to do on *Angels in America,* he couldn't give the closing speech in the cavernous Castle as scheduled. John Preston was asked to replace him. As hoarse as he was, John accepted the challenge. It was his farewell, although nothing in the speech admitted this. He spoke of the anonymous but now-notorious traveling salesman in Hartford who had initiated a joyful young John into gay sex, telling him never to be furtive or ashamed about his desires. He spoke of entering a snobbish university where he was derided for his honest New England accent, and how he rolled with the punches (but did change his speech). He spoke of many things in his life leading to his presence on that platform that night, and how he felt about life in general, himself in particular, and how he had tried to serve the gay cause, particularly in literature. Particularly in pornography, of which he was proudest. He told us to never be afraid again. He was eloquent, his voice striving against the crippling hoarseness afflicting it. In his own way, he told us good-bye. Sitting with me, a friend who had flown in from Amsterdam for the conference was moved to tears at what John had overcome. I was moved not by what he had overcome, but by his accomplishments. John Preston was the last person I could ever think of as any kind of victim, anytime. John's speech closed the conference, and we returned to where we came from.

Later that month, Jim, who had been in far stabler heath than Guy, fell abruptly into illness as if he had been dropped through a trapdoor. In the days that followed, every system from circulatory to digestive to kidneys to lungs began to fail—all except his mind. He watched all this almost with bemusement: a frantic Guy, who had a bed put beside his in the hospital, his mourning gay family, his dependents. One day near the end, in tears, I asked him how he felt, what to do, how to cope. "My doctor says Mylanta," he answered with a grin. He asked that all medical heroics be stopped: take out the tubes, remove the machines, let him go. It was done. Little by little he went from us. For a while we could call him back, but finally the door closed. Guy was always there, soothing, rubbing, fetching, holding; heartbroken. Jim never wanted to be the survivor, though we had expected Guy to die first. He died in November. One of our family got the news as he chopped wood for fuel on his homestead 200 miles north. In the –40° degree weather, his eyelids froze together when he wept, and his lashes broke off as he rubbed them open. Jim was cremated, and his ashes were scattered up at the cabin in the snow. We limped through that Thanksgiving. Shortly before Christmas, Guy gave an open house attended by several hundred people, in tribute to Jim's life. He knew that this was his good-bye, too.

John was busy getting his projected books launched, and this was reflected in the several letters I had at the end of 1993 and into 1994. These concerned changes in manuscripts, plans for the books: technical details. As usual, there was no word at all about how he felt or the state of his health. He was too busy for trivia of that kind. But in mid-season there was a hint of fatigue. "How are you doing?" he wrote. "Winter is always so romantic in the beginning of the season here in Maine, but by February, it becomes very, very tired. I had thought of going to Miami Beach for a break in the assault, but let the possibility pass. My mistake."

Guy hung on, legs swollen and painful from peripheral neuritis, losing weight, wracked with diarrhea, "still putting one foot in front of the other," as he would say. Guy was troubled by episodes of uncontrolled, racing heartbeats. "I hope it just stops," he said simply. In January he gave a birthday party for me at the house. In March, for his own birthday, I wished him more. He thought a minute, then said, "I *would* like one more." Then he added, "We'll see." In mid-April he called me one day and asked me to take him to the hospital because his breathing was getting increasingly worse. I knew that for him to ask to go to the hospital, things must be bad indeed. While we were in admissions waiting, Guy on the gurney, I stroked his hand, looking at its fine structure, wondering when it, too, would be put in the fire.

At that same time I received a note from a friend of John's

and mine: "Yes, it's true, Preston had a 'motor seizure.' The doctors thought he would not survive & then after 36 hours of sleep sat up & ate an egg, according to one of his helper/protégés. That's all I know. We're told to still write— phone calls not advisable. I'm sorry about your friend Guy. It's all the same, isn't it?" Then a letter came from Portland telling me that a seizure had "effectively ended John Preston's productive career," also advising me not to telephone but that letters would be welcome. Usually a procrastinator, I wrote at once, wishing John well and telling him how much he meant to me as a friend and as an editor. I shall always be glad I did. The words that his productive career was "effectively over" were almost unbelievable. How he would have hated such a sentence, I reflected.

Guy lasted ten painful days, gasping his life away with pneumocystic pneumonia, dying on April 28. Under a spring sun, his ashes were scattered up at the cabin with Jim's. Several days before that, a letter arrived from a New York friend containing John's obituary from the *New York Times* along with the tribute to him in the same paper, the same day, from Anne Rice. The date of John's death was April 28. I felt as if something in me had been amputated. I could mourn Guy; I was there. I didn't know whom to write to or speak to about John; I had no further information. I could not close; my sense of remanence grew acute.

A month later, I received a telephone call at home. To my surprise, it was John's mother, Nancy Preston, and she was in Anchorage. Mrs. Preston had come to Anchorage to attend an international meeting of city personnel; she has been the town clerk in Medfield for over twenty years. She had read my last note to John and had written down my address because she was coming to Anchorage and wanted to call me. The evening we had dinner, John's mother told me calmly about his last days. They saw that John was going, and they chose not to burden him with heroic measures, which he didn't want. Mrs. Preston brought the extensive obituaries from the local papers along with the grand program of his funeral at the Episcopal cathedral in Portland, with the eulogy by the bishop of Maine and "Amazing Grace" sung by Jessye Norman. Nancy Preston's sorrow, and her pride in her son, was as serene as she. "After all, my mother will tell you," John wrote, "I have written books, and let the contents be damned! They may have gay themes, but her son is an author and, while she might not have discussed my homosexuality very lavishly in the old days, I don't think her pride in that particular achievement can be underestimated now. She attends my readings, brings her friends along, passes out photocopies of my reviews." And in her I could see the mother who, he wrote, "would made hot chocolate and fresh doughnuts (from scratch) for all the neighborhood children" when he was young and winter snowstorms came. At last I was able to share my feelings with the source, so to speak. It was a relief I had not expected, and I was grateful.

Summer has come. Here, in its brief season, it bursts with green fragrance. The light lasts almost until midnight. Against a wall of birches, spruce, willows, cottonwoods flashing in the sun, my white dog crouches in the unmown grass crowded with dandelions. Nearby, a clump of lilac bushes bends with blooms against a patch of sky. The air is cool, and a silvery haze hangs against the distant mountains. There is a sense of expectancy; I feel as if I am about to start on a journey. It is an instant of knowing this minute, being grateful for breath and for the light of day, being part of it, sensing the vibration of life. I think of Jim and Guy. I think of John.

MY BRUNCH WITH
JOHN PRESTON

William J. Mann

What does one wear to brunch with a pornographer?

Should one dare to provoke? Should the T-shirt, for example, be a tad too tight, delineating the pectorals? Should the jeans hug the butt, or should they hide it? The 501s clone look or the baggy hip-hop boy look? What would please the pornographer more?

I settled on a sweatshirt and a pair of shorts with work boots, laughing at myself. This is a casual but professional meeting, I scolded myself silently. Don't get caught up in the image.

But John Preston was much, much more to me than a professional contact. Not that he knew it. Not then. He, I assumed, regarded me as little more than yet another editor, and at that, an editor he was doing a favor for by allowing me to publish his work in *Metroline,* the queer Connecticut-Massachusetts magazine I publish. Certainly he wasn't dependent on the meager $30-a-column check he'd receive from me twice a month in the mail. On the contrary: I was dependent on *him,* and other writers of his stature, for adding legitimacy to my publishing venture.

When I'd met him the night before, after a reading he gave of his work at the Fine Arts Center in Provincetown, I'd known he'd been sick. He looked thinner than his photographs on his books—older, too, and wearier. But that didn't diminish my attraction to him. Still, I suspected that this latest rally of his immune system was perhaps the last of what I'd heard had been many: I'd known too many others in their last months for me to believe otherwise in this case. So there was an urgency to my attraction, to my desire. And to understand that, one would need to flash back several years, before I was an editor, before I was queer—in fact, back to a time long before I ever had any hope of meeting the pornographer of my wildest dreams.

But first: a year before his death, I interviewed John Preston. Over the phone. Nervous as hell. (Me, not him.) He said to me then; "In our march toward respectability, we sometimes lose sight of what it is we are trying to win."

Back in 1984, I knew exactly what it was I was trying to win: my right to fuck in the way I wanted to. As a college student, I wasn't queer, hardly even gay: a nascent, budding homosexual was perhaps the most to which I might lay claim. Sure, I'd fooled around with a few guys, thought of myself as bi for a time, now even called myself gay (in certain circles). I was certainly aware that I liked cock since the fifth grade. But to see myself as somehow part of a transformative movement, as something so intrinsically "other" that the world I perceived was fundamentally different from that which was perceived by others, was not part of my understanding. All I knew was that I wanted to find the freedom to fuck other guys and have other guys fuck me, and to explore the kinds of desires that I'd never heard talked about: except in a couple of books I found by an author named John Preston.

He scared me. He really did. But God, did he ever excite me! It was through *Mr. Benson* that I first encountered Preston's work, followed soon after by his *Master* series. This was long before—*eons* before, in virtual if not literal truth— his *Hometowns* and *Member of the Family*–style anthologies. This was John Preston as unadulterated pornographer, and the pornography he produced was like nothing I'd read, before or since.

Take away the SM label, just as Preston himself generally stripped off the SM paraphernalia in his stories: no slings or bullwhips here. Instead, what Preston did—and why his pornography resonates even for those us not thoroughly "into" sadomasochism—was explore the limits of passion, of the abdication of control, of the liberation of power. He asked the questions—and offered possible answers—that probed the depths of our consciousness: what happens when one totally surrenders one's will? What is the meaning of trust? And through it all, where does the erotic begin and end, if at all?

For me John Preston became an icon: an icon of passion, of honesty, of why we should, after all, enter that great big fight called gay liberation. At that point in my life, to meet him, to talk to him, to actually *have sex* with him, would have been unimaginable. His dark, mysterious visage on the cover of his books invited me into to his world, a world where the erotic imagination reigned with the divine right of kings (or queens). In all of the debates about pornography's merits (or lack thereof), Preston was always precise: don't erect barbed wire around the place where the imagination might range. In my own quests, my own personal exploration of sex, I was often timid; yet, in my fantasies, I became the voyager on one of Preston's hero's journeys, a traveler in search of himself and his dreams.

Preston awoke a passion within me that I believe is basic

to all humanity, a gift we all possess, but too often suppress in its stirrings: out of fear, out of a misguided belief that these most basic, these most human, desires must be wrong. Every time we engage in queer sex—sucking cock or licking clit—we are taking a leap of courage because the sexual expression of who we are is devalued, denounced and demeaned in this society. "Passion of any sort is no longer valued," Preston told me in that same phone interview. "To be passionate is perceived as being out of control. We seem to be developing an ever-increasing list of prohibitions when the whole point of our lives was to crush inhibitions."

That's what I came to understand, eventually. But in 1984, all I knew was that I wanted to be free to get my rocks off with other guys.

Same thing, John Preston would say.

So back to our brunch. I met him on the front porch of his guest house (a guest house, I later learned, that has a fully equipped dungeon in its basement—the things I learn too late.) He was dressed simply: white shirt, beige pants. We made pleasantries about the day, about the reading the night before. He'd noticed I'd come in late. "I'll send you the full text of the reading," he promised.

Purely professional, I told myself. He's being purely professional. That the reading included a pitch for men to contact him for sexual inspiration had nothing to do with his sending it to me: I believed that as I thanked him for his courtesy.

Of course, what I wanted him to suggest was that we go back inside his guest house so he could tie me up to his bedposts. But instead he suggested a place for brunch and what did I think? "Sure," I said. "Sounds great to me."

We talked about lots of things over orange juice and eggs Benedict: the mystifying (to him) respectability to which SM groups were now aspiring; the new alliances among gay men and lesbians; the word "queer" (he liked it, after some initial discomfort). But it was as if we were two academics for whom sexuality—at least, our *own*—was an irrelevant, arbitrary thing; instead of owning the reality of what we were, which was pornographer and disciple, teacher and student, man and boy (chronological age has nothing to do with it; perception does), master and (dare I say it?) an at-open-to-the-possibility (at least for a day) slave.

But on another level, anything else might have bordered on the inappropriate. Yet, if rewriting the rules is the goal, who is to set the standards for appropriateness? Us? Or them? "Them" would have said we behaved absolutely appropriately: publisher of small gay publication meets with respected writer and contributor. Of course, under those rules, brunch had to be on me. And so it was. Preston was uncomfortable with my picking up the check. So was I.

Because let's face it: despite even Preston's protestations that nobody ever confused him with Franny, the Queen of Province-town (his drag-queen creation) yet *always* assumed he *was* Mr. Benson (the SM master), there is not one person who has even a passing knowledge of gay lit who can't tell you what John Preston liked to do in bed. That's not to say he was never a bottom, or never enjoyed vanilla sex, but come on: John Preston was—is—the master, and he never really tried to hide that fact.

What happened next was, I'm convinced, an act of fate. A few weeks later, after we'd shaken hands and very professionally said our good-byes, I spotted a well-placed personal ad in the pages of the *Advocate Classifieds,* with no attempt to hide the fact that the person who placed the ad was, in fact, Mr. Benson himself. Come teach an old pornographer new tricks, the ad basically challenged, a dare Preston had thrown out at the end of his reading in Provincetown as well.

It was destined: I couldn't resist writing. "Truth be known," I wrote, "that's always been my fantasy. I just didn't think it was appropriate to say so." When I dropped the letter in the mail, I knew I had broken a few rules—yet so conditioned was I that instead of exhilaration about my honesty, something that, on the surface, at least, I aspired to feel, I had the sinking feeling that comes from giving in to impulse. It was a moment of revelation: the risk-taking had meant a surrender of control, and I was not comfortable with that. For embracing passion is not an easy step; rewriting the rules takes rethinking one's life. Had I been able to retrieve the letter from the box, I would have.

And so, a few days later, came back this letter from John Preston:

Ah, human life. Now look, the whole rap I was giving you at lunch in Provincetown was an attempt to seduce you. I didn't want to be any more up-front about it because we were talking about business and I didn't want it to get mixed up—unless you picked up on it and it was obviously spontaneous and mutual. There I was, talking about how terrible it was that I couldn't get this other young man into bed, hoping you'd take the cue, and all I got back was advice to "wait for him," that he'd come around. An ultimately frustrating experience.

He ended the letter offering to teach me the basics of SM: "Just let me know. I'm pretty good at the introductions."

Looking back, I see the folly of any advice that advocated waiting—especially in Preston's case. But that's what I did: I waited. Consider the effect of such a letter: how might some straight girl who'd grown up mooning over the Beatles react if, years later, Paul McCartney wrote her to say: "Sure. Let's do it"? She'd probably do what I did, at least at first: nothing. But I thought about it. Near continuously. Good thing my lover and I have an open relationship. He was quite accommodating, in fact, and we even talked about his coming along. (Preston had actually encouraged couples to respond to his appeal.) Yet I had to ask myself: Was all this real? Was I now going to actually plan a trip up to Portland so John Preston could take me to the depths of my erotic soul?

Sure I was. I'd come a long way since 1984.

Or maybe, the world had. At least, the queer world. What we were about—or what we were in the process of becoming—was a force that had the power to transform (the sprouting of new Log Cabin Clubs every few months or so notwithstanding). We were rewriting the rules because the old ones didn't make sense for us. Maybe publishers should *never* sleep with writers, no matter how famous, but they do; and maybe men in couples should *always* be monogamous, but they aren't. Maybe those who are HIV-negative are crazy to sleep with those who are positive, but isn't that all just a bunch of crap fostered by an antisex "safe-sex" campaign? Wasn't John Preston, by remaining sexually active (or at least, openly desirous) through the last months of his life, debunking the myth of the sexless PWA? Rewrite the rules. And anything can happen. Even adolescent fantasies might come true.

Yet so long had I taken in my astonished calculations that I received a postcard from Preston before I had a chance to reply. On the front was the picture of a very hot muscle man in black leather vest, chained between two columns. On the back he had written: "Scared you off? I hope not."

"Not at all," I wrote in reply, but I don't know if he ever read my letter. I heard that week that he'd taken ill again. A month later, John Preston was dead.

Passion. When I think of John Preston, this is the word that comes to mind first, like no other. He lamented its invalidation in our culture, especially in gay culture. "Look," he said to me in that phone interview that runs through my mind periodically like a tape loop, despite the fact it was erased, by mistake, long ago, "I'm the ultimate AIDS educator. I'm not talking irresponsibility. But there's a sense among people that being irresponsible comes from uncontrolled lust. One of the biggest things we've always fought against is the idea that gay men are only lustful; that that's all we are. But in our attempt to deal with that, we've gone too far in the opposite direction. We've denied that being lustful is good."

And so it was with sadness and not a small degree of anger that I read the obituaries of John Preston: the ones in the straight papers, like the *New York Times,* that lauded his achievements in ways unthinkable for queer writers just five or six years ago, but also the ones written for the gay press. For all of them, down to the very one, did to him in death what he fought against so strenuously in life: they made the erotic incidental. They lauded *Franny* and the so-called "straight" (isn't that ironic?) anthologies: *Hometowns, Personal Dispatches*, *A Member of the Family*, and others. Most at least mentioned the "erotica" (Preston preferred the term "pornography") but they frequently failed to even mention the names of the books. As wonderful and as important as the anthologies are— and I have an essay in one of them—shouldn't John Preston nonetheless be remembered more for *Mr. Benson* and *I Once Had a Master*?

And isn't that the way he would have wanted it? At least, that's the perspective he had by the time of his death. I can't claim to have known Preston beyond my one brunch, my one interview, and our series of letters; so there may have been a time he yearned to move beyond the label of pornographer. But sitting that afternoon on Commercial Street in Provincetown, when he insisted on buying me a soda since I had paid for brunch (I didn't refuse: how could I?), we watched the boys go by and Preston said to me; "I want people to know what I'm trying to say. I don't want my message distorted. We can't lose sight of what gay liberation is all about." What *is* it all about? I asked. "Self-definition," Preston responded. Gay liberation is about breaking rules, he said, about crushing inhibitions, about being able to love not only *whom* we want, but *how* we want. In a letter to me written in the November before his death, Preston had this to say: "I think the upcoming publication of *My*

Life as a Pornographer, and the realization that I'm always going to be perceived as a pornographer, no matter what else I do, has changed things a great deal for me. It's what I'm all about. It's about being able to say the final fuck yous; take it on *my* terms."

Preston had high hopes for *My Life as a Pornographer,* that it might finally enable people to grasp what it is he was trying to say behind all the hot stories of masters and slaves. It goes back to those odd stirrings of desire I first felt in 1984, to push myself, to break the limits, to bend the rules, to find the courage John Preston displayed the very first time he, as a teenaged boy from a small town in Massachusetts, stuck out his thumb and allowed himself to be picked up by a passing motorist. The courage that it took for me to write that letter to him, admitting my desire—finally, but too late, and that's one more reason for me to hate this damned, despicable virus. The courage it takes all of us to be queer, and especially the courage it takes every time we fuck, every time we enjoy the kind of sex that lives in our deepest desires. For it is true that John Preston, beyond all his undeniably important contributions to that collection of words he sometimes sardonically called "literature," left us another, equally important legacy: to remember who we are, and how we love, and why we started fighting in the first place.

THE LAST VISIT

V. K. McCarty

When I arrive the last time, John is sleeping, ensconced neatly in the headquarters he has recently set up for himself out in the living room, with the bed now pressed into the front bay windows. Rolodex and phone on one side table—and cigarettes. Faxes and files on the other side in a box under the table—and on it, more cigarettes. It's all so achingly familiar.

The apartment has changed, though. There are mahogany bookcases now. And a nifty recliner. And a highboy for his china with curved glass doors. And a formal dining-room suite. Mind you, there were several happy years in this place before any of these beautiful things arrived. Years of radical freedom, mattress on the floor and much exulting in the view down Park Street.

And before that, in two other apartments, the first with a view of the ocean and little glints of dawn light sparkling right through the wallboards. The sense of freedom there was bright and bristling, coming up the stairs past the potbellied stove on the landing and into the sandy open space. It was further invoked, exquisitely so, by knowing that up the steeper stairs in the back was John's scene-space, with two-by-fours erected over a bed frame. And rope in piles. And a pillow for Jason made of dirty socks and jockstraps. Sea smells and moonlight came right in; it was my first view of Portland.

And yet, for all the rebellious joy of his bohemian Smith-Corona days, I remember how proud John was the day he finally bought the bed, the day the dining-room furniture arrived, each time he purchased a piece of Portland glass, the day Tom put the bookcases together. His home has become filled with the symbols of mainstream success.

John has changed, too. He is napping wearing glasses; and he has suffered through the winter. Sleeping, he is peaceful and childlike; but the moment he wakes up, he's still driven and arch and laughing; and coughing and wry and sexy as ever. And completely ordering about a cadre of home caregivers and nurses, floral delivery boys and laundrymen. Between naps he has intense agendas for everyone present, with faxes flying and phone calls galore.

At his request, I am sitting nearby in a high-backed chair—wearing lots of eye makeup. And pearls. For some reason, John loved me in pearls and often pressed me about doing up my eyes. Made a big point of it many times, but once in particular for a televised black-tie Human-rights benefit dinner at the Boston Ritz Carlton, he was quite incorrigible about it. Back and forth to the bathroom with him in the bar as he demanded more. I think it reminded him of his debutante days. If you can believe it, he was truly known as one of the college men around Chicago who possessed proper evening clothes and could be counted on as a reliable deb escort for the grande Lake Michigan coming-out parties. So now, on this emotional journey, when I might have been more comfortable in a flannel nightgown, I'm in eye makeup and different pearls every day.

Friends and lovers drift in and out, visiting editors and writer-protégés on pilgrimage, his therapist, his lawyers; and nearly every day, in matched silk and tweeds, Miss Frannie Peabody, whose name I now realize is pronounced Pee-b'dee down east here.

Much of my fascination with things down east I owe to John. Even though I was born in Boston, my family left so soon that I consider my having grown to enjoy the brisk pleasures of the New England coast to be John's personal gift, imparted persistently and generously over the years. He insisted that I experience Boston his way. After all, being from there, he wanted me to know his good friends in the area, and life in his favorite hotels. He had, for example, a pair of very Victorian Tufts University chums with a coffin in their parlor; I was so enamored of them I'd pack an extra suitcase just to be able to change clothes suitably often enough when we dined out or visited them. John showed me where to have downtown Sunday brunch with violins playing, and how they send roses by every day you stay at the Parker House. He showed me the leather bars, and even introduced me to a foxy political pal who carried us off to Mrs. Jack's little museum-manse, Fenway Court, with her very own John Singer Sargent portrait.

John insisted I experience Medfield and his sister's wedding, and I must meet his marine brother. And I must understand that he grew up in a house that was built in the 1700s, not 1800s, and how to tell the difference. And know that my baptismal certificate looked exactly like his. At that time, I wasn't sure he'd understand the faith-wrestling I was going through, but he'd been through similar struggles and was very helpful. So much so that it seemed only natural to ask him to be my godfather when the time came, even though it meant traveling upstate to my convent for the service. It shouldn't have surprised me either to discover that he'd been called to so many jobs in church counseling, and in the service of the altar; he was even a subdeacon.

John insisted, too, that I experience Provincetown. Frankly, it didn't seem as if I'd be able to enjoy P-town, what with the sunshine life and the dunes and all, but John had that all figured out. A year before he finally got me there, he kept telling me about "The Captain and His Ship," this incredible yellow Victorian where he was so happy, and more wonderful friends who took care of him. They let me stay in their high-ceilinged dining room, and I went back for ten Septembers after that.

On holiday with John, life followed a rather Victorian pattern. Late morning we breakfasted—trust me, very late morning. Always someplace with good coffee and a bar, where he was known and fawned over. He wanted a drink, but lots of good fresh milk, too. On the walks afterward, he showed me shops his friends had developed; and, passing the ferry, he always had cathartic stories about relatives to share. Perhaps these streets reminded him of the textures in Medfield or where he wandered as a restless teen on the bus, hunting for ravishment and reconciliation.

In the afternoon, we sunbathed. We accomplished this rather (for me) amazing feat at a motel-cum-spa that the men who lived next door had right across the street on the beach. John had them put me in a peacock chair under an awning so he could sun on the deck with me beside him in the shade. Later it became a restaurant, but those were halcyon afternoons that first late summer. I'd change into whites, open a bottle and a parasol, and walk along the sunning boys on the deck, passing champagne; then drift down to wade in the bay, and back to the shade of the peacock chair—and John.

At four, all the folding chaises were stowed and the tea dance began on the deck. Often we broke out a little leather for this. John mixed his cruising with magazine networking; I did mine dancing. Then we napped; he up the ladder in his loft, and me in the dining room. Later we dined, sometimes taking in a drag show or a cabaret singer's performance along the way. It was one lobster place after another; but, disdaining the lobster, John always wanted steak and scotch. Later yet, we promenaded with the friendly—or not-so-friendly—crowds on Commercial Street near the ice cream and pizza shoppes, stopping at various haunts, but usually ending up in the leather bar over the A-House.

In Old Orchard Beach, John had dear friends who tended their employer's beach house, making an admirably orderly home of it between his visits. It was right on the ocean, with histrionic waves breaking beyond the picture windows during storms. I loved resting and recreating there, smoking and drinking and feasting in happy dishabille. And enjoying all the boys who dropped by and inevitably ended up confessing their sexual histories to John, sometimes staying to spend the night in his bed.

We often drove in to party at the bar a couple of his cohorts had opened there, but we shared only one weekend in Ogunquit. It was unabashedly memorable, though. Some man courting John had just purchased an amazing home, with all the furnishings included, out on a rocky promontory of Maine coast. And he'd arranged an extraordinary Fourth of July celebration during which John and I continually giggled about living out all our Great Gatsby fantasies. Each meal was more elaborate than the next, but the highlight of this fête galante was a lawn party under an immense tent that boys came and built the last afternoon. Caterers filled it with ice sculpture and shellfish and extravagant spreads of crudités and pastries. Though to be perfectly honest, I never did understand where all the guests came from. The entire weekend climaxed with a magnificent fireworks display, and for me at least, with the startling experience of spying John having sex.

Because I had crept down the staircase in a nightgown, hearing gasping in the living room when I was in the bathroom, I couldn't escape the odd notion that I was glimpsing the forbidden sight of Santa Claus performing his conjugal duties. Actually, it was the second time I'd heard sex from the bathroom that day; in the afternoon, I was absolutely riveted to the bathroom wall listening to long stretches of smacking and gagging and sighing I would have sold my soul to see. This was much tamer, though certainly beautiful in the flickering fireplace light.

Our travels were great fun, though often exhausting, and we drove hung-over a lot. Sometimes I remember not exactly knowing where we were headed, though it was always P-town or Boston, one end of the Cape or the other. Many stops at friendly watering holes blend together, but many of them had similar elements of charm and synchronicity. Someone would spot us as gay, or perhaps we would spot someone as delectable, or submissive, and we were off and running; hearing the tall tales, making threats, spinning seductions over the bar.

But now this morning, under crystal skies with brilliant early-morning sunshine pouring down on the plant-forest in the back window, I'm transcribing changes for a new edition of *Franny, the Queen of Provincetown*. This was actually his first published full-length piece, the thing that earned him his first ABA Convention at which he could call himself an author, after all the years of magazine writing. But today it's one of three books John is anxious to develop or revise in these last days, with each episode of cognizant waking precious. And now so much is unspoken in the blaze of eye contact.

John had me called out of bed before the *Today* show and has run us, chain-smoking, on yet another dawn course of message-dictation and, ignoring the awkward pathos hanging between us, we're doing copyright assignment and gift giving and editing, which is now filling my notebook. We're even working on reassigning his frequent-flyer miles to one of his protégés. Home-care deliveries and nursing protocols have finally brought this onslaught of work to a temporary halt and now, in a gesture of normalcy, like anyone else performing the same function, John has called for the Boston morning paper. A trio of favorable reviews in the last week's newspapers truly pleases him.

To offer him privacy while he's being bathed and nursed, I've retired to the office/boudoir that has become his publishing control center over the years in Portland. The high walls rise barren now up to the green-and-red landmark ceiling reliefs; all the posters and memorabilia and boy-meat calendars have been sent to John's amassed archives at Brown University. On his desk three glazed blue-and-buff vases hold pens and pencils, a brown pot contains Badboy lapel buttons. Two shallow Canadian Seal pots hold paper clips in two different sizes. A tin box from Decatur House contains hanging things. Several adding machines and a futuristic-looking mechanical stapler stand beside the large brass shaded lamp.

On a side desk, a two-gallon crockery pot, of rubber bands. Beside it, a bookcase with a dozen Rolodexes bunked together, and the *Literary Market Place*, software boxes and manuals, *Timetables of History*, *Reader's Catalog*, *Webster's*. On top, *Random House Dictionary of the English Language*—the big one, and *Physician's Desk Reference* for 1990. And above that, appearing austere against the now-naked wall, a half-gallon Eight O'Clock coffee tin from between the wars. How many of us have taken him A&P coffee on our visits down east to see him?

Tucked in by the lamp are the printed cards with quotes that used to be in various configurations around the wall. Now piled together, they seem in their random order such intense bedfellows: Colleen Dewhurst and Federico García Lorca, Dante and Isak Dinesen, Camus and Saint-Exupéry, Yourcenar and Paul Monette. Righteous indignation and wise observation born of genius and suffering mingle in these brilliant messages.

Behind the desk, the communications headquarters. Hewlett-Packard LaserJet III, Zeos 486 hard drive, NEC Multi-Sync 5D monitor, keyboard with WordPerfect 5.1 for Windows key guide, AT&T answering machine on auto. And above, one sad memento still hangs on the wall: a life-size poster of a vizsla, just like his beloved puppy, Vlad the Impaler, now gone.

How will I say good-bye to John? The question has haunted me continually on the plane, and every minute listening to him, and especially watching him sleep. And yet, even with him resolutely veering away from emotional topics, it seems in a way as if we have spoken of nothing else, and I think we have been making poignant—if oblique—farewells all through this visit. I treasure the memories he has shared with me, but it makes me heartsick now to realize how often we have joked about my relishing the sound of his whimpering. He would struggle for a few moments, and then grin and ask me if I enjoyed it. But by the last day, he's been suffering so badly—and slipping—and a new protocol of painkillers is being devised.

His sister had called me early the first day to come as fast as I could. I had changed my flight and walked directly out of the office to the airport, but now I was leaving early, too; there was a resonant sense that our work was completed, and we had said our good-byes. And John was fighting painfully against drifting off to sleep with me there. Yet I was so afraid—I think all of us were— that it would be the last time. It wasn't, though. John had other moments of waking and sharing, but for me this was the last.

Herewith the printed quotes that were thumbtacked up on John's office wall:

Will someone please talk about our children? They are being deprived of sex and love. What will happen to a generation that lives without those miracles?
                                          —*Colleen Dewhurst*

Why should one struggle against the flesh when there is the frightful problem of the spirit to be faced?
                                          —*Federico García Lorca*

Women around me whisper relentlessly, "Why are the men always so concerned with blood and violence," they wonder. But I think I know. If Gertrude Stein had been taken to a lonely road and shot, that would be a subject of our women's poems. You bet it would. It is a matter of history, and of experience, it is a matter of tradition.   —*Judy Grahn*

In the middle of the journey of
our life
I found myself within the
forest dark.
For the straightforward had been
lost.
                                          —*Dante,* The Divine Comedy

One must, in this lower world, love
many things finally to know what one
loves the most....
                                          —*Isak Dinesen*

If you are attacked as a Jew you have got to fight as a Jew, you cannot say, "Excuse me, I am a human being."   —*Hannah Arendt*

It is not a question of sublimation, which is itself a very unfortunate term and one that insults the body, but a dark perception that love for a particular person, so poignant, is often only a beautiful fleeting accident, less real in a way than the predispositions and choices that preceded it and will follow it.

—*Marguerite Yourcenar*

All I maintain is that on this earth there are pestilences and there are victims, and it is up to us, so far as possible, not to join forces with the pestilences.

—*Albert Camus,* The Plaza

"Men have forgotten this truth," said the Fox. "You become responsible, forever, for what you have tamed."

—*Antoine de Saint-Exupéry*

I wish to leave a proper testament of what my people have gone through.

—*Paul Monette*

But I forget; why sweat I out my braine In deep designs, to gay boys lewd and vain?

—*John Marston,* The Scourge of Villainie *(1599)*

If you think there are no new frontiers, watch a boy ring the front doorbell on his first date.

—*Olin Miller*

I am a poor passionate and silent fellow
who…carries inside himself a lily that
cannot be watered, and to the simple eyes
that look at me I show a rose reddened
with the sexual shading of the April
peony, which is not my heart's truth.
—*Federico Garcia Lorca*

A culture without dreams is finished. It has nothing
to motivate it.   —*Joseph Campbell*

To endure, a people must treasure the image of itself.
—*Pearl Buck*

According to the scholar Salimbene, the second folly
of Frederick the Great was "that he wanted to find out
what kind of speech and what manner of speech children would have when they grew up, if they spoke to
no one beforehand. So he bade foster mothers and
nurses to suckle children, to bathe and wash them,
but in no way to…speak to them, for he wanted to
learn whether they would speak the Hebrew language,which is the oldest, or Greek, or Latin, or
Arabic, or perhaps the language of their parents….
The children all died for they could not live without…words….

PRESTON THOUGHTS

Samuel R. Delany

How many people do you know who have died of AIDS-related complications?

It's been a strange experience to watch the answer to that change over the years. When I wrote my first novel about AIDS in 1984, it included an account of a 1983 brunch conversation that took place among some friend of mine, Frank, Ralph, and Harvy, in which we talked about the fact that we didn't know anyone yet who had it.

Three years later, Ralph was dead of AIDS.

A dozen years after that brunch, and AIDS has become the largest killer among those in my personal circle—beating out cancer, suicide, and heart disease combined.

This year it took John Preston.

The first time I saw John was at a reading he gave at the Food for Thought Bookstore in Amherst, Massachusetts, the town where I teach—but we did not meet. What stays with me even more than the reading itself, however, is the enthusiasm of the young people who ran the store in the weeks before John was to come. He was very much a man who traveled with his own myth preceding him.

When we actually met—at the 1992 Lambda Literary Awards Banquet in Miami—John chided me for not coming up and introducing myself back at Amherst. Over the drinks we were having in the hotel lobby with our mutual publisher, Richard Kasak, John even seemed doubtful that I had actually been there....

We met again—the second and last time—at the 1993 OutWrite Conference in Boston, where John substituted as a last-minute speaker for Tony Kushner, when Kushner couldn't make it. Again, the meeting was a genial group of people sitting around a table, drinking in a hotel bar, much like the first.

To say that Preston was tall, easygoing, witty, and well-spoken—well, many people knew him better than I; they can catch the nuances to those aspects (certainly the ones that first struck me about him) better than I can.

I'd been hearing of *Mr. Benson*—John's best-known novel—for years; but I'd read it only when Badboy Books republished it in 1992. It's an extraordinary performance. Something is going on there that you don't find in most porn—made the more unusual because it's so hard to put your finger on exactly what it is.

My favorite book of John's is (and probably will remain) his collection of essays, *My Life as a Pornographer.* (*Hustling* is also a charming how-to book.) I wonder if this isn't finally what holds the key to *Mr. Benson.* John lived a highly active sexual life. The fact is, you learn things about sex from doing it lots, with lots of people, that measurements, film, strong lights, or written reports will never teach—things that have to do with the way sex connects to the social world around us. There are things known to the person who has had sex with two or three thousand-plus partners that will never be known to the person whose sexual experience has not exceeded fifty—even if four or five of those fifty have been long-term relations with thousands of sex acts apiece. As one reads sexual commentators from Sigmund Freud to Camille Paglia, again and again one comes across coruscating naïvetés (naïvetés one never finds in, say, Sade) that make the sexually experienced reader sigh: if only they'd done a bit more of it, with a wider range of folks, such idiocies might not have been uttered.

I've said you don't find that sort of naïveté in Sade. You don't find it in Preston, either. Preston's essays are rich in sexual insights. For all the element of pornographic exaggeration, a background knowledge of the workings of the real thing is evident throughout *Mr. Benson.* And that is the *real* authority the book emanates.

After John's death, on the day before the memorial reading for him at The Lure on West 13th Street, I was on the Broadway subway that morning, heading downtown, when I glanced at a woman sitting a bit down from where I was standing. She looked Hispanic. Her denim jacket sported a fair amount of silver and fringe. Her earrings were large, bright, and dangly. She had a big pocketbook on her lap. Propped on it, the paperback she was reading was *Stolen Moments,* the fourth novel in John's *Alex Kane* series.

In New York, there's a kind of writerly myth about books on the subway. To see a reader with a book on the subway is to know it's achieved a certain popularity. Back in March 1893, when Stephen Crane had his first novel, *Maggie, A Girl of the Streets,* printed at his own expense, he hired three of his art-student friends to sit with copies of it on the Third Avenue el all day, riding back and forth, pretending to read it with great enthusiasm—the best advertising he could think of! The 1965 was the first time I sat down on the train, looked across the aisle, and saw a youngster reading my just-released novel. Far more than the author's copies in the mail, that marked the moment from which I believed that possibly I might be a real writer. In my stolen glimpse of the reader of *Stolen Moments,* the timing was certainly propitious. At the Lure reading the next night, it was warming to be able to tell those gathered in memory of John what I'd seen. And when I was leaving The Lure, walking back to the subway, someone shouted at me from the back of a motorcycle, vrooming past, "Hey, thank you!" I'd like to think that's what they were thanking me for; as I would like to think it means there's a chance of John's work persisting with a certain audience.

The anthologies John edited, on hometown experience and coming out, will be a treasury of information on the reality of gay life over the last decades for years to come.

The intelligence of actual sexual experience that informs the range of his work, whether fiction, pornographic fantasy, or nonfiction, gives it a rare immediacy.

Cherish it. It's a sterling quality.

FACSIMILE TRANSMISSION: ONE LAST PAGE

Patrick Carr

TO: John

FROM: Patrick

And so it's *adios* via fax, your favorite. And did it not always serve well, delivering those monologues. *But you know,* I said once, *faxes fade. They gradually fade away to blank pages.* Yes, you knew. You have to make copies of them before they disappear.

But who'd have thought there was a need to save them all up? Curls of weird, slick paper—why bother? What did we say, after all? All that clogging of Ma Bell's synapses— saved for posterity? I can imagine you chuckling at the thought.

And don't they all blur in my mind now. Fade, yes, but only at the edges, where they come together, finishing my picture of you. Messages of encouragement, direction, advice

—through them you became what you most wanted to be: a guide, a motivator, a supporter of strange young men whom you thought deserved encouragement.

Even for that, you'd probably rather have a piece of fiction dedicated to you—but our casual sheaves of paper? *Patrick, really*...you'd say...*recycle them.*

But then there were the personal notes that passed between us as friends. My ramblings—your concise, witty replies. The gossip that was our secret sustenance. Inside jokes. And again, your advice.

So now—let the words fade, I suppose. They were merely the wrapping around what you actually gave, with the offhand generosity that always distinguished you. They did their job—made you present, and important, and unique. Let the nouns and verbs disappear. Care does not require them.

But enough with the seriousness. We were never so dour. If our correspondence is over, let it end on a note more typical of our too-brief friendship—

How cute was that young monk who served at your requiem mass?! You picked him out from beyond the grave, so help me. And how alive that chapel was, how perfectly alive. Because I knew you were loving it.

Until later,
Patrick

A FEW SIMPLE, ORDINARY THINGS

Agnes Barr Bushell

Editor's note: This is a story written in the spring of 1984, about six months after Ms. Bushell met John Preston. She took Preston out of his Park Street apartment, complete with all the trappings of his SM world and put him into a longer work contrasting and comparing the various forms of love she had been witnessing among her friends. The character of Charles, dialogue taken from John's own discussions with Bushell, is clearly a strong fictional portrait of Preston. Unfortunately, the subplot containing him did not survive the final editing of the novel Local Deities, *and this became the only appearance of Charles/John in her work.*

Rick Adams, born under the sign of Mars and a different set of names, wearing, on this glum Tuesday morning, shades, black leather jacket, white scarf (coffee stained), jeans, boots, and a Camel nonfiltered, stands on the corner of Commercial and Moulton at the edge of the

steep cobblestoned incline that marks the natural bound-
ary of water and land. Not that natural boundaries mean
much anymore, in any sphere. Over a century now the
sea has been covered over by the stones, cement and rail-
way tracks, but still it snakes under wooden docks, nibbling
away at the pilings with a memory for its territorial rights,
ancient and inviolable. Eighteen fifty-two it happened.
Mammoth crime against nature and nature's god. Hence
the rampant perversity in this part of town, unnatural acts
committed daily, nay, hourly, on these very streets which
should be densely populated by fishies and other
unearthly phenomena.

Flicking cigarette onto the pristine sidewalk, stuffing
hands into pockets, Rick Adams saunters across the cobble-
stones and tracks without glancing left or right. Cultivate
the saunter. The gay gait. Head up, shoulders back. Cars,
trucks, bicycles grind to a halt. When you walk into the sea,
it either parts for you or it doesn't. And don't forget to scowl
at the lawyers, packed in here like sardines now, smug as the
streets they walk along. Ah, Rico, how they wonder what
you are. Or as Charles once put it as we cozied up to some
bar, "We got 'em puzzled all right. They can't figure out
whether you're a dyke or my effeminate boyfriend."

What I really am is a spy in the house of love.

Safely across Commercial Street, through the door, up
the stairs, inside the relative safety of the studio, Rick aban-
dons shades, jacket, scarf and ambiguous sexual identity for
paper, pen and ink. The writer must be an androgyne, says
Virginia Woolf. Both genders or neither. A manly woman
or a womanly man. Have sex with all persuasions. Assume
the sex of all persuasions. Be a gender traitor. But first learn
a little tae kwon do.

I like you a lot, Yves said, opening his belt.

Don't you love me a little?

Love is a word reserved for those you would die for. If I
were willing to die for everybody I fucked…

For some people, this is still a definite consideration.
Not for me, sugar.

This is the testing ground of love. Everybody is failing. I
am doing a survey. The prognosis is not good. Worse, I've
become stupid. Can't get the dialogue down straight or
remember the simplest things: the proper use of household objects, the names of poets and characters in books,
party lines. Voltaire was serious, Yves says to me. This is
the best of all possible worlds. Staring at him, empty-
headed. Cannot rejoin. Missing neurons, too much reefer,
or maybe it's cigarettes. Like sugarplums, they dance
away—Marx, Kropotkin, the Port Huron Statement, the
Sermon on the Mount. Instead he offers me ancient
wisdom from *Kung Fu* reruns: Do you think you can take
over the universe and improve it? I do not believe it can
be done. The universe is sacred. You cannot improve it. If
you try to change it, you will ruin it. If you try to hold it,
you will lose it....

And lose it I do, daily. Because you want to hold onto
it, Yves says, his dark eyes moist with sincerity and reproof,
because you insist that everything make sense. Because I
don't know what love is anymore, I reply stoutly, or why
simple things have to be so difficult. Anyway, what's wrong
with holding on, I ask him. What's wrong with making
sense?

The problem is that desire comes as a shock. That's its
nature: shocking. And I have been insulated, hibernating
with my own kind. We speak in codes, having already
divided the world neatly into good and evil. We hover
above it all, ancient, cynical and removed, chained to irony
as to a kind of karmic guilt. But Yves is too young for cyni-
cism, too innocent for guilt. He floats like a cloud. If he also
had compassion. But maybe he does. Maybe he pities me
my chains.

The role of the angelic being, he announced to me, is
to free others and move on.

We were arguing about a character in a book. He was explaining to me that the book was a tragedy because the protagonist stayed with his lover instead of moving on to save someone else. How many people can you expect to save in one lifetime? I asked him. He only smiled at me.

Yes, he pities me my guilt and my chains. So, out of this pity, this detachment, he sometimes allows me to love him.

Sex with Yves, sex with a cloud. He surrenders his body to me, yields like water yields to the shape of gorges and rocks. A form of passive resistance. It broke the British Empire, but I am an emotional Stalinist. If they lie down, fuck 'em. But I leave him every time feeling like a rapist or a succubus. I close his door and think, never again. He is turning me into a monster. Then I think (noting the irony), No. He's turning me into a man.

The testing ground of love is mined. Enter at your own risk.

I have not seen him in a week. Whenever tempted to use the phone, I take a bath. I am so clean, I squeak. I have also been sleeping a lot. I dreamt small mythological animals were coming out of the spigots of my sink. I read *Buddenbrooks* and decided to go to the dentist immediately. I had a long conversation with my dead mother during which she recommended that I move to Peru. My mail consisted of nothing but notices of bounced checks.

The best of all possible worlds should at least have provided us with a guaranteed annual income, free tobacco and mutual love at first sight.

But think, I say to him, touching the scar on his big toe, in another time or place I'd be risking my life just being in bed with you.... What happened to your toe?

A lawn mower.

Weren't you wearing shoes?

You sound just like my mother.

I can't help it. It's a habit. Were you?

What?

Wearing shoes?

Of course not. I was just mowing the grass. Why wear shoes?

So you wouldn't cut your foot off.

But I didn't cut my foot off. I only cut part of my foot off. Not even. Anyway, it was ten years ago. Ancient history. But I'll tell you. I'll remember that lawn mower for the rest of my life. Power tools and lovers—it's always the ones that hurt you the most that you never forget.

Rick Adams glances down. The page yawns open, rumpled and forlorn as an empty bed, creased by a few scribbled lines of pathetic half-remembered conversation. Charles insisting that nobody but a fool ever writes except for money. And he's right, though not for the reason he thinks he is. It's because money, like marriage, legitimizes the otherwise unacceptable—prurience, petulance, self-indulgence, ego gratification, and other forms of crass and lewd behavior usually considered tasteless or impolite.

Bah! says Rick Adams, throwing down pen and readjusting drag, emerging brazenly onto the brick sidewalks, sauntering with cultivated grace up from the waterfront and, studiously sidestepping all beautiful angelic presences, arriving at last at the door of a friend.

"I think I've recovered," I announce to Charles, after letting myself in with my key. I have a set of Yves's house keys too. I can walk right in on both of them. And often do.

"I didn't even know you were sick."

"Lovesick. But I've recovered."

"So I see. You're back in uniform. I was wondering how long the dress-up phase was going to last. Well, it's nice to have you back, Rick."

He was still in bed.

"Want me to make coffee?"

"Just put the water on. I'm getting up."

Out of the corner of my eye, I notice that besides the usual can of Crisco there is a small paper bag of clothes-pins next to his mattress. He notices that I notice.

"I found Eddie again."

"So I see. Am I going to find him chained up in the kitchen?"

He rolls his eyes at me.

"Just go put up the water."

"Yes, sir."

I go into the kitchen, fill the kettle, put it on the stove, fiddle with the knobs. I have done this for Yves of a morn-ing as well. I am the official coffee-preparer. Typical.

He comes in yawning, buttoning his fly, a foot taller than I am, steel gray hair shaved down practically to the skin, lean as a cat, cigarette already dangling out of his mouth.

"Where is he?" I ask.

"I sent him home last night. I don't sleep with them, you know. Never get a good night's sleep when there's someone else in the bed. Besides, it's Tuesday."

He says it without emphasis, as though he were saying, Besides it's raining. What he means is that his Tuesday morn-ings belong to me.

"So, Adam," he says. "What's new in the orchard?"

I scowl up at him.

"The Adam-and-Yves routine is getting a little tired," I say.

"Hey, you were the one who told me you were playing yang to his yin. So what happened? He finally fessed up and told you he was gay, right?"

"Wrong. He just doesn't love me."

"So why does he have to love you? He puts out, doesn't he?"

"But he doesn't have his heart in it."

"His heart? His heart! Doesn't he fuck with his cock like everybody else? Who cares where his heart is?"

I watch him spoon coffee into the filter. He never counts,

does it by sight. Pours water by sight, too. Sometimes his eye's a little off and we wind up sipping high-caf mud. Then we're so shaky we have to drink martinis for lunch. And there goes another Tuesday down the tubes.

"You're not serious," I say.

"Of course I'm serious. Just tell him you don't give a shit about his heart, you just want to get laid."

We sit at the table, clear some space for the cups from out of the clutter of Swedish pornography, *Drummer* magazines, leather-club newsletters, lascivious fan mail, and a week's worth of *Boston Globe*s. I'm used to the pinups on the walls, the naked young men gagged and bound in rope, simple, ordinary clothesline by the look of it, though occasionally a new, particularly enormous cock swathed in leather will hold my attention for longer than thirty seconds. I'm used to the letters he gets, mostly rather pathetic, from men begging to travel hundreds of miles to be tortured by him for a night. The responsibilities of a self-professed sadist are sometimes overwhelming. But as far as I can judge it, none of it has anything to do with his reality. He smokes too much and drinks too much and writes too much crap, but I understand—it pays the bills. However, when the man starts talking to me in Martian, I begin to get annoyed.

"Charles," I say, "I don't know what planet you come from, but here on Earth people don't go around telling other people that all they want to do is get laid. For one thing, it's hardly ever true...."

"Gay men do it all the time."

"Gay men are nuts."

"Straight men are nuts."

"Why don't we just say all men are nuts? I'll agree on that point."

"Straight or gay"—he sucks a last lungful of smoke out of his cigarette—"men are not worth it, period. Take it from me. I've had twenty-five of them, and they're just not worth it. You should find yourself a nice dyke."

"Eat shit," I say as sweetly as I can.

"Well, was he that good?"

"He's beautiful."

"That's not the question."

"That's the answer."

"So, it was small, was it? Did he apologize? Did you have to reassure him?"

I just laugh at him.

"It was, wasn't it? Tiny. Like sucking a toothpick. You could barely see it. Such a beautiful face, such a minuscule cock. No wonder you feel like Adam."

"Actually, he's perfect. His body is perfect. He just resents it that I love his body."

"Of course he resents it. Straight men can't tolerate being sex objects. They have to be the pursuers. They have to conquer."

He lights another Tareyton and raises an eyebrow at me. The raised eyebrow doesn't mean he's quizzical or even incredulous. And Charles is never merely curious. Charles moves from nosy directly into inquisitional. No, the raised eyebrow is a flourish, a grace note, a curlicue. It is his only affectation, the only place he allows the fugitive queen inside him to act out. "I hate to tell you this, Erika," he says, "but you're not over it yet."

Then he squints at me through his smoke.

"Did it ever occur to you that he might be a closet case? Because with your track record..."

"Will you please stop projecting yourself onto the world? Just because you can't understand why any man in his right mind..."

My voice is sounding uncommonly brittle so I stop talking and light my fifth cigarette of the hour. Packs disappear in my hand now. There are many kinds of suicide, and they're all unethical as hell. Many kinds of lies and ditto in the ethics department. But hell is other people, as M. Sartre remarks so pithily, and so you must defend against all comers with smoke screens and leather jackets even if a marshmallow resides within.

He is asking me how I feel. A question Yves never asks. Yves assumes he knows how I feel every moment I'm with him, and since I become emotionally transparent in his presence, he is usually absolutely right. But Charles is a writer, a pornographer, to be precise, and so cares about everything in minute detail. (The exact size of the cock, the precise number of thrusts per orgasm, *et cetera ad nauseam.*) Still, I lie to him. He wouldn't understand the way I feel—how could he? Like something died in my arms, an infant I lug around with me, a bag lady with a dead baby or Medea who did it herself.

"I feel old," I say, which neighbors on the truth. "I feel like Horace. Come, now, last of my loves. *Age iam, meorum finis amorem, non enim post hoc alia calebo femina…*"

"Oh, stop it! If you're old, what does that make me?"

"It's different for men."

"Tell me the truth."

"You're old, too, Charles."

He glances at the clock.

"Ten-thirty. Are the bars open yet?"

"You haven't had breakfast."

"Bloody Marys'll do just fine."

We go outside. The weather's changed. Now it's sunny and warm. Spring. There are so many old people on the street. I wonder how they can stand it. I wonder what I'll do when the full realization fits me, when I finally know for a fact that I'll never hold him again. Like I know for a fact why women humiliate themselves for men, why they put up with beatings and abuse, why they prostitute themselves, give their men money, babies, careers, their lives, and hopelessly, stupidly, getting nothing back but a body, a taut, strong body to hold for a few minutes in the dark.

Rick and Charles, under pseudonyms, enter the leather bar around the corner. More naked bodies plastered on the walls. Is there to be no end to this? Joint's dead at 10:30 A.M., dyke's behind the bar. She doesn't even glance at me anymore. I'm Charles's woman, a puzzle to everyone. Not good for his image as Top of the Town or mine as Mother of the Year. We sit at a table and Charles digs out some change and goes to the jukebox. An hour's worth of Billie Holiday, punctuated by "Girls Just Wanna Have Fun" and "Sweet Dreams."

"I know you're tired of hearing this," he says, sipping his Bloody Mary, "but I really don't understand why there are any straight people left in the world."

"You want another harvest of sixteen-year-olds to seduce, don't you? Where are they supposed to come from?"

"How long do I have to wait for yours?"

"Eleven years. You'll be dead by then."

"Is this maternal rage I'm hearing?"

"No, this is Xanthippe's revenge. We call it AIDS. Just will me your typewriter."

"Like hell I will."

"If you don't, I won't croon at your wake."

"They'll be enough gay boys crooning at my wake."

"All twenty-five hundred of them? You'd better book a cathedral."

"You're just jealous."

"No, I'm just choosy."

"Yeah. Real choosy. Featherheads. If I put myself through the mill like you do for every man I fucked, I'd have been in an asylum by the time I was twenty. They're not worth it. Believe me. They're just bodies I play with. The only thing that matters is what you can get out of them. If you can get a good story out of it, fine. If you can't it's a waste of time. Go home and write and stop wallowing. Some day he'll eat his heart out."

"Yeah. And someday I'll hit menopause."

"Erika," he says, "will you please wake up."

But waking up is hard to do. You may wake up from one dream only to sink into another far deeper and therefore far more dangerous than the first. Shedding disguises is easier. Or so Rick Adams believes, stripping off leather jacket and jeans, slipping on skirt. A little color smeared tactfully on eyelids and cheeks. A gold wire eased through the earlobes. A white silk blouse, stockings, heels. But I keep hearing Charles's voice in my ear, the other disguise, the deception of words. Martian he speaks to me. Martian defends him. The size of an organ takes precedence over any quality of soul. As though he believed a word of it. As though he didn't know how transparent his disguise really is.

I walk home from my studio on the waterfront as the streetlights go on. I have written four pages of fiction and a letter to my husband telling him who I think I am. It is a letter I will never send. Tomorrow I may think I'm someone else. I don't trust myself or the definition of terms.

We are all wary of each other. On the street. In our own homes. A strange wariness, all afraid, all afraid of each other. I don't understand this.

Or maybe I'm the only one they don't trust.

"It's very simple," Charles said. "Any woman who would cuckold her husband is ipso facto untrustworthy."

Cuckold. I thought that was one of those words that had gone out of circulation in this country, except in translation.

"Do wives get cuckolded too?" I asked him.

"No," he said. "Wives get what they deserve."

He'd disapproved of Yves from the beginning—too light-weight for me, too young—and Charles is not the sort of man who enjoys having even his unsolicited advice go unheeded. Of course, Eddie is even younger, but I don't mention this to Charles, who would dismiss it anyway as one of the prerogatives of his particular calling.

"Your husband," he had pronounced at the time in his most pontifical voice, "is handsome, faithful, pays the bills and cooks you dinner. Do you realize how many gay men there are in the world who would kill for a husband like that?"

But had I stopped to consider this collective gay yearning for my husband before I dived headlong into extra-marital anguish? No, I had not. Or was it Charles's own yearning that I had ignored? Under all the bravado, did he really want the very handsome, faithful, breadwinning cook I was abandoning—or a gay version of it? While I, on the other hand, did I really want to beat men up and decorate them with clothespins? Was I living his fantasy while he was living mine? Was this why we were friends after all, because we were a living, breathing embodiment of the inevitable and sublime attraction between the diametrically opposed? Thesis and antithesis? Matter and antimatter? Fish and fowl?

I gazed around his apartment, furnitureless except for the barest essentials—a table and four wooden chairs, a mattress, an IBM Selectric and a desk. He didn't have a TV, a stereo or a phone. He couldn't pay his rent. All he had really were those pictures and the boys he would beat but refused to admit he could love.

"You have no idea, Charles," I sighed, "how regular meals, financial security and connubial bliss can wear on a woman."

"Erika," he said, "go home."

Yves lives on the top floor of the tallest building in his part of the city. Walking home in the evening, I could gaze up and see his bedroom window and the light shining out, through fog and storm and darkness, drawing women to him like ships to rocks. I would go to his door and knock. He would open the door and open his arms and I would step into them as into a dream. In this dream, we don't have to say any words, make any promises, worry about husbands, children, saving the world, or whether it's time for dinner. In this dream, the sea takes me. I drift out on the tide, lose my life jacket, my grip. I lose everything in this bed, this dream. If he let me, I would self-destruct.

That he doesn't let me I take sometimes as a sign of love.

I walk home through the park. It's there waiting for me on the other side of the trees—husband, children, cats. It is mine, made by my own hands, the way Charles has made his life or Yves has made his. It isn't only mine, though. It belongs to three other people. I can't send them packing when I'm finished playing with them. I can't send them home; they're already there.

I reach the front porch of the house. Inside, children are laughing. I fumble with my keys, but in the dark I can't remember the shape of the one that opens my own door.

A child comes running. I hear his bare feet slapping against the wooden floor, the bounce of his laugh. Mommy's home! he yells. He pulls the door wide open and leaps at me without warning, trusting that I'll catch him. Light pours out from the doorway, light and warmth, the sound of the TV, the smell of food cooking on the stove, but I can't pay attention to any of that because he's already airborne, flying right at me, and I have only this split second to brace myself, catch him right out of the air, hold him safe, and he's giggling, wrapping his arms and legs around me so I can't move, can't even breathe, squeezing me like a boa constrictor, so hard and so tight I think my heart will stop. Then he wriggles free, slips out of my arms, and charges off down the hallway to announce my arrival, joyfully, easily, as though nothing in the world could be simpler or more wonderful.

FRANNY, THE MATCHMAKER
Will Leber

Author's note: I made a pilgrimage in April 1994 to visit John Preston at his home in Portland, Maine before he died of AIDS. When I arrived, he felt that death was in him and he was in a race to finish his work. His friend Agnes Bushell described some of John's last days (days in which I was so fortunate to share) in the Boston Phoenix:

John died with books in his head that he never had the time to write, books half-done, books whose contracts he was still waiting to sign. Literally, on his deathbed, chain-smoking as always, he signed some of those contracts, and he dictated the epilogue to the new edition of Franny, *which he always said was his most-beloved book...*

He was concentrating on what Socrates says is the only thing that really matters to men: their immortality. John was a writer, and so for him the only immortality he could count on was in his books. When I walked in, John was lying on his bed in the middle of his livingroom. His longtime friend, V. K. McCarty, was sitting erectly beside him taking down the dictation (which Agnes describes deftly) of his novel, Franny, the Queen of Provincetown. *Like John, she is a well-known writer of erotica whom I admire greatly. John had included my first published story in his* Flesh and the Word, 2 *anthology and brought me out as a porn writer. He had also named me among the "young writers" to whom he dedicated his recent book,* My Life as a Pornographer. *I had come, in part, to thank him for his important contributions to my life and career.*

When I told him how honored I felt to be included in that dedication, he replied, "You may not be thanking me when you want to be an English professor someday. And not to diminish the importance of pornography, but look where I've returned to now." To Franny. *That novel held great importance to John because it captured the lives and preserved the histories of a group of gay men who had literally rescued him as a high school boy off the streets of Boston. John often told the story of how, back then in a hostile world, a bunch of flamboyant drag queens had helped him to survive and ultimately find his way as a gay man. He also never failed to point out the crucial and visible role of queens in the gay-liberation movement. His novel,* Franny, the Queen of Provincetown, *represented, on some level, a payback to all the queens he had ever known for their kindness and activism. I believe John wanted to make sure that debt was paid fully before he died.*

John passed away at the end of April. In July I visited Provincetown, following the Stonewall twenty-fifth anniversary celebration and March on the UN in New York City. I was there over the July Fourth weekend. John was very much on my mind, as was his novel—so much so I began to see his character Franny around town. And he started talking to me.

This is how I came to write "Franny, the Matchmaker": One night in Provincetown, as I lay on my lumpy guest-house bed, the events I have outlined conspired. I had a dream in which John was still alive and Franny and his entourage had come to Portland to tell John, V. K. and me a story. I understood then that I had to write down this story.

Some readers will recognize events and names that are familiar in the narrative that is attributed to John. While I chose to use real names, there should be no mistake that this story is fiction, even though, like our dreams, it originates from true-life experiences.

Finally, I confess to plagiarism and imitation of John's work. I have stolen some of his characters. I have not, however, attempted to copy his singular style. I hope only that his spirit has survived in these pages. If it has, then I have succeeded.

The Living Room

JOHN:

Thank you for coming, V. K. Yes, I knew you would. We accomplished a lot yesterday, but there's so much work I still have to get done. Yes, the lilies are beautiful. Anne sent them. No, you cannot force them. Don't touch them. Leave them to open naturally. They've got to last through Monday. I have guests coming. Yes, they are rather like a vagina. Not that it is the first thing that comes to my mind. Don't touch them. Of course it's an order. I know you're used to giving the orders. So am I—which is why we're such good friends. Neither of us ever listened to the other, at least most of the time.

Could you put another pillow under my head so that I can see you better? Can you believe I've come to this? I can only move my arms and my head. From my chest down I'm nothing but pain, totally immobile. I can't write. I can't do anything for myself. Are you shocked at how I look? You haven't said anything. I am not beautiful. Ha! I am particularly not beautiful in my soul. You of all people know that. Remember the things we used to do? Unmentionable things...

You didn't wear your dominatrix drag for me. You brought your entire makeup kit over? Of course I remember how I'd suddenly demand that you go put on different colors of eye shadow to fit our changing moods. No, the color you have on is fine. Your face is flawless.

Even in your corporate power attire, you have that certain savoir faire. You look a bit corseted; the fit of the jacket. And the brooch at your neck—is it antique? Of course, it was your mother's. Hand me my cigarettes and the lighter. Now that you're beside me, I can smoke. Tom won't let me smoke unless someone is watching because I might doze off and drop the ember. He doesn't want to go up in a blaze of fire. Me, I might not mind. He's studying to be a nurse. He probably has had more training helping me than he'll ever get in school.

I had the visiting nurse increase my morphine again. It's such a struggle because I have so much to do. I need to stay conscious, but the pain reached such a point I had to have morphine. Let's get to work while I can. They are going to tell us another Franny story. I know you were surprised when I, a pornographer and leatherman, first wrote that novel celebrating Franny—a queen with a golden heart. You've been so great taking down my dictation. But this time, they're going to talk. Did you bring the recorder? And you can work it? I know you are extraordinarily capable.

You've met Will, right? I'm glad you had breakfast together. It's my favorite meal, the fuel for the day ahead. Will always sends me neatly typed manuscripts. He'll transcribe the tape. They're all here. They're just going to tell the story the way they want. You know a writer's characters are like his children—they eventually leave you and go on with lives of their own. But, if you're lucky, they come and visit.

Will, sometimes you might have to interject some notes in the margin, tag the time and place and who is speaking. V. K., hit the record button. Ah, yes, I can see it now, the New England charm of Provincetown, that beautiful crab-claw-shaped bay, that colony of queers…Franny's town. Listen!

Provincetown, the July Fourth weekend, 1994
Dick Dock, 2 A.M. Saturday morning, July 2

ADAM:

Franny says to just tell the truth. He says that there have always been just too many lies. So the truth is that we met at Dick Dock. We met at 2 A.M. under a clear and starry sky.

FRANNY:

That's right. He was just going around and around underneath that pier. He was ducking in and out of the pilings, shuffling through the sand, spinning around those poles under the dock. One point he was going around so fast, so often, I was sure he was going to turn into butter.

ADAM:

The tide was only partway out. You could only stand up under the dock out near the water's edge. And that's where the action was heaviest, the men packed most tightly. I wanted to be a part of it. I needed a man. I'd been in Provincetown for two days. I'd been to tea-dance and in the bars at night, and nobody talked to me.

FRANNY:

You were desperate.

ADAM:

I guess it showed. Maybe that's why I couldn't get lucky. I thought I was hiding it, but I guess my need was too obvious. It scared the guys away. I was losing my cool. I couldn't remain aloof, like all the muscle boys. I couldn't keep up that facade.

FRANNY:

He hit his head on one of the cross timbers as he came out from under the pier.

ADAM:

You could stand up underneath the dock in between the rafters. They were spaced like three or four feet apart and all the guys were bunched up in there doing the dirty. Nothing unsafe, you know, JO and some sucking. The whole scene wasn't solely for sex, either, there were all kinds of guys out there in the shadow of the moonlight along the harbor's edge. Guys were meeting and talking and kissing. I figured there had to be someone there for me.

FRANNY:

It is kind of romantic. Provincetown at its finest…moonlight, stars, the glass-smooth water reflecting the lights swagged along the masts of a cruise ship out in the harbor.

After the bars close and after cruising quiets down on Commercial Street, it's the last stop of the night. Dick Dock is the last chance for romance. That night, I'm sitting on the spectators' bench—a creosote-soaked log stuck in the beach about fifteen feet over from the dock—smoking a joint. Drag queen that I am, I love cheap entertainment. I've become somewhat of an insomniac. A peril of age. You need less sleep.

There is always a place in my heart for the wounded. A dazed boy with a knock on his noggin was too much, just too touching. I can call him a boy. He's gotta be under twenty-five, and I'm in my sixties. My purpose in life nowadays is helping people with AIDS. So I appreciate every year. I appreciate the gift of every day. I had to rescue him. I jumped up, ran to his side and ushered him over to the log. "Poor baby, come sit with mama." I rubbed his head.

ADAM:

You were wearing a simple house frock with a chartreuse cardigan sweater.

FRANNY:

And you wore a tight tank top and cut-off jeans. "What's all this trinket trash around your neck?" I asked.

ADAM:

One man's trash is another's treasure. I had the ring my ex gave me hanging from a gold chain, my dog tags commemorating the '93 March on Washington, and gay freedom rings I just bought the previous weekend in New York at the Stonewall twenty-fifth anniversary march.

FRANNY:

"Who gave you the ring?" He was shivering. And he was plastered.

ADAM:

"My long-lost ex-lover. He couldn't keep his dick in his pants."

FRANNY:

I rubbed his bare goose-pimpled arms and he flexed his muscles for me. He has very nice biceps, resilient, young flesh and firm muscles. He isn't a gorilla, like some of the gay boys these days. You know the ones who go down Commercial Street without any idea what to do with their hands. The hands just kind of flop around at the end of those bulbous limbs. And those big muscle guys have all taken to shaving their chests and their arms and legs, too. And they call me a queen! I wouldn't be so hard on them, but some of 'em look down on the nellies like me. But they wouldn't be out there struttin' if it weren't for us queens. We led that Stonewall riot. Queens, perverts, misfits! But there—shivering in my arms—I had my own nice gay boy. He wasn't like those others. He showed appreciation. I petted him, and he said:

ADAM:

"Thank you. Oh, man, do I feel dizzy."

FRANNY:

"Suck," I shoved the joint in his mouth, "It'll make you feel better."

ADAM:

And then you took me home.

FRANNY:

You needed to go to bed. You was a mess, child. No telling what might have happened to you if I'da left you out with them land-sharks. We sashayed away from the dock to a serenade of catcalls and whistles. See, in a small town like this, everybody knows your business. Miss Rose Kennedy was relaxing along with a cadre of other townies at the end of our log. As we passed, Adam clinging to my arm, he pronounced, "Good evening, Franny. Don't let him keep you up too late. Do remember we have a date for tea tomorrow afternoon." As we neared the end of the beach, I could hear the weary complaints of waiting friends. "Johhhnn... hurry up! You've been in there for almost an hour.... Let's go or we're gonna leave you." And the crisp night air filled with little cries, and then an exceptional loud, long moan of relief. The sideline queens laughed and called out, "You go, girl.... You just go!"

ADAM:

I woke up in your arms.

FRANNY:

Wrong. *I* woke up in *your* arms. I had made a cot up for you in my boudoir. I didn't have any rooms available in the house because we were full up. So I made up the cot, but by the time it was ready, you had already crawled into my bed. I wasn't about to sleep on a cot. Not at my age. When I woke in the morning, you were snuggled up and with a hard-on pressed against my backside. And I said, "That's a cute way of saying you love me."

ADAM:

"Cute?"

FRANNY:

"Would you rather I say 'urgent'? It's not. Should I say 'monstrous'? Would that soothe your ego? All you men. You're so worried about slights of your manhood. Size. Readiness. Hardness. Honey, you might as well get used to it. I call it like I see it."

Presentation!
Sunday afternoon, July 3

TERRY:

"Have you heard Mickey's story?" I asked Franny and Isadora. We were up on the porch out of earshot of Mickey. He was down on the lawn attaching a banner to his car. "He told me about his miserable Catholic childhood, and his boyfriends who wanted to pretend they were straight, and a lover who beat him up. You think the world has changed, and then you meet somebody like Mickey."

FRANNY:

We've heard it all.

ISADORA:

In detail.

TERRY:

Makes me fighting mad. I just want to protect him from that ever happening again.

FRANNY:

It breaks my heart. You hear stories like Mickey's, and you realize our people are still fightin' them same battles we fought decades ago. Still bein' taunted for the clothes they wear, the way they walk, for livin' with another guy. Still bein' forced to pretend they are straight. Billy, a member of the family and our head gardener, heard us raising our voices and wheeled over. He stopped in front of us, waving a newspaper in the air.

BILLY:

Worse yet, and this really gets my goat. We are still fighting ourselves. Let me read you a personal ad from the *Boston Gay News:*

Straight as an Arrow
Young GWM seeks GWM under 30 yo. YOU: straight-acting, straight-appearing, HIV– financially secure, boy-next-door, no smoke or drugs. ME: same.

Tell me…doesn't that ad depress you? I'm a middle-aged GBM, limp-wristed and swishy, financially wrecked, and I've got AIDS. I don't expect to be loved for my illness, but that "straight-acting and -appearing" stuff really irks me.

ISADORA:

Infuriates me…I see all these lucky boys, they come here on vacation. They young. Some of 'em, they weren't even *born* before Stonewall, twenty-five years ago. Those lucky boys, I am tempted to say, them lucky white boys—but a lot of 'em ain't white. Lots of 'em had such advantages compared to when we was young. Maybe they grew up in a big city, got to read books about gay people we never had, see plays about gay people that never existed, go to organizations there'd be of gay people we never imagined. And still, they wanna be straight? I hear 'em talk. They take so much for granted. You can't blame 'em, I guess. For them Stonewall is ancient history.

FRANNY:

But to old queens like me and Isadora, it could be yesterday. And the day before yesterday, we had no gay rights, no gay books or plays that said good things about us, we had no gay flag or gay organizations. The day before yesterday, boys couldn't dance with other boys. And then one day, we said things was goin' to change, and from that day forward we didn't turn back. But that day is today, and every day. When you get to my age, you know that twenty-five years ago was only yesterday.

ISADORA:

You hear some gay guys say they just want to be accepted by the mainstream. What in blazes is that? And where do they get these ideas?

FRANNY:

I'll tell you. Do you ever watch TV and really listen to all those commercials, those ones that are trying to sell you something bigger than a hamburger or a bar a' soap? You know, those commercials like got Ronald Reagan reelected, full of shit and nostalgia?

They go like: "It's morning in America…and all you women better get your butts back in the kitchen and all you men better shave close, put on a tie and get to work and you kids better be white and clean behind your ears and pray before bed and everybody better remember how good it use'ta be back when, how wholesome the world was before and how clean and safe the streets were when everybody was the same and behaved and lived in fear of being out of the norm, remember?" Message is, if you want to be accepted, to be a part of America, then toe-the-line, color inside the borders, don't stand out, don't stand up. All spoon-fed to us disguised like cherry cough syrup, breakfast cereal, and the cream in your morning coffee.

Every day I get up ready to fight because things weren't better for me yesterday, but I want things to be better for

me and for my family and for my boys and for everybody today. And better—even better—tomorrow!
ISADORA:

Amen.

Line Up!
The Fourth of July

FRANNY:

Terry roared up to the house on his Harley right at ten. Mickey was on the back behind him. It made sense that Terry would give him a ride over since Mickey'd left his car here—it being decorated with a big banner on both sides: THE QUEEN OF PROVINCETOWN. I couldn't help hopin' they'd spent the night together. Terry didn't get a leather collar on Mickey, but he did get a metal-studded black band on his right arm. And Terry had a matching one on his left. Back in the old days, that used to mean bottom and top. But I'm not sure they'd even been side by side, except in Terry's imagination. Terry had also got Mickey into black leather chaps. They looked fine on him! And Mickey had no shirt and wore his baseball cap, of course. Terry was completely decked out in black leather, including gloves and a cap.

"Hello, my dark knights." I waved at them from the steps.
TERRY:

"My Queen." I took off my hat, bowed and dropped to my knees. "May I be at your service? You look divine!"
MICKEY:

She looked like royalty for sure. She had on a big gold crown. Her gown was pearly white. There were big diamond rings on all her fingers. I bowed, and I don't do this for anybody, but for the Queen of Provincetown, I took off my cap.
TERRY:

Secret is, he has a bald spot.

FRANNY:

Jimmy arrived wearing a white tuxedo with tails and a top hat. He was carrying a whole armload of signs he'd painted up in red, white and blue. "Aren't you a looker!" I whistled at him.

JIMMY:

I tried to figure out how I could best dress to be the Queen's servant.

FRANNY:

Well, I've found a nice, young man who volunteers for the Project to help you carry my train. You're going to love him—He's sweet as bubblegum. At this point, we was beginning to run late. Miss Stevie had been held up in the bathroom for over an hour. Alan was sittin' over in the front passenger seat of the Cadillac. He kept honkin' the horn. "Come on, Stevie!" And then she came out with Erik on one arm and Adam on the other.

ERIK:

Stevie looked like America gone wild. The dress was all sequins. The bust was a blue background with white stars and the body of the gown was crossed by shimmering stripes of red and white sequins. White gloves stretched up above her elbows. And she wore diamonds at her neck. She took the porch like a runway and rolled her bare shoulders side to side as she walked. She was stunning—the flag gone Hollywood. Then Adam started singing.

ADAM:

"There she is—Miss America! There she walks like a star! There he is—our friend Stevie...the wickedest drag queen of all!" I laughed so hard, and so did Erik.

STEVIE:

"Cool it, boys," I chastised them. "You'll give away the surprise."

FRANNY:

Enough! We're already late...grab the muffins and coffee. We got to get to the parade!

MICKEY:

Franny hopped in the Miata with me. We stored the canteen of coffee and the platter of muffins behind the seats. She held a big rolled rainbow-striped bundle in her lap. "What's that?" I asked.

FRANNY:

"That's my train."

MICKEY:

I felt so dumb when I asked Terry about it later. I thought she had a little engine and caboose all wrapped up in there, which I thought was strange. He told me later that a train was that capelike thing Queens and brides wear.

FRANNY:

We led the way out to Bradford Street to the assembly area. Terry drove the pink whale. Stevie, Matthew, Billy, Erik, Adam, Jimmy, Adele, and Alan piled in the Cadillac, some of 'em on each other's laps. Isadora, her boys, Rose, Nightstar and Lydia and her family was meeting us there and so was a bunch of others. When we pulled up to the throng on Bradford, I started looking for Bull Muñoz. He's the chief of police, and one of his unofficial duties is organizing the Fourth of July parade. He's kind of a stout guy, a descendant of Provincetown's Portuguese fishermen and Italian merchants. I spotted him right off running around with his hands in the air. He was in uniform. "Bull…Bull!" I yelled. Then I told Mickey to beep the horn. He walked over to us.

BULL:

"Whatsa this? Whatsa goin' on here? The Queen of Provincetown? Whatsa that?"

FRANNY:

"That's me, Bull. Doncha recognize me? Franny!"

BULL:

"Franny. So yeah, it's you! I didn't know you were in the parade. But you look nice, real nice. I tell you something. I don't know about this town. Nobody is ever on time. I tell 'em where to get in line and they screw it up. If the parade starts an hour late, they think it's on time."

FRANNY:

"You're probably hungry, too. I brought muffins and coffee. Help me outta here, and I'll get you some."

BULL:

"Might as well take a break. The veterans is supposta lead the parade, and you see them? No. This parade's it's not goin' nowhere. This is my last year, I tell you."

MICKEY:

Franny had to slide out—that's the only way to explain it. You couldn't open the doors, of course, because of the signs and decorations. Gowns aren't made for climbing over the side of a convertible. And when she got up to sitting on the top edge of door she fell out into the chief's arms.

FRANNY:

"Whew...I feel like my crown is crooked. Bull, could you be a dear and straighten it?"

BULL:

"I can't reach it."

FRANNY:

"I'll bend down. There. Thank you. Now coffee."

MICKEY:

I pulled out the coffee and muffins, and we set them up on the trunk lid. Franny poured some for the chief and handed him two muffins. Our crew piled out of the Cadillac and came over for coffee.

BULL:

"No offense, Franny. It looks great. But, I don't get the idea. Queens and princesses in the Fourth of July parade?"

FRANNY:

"Well, it's Independence Day, right? Come over here and let me read you the signs: 'Franny's Hospice and the AIDS Project Celebrate Independence Day. Neighbors Helping Neighbors to Lead Independent Lives.' Do you get it?"

BULL:

"I think so. All of you do good work for other people. You touch my heart."

FRANNY:

"We're showing that all us queens—gays, dykes, queers, whatever—got a right to have the freedom to be who we want to be. We've got the right to be independent and the responsibility to help our neighbors to have freedom."

BULL:

"Here, in this town, everybody is independent! I gotta go find some kids to run along and scoop the poop behind the horses. And I gotta find a place for you...behind 4–H, in front of the high school band, maybe after the fire trucks? Thanks for the muffins!"

FRANNY:

I sent Mickey over to offer the Senior Squares some muffins before our crew had at 'em. They were cranking up the country music and preparing to practice. When he came back I grabbed one off the half-empty tray. The first bite, and I knew why Erik and Adam had been so happy all morning and I was a little worried about what we'd done to ole' Bull. "My God!" I grabbed Terry's hand as he was about to take a bite of his muffin. "You can't eat that—you're driving. I can't believe what I've done. Somebody switched the labels—those are the marijuana muffins, and we just got the chief of police stoned!"

TERRY:

About that time Isadora arrived with Rose and Ricardo and the boys. The Love Shack dancers, all with chiseled pecs and stomachs of stone, carried her on a litter. They wore gold bands on their arms, the Love Shack towels around their waists and golden sandals. The litter was painted gold. Isadora wore the white silk smoking jacket, and long dangling strands of pearls from her ears. She'd changed her hairstyle; it cascaded from the top in a frizzy shoulder-length waterfall. Rose, posing as Eleanor Roosevelt, looked truly of another era next to that crew.

FRANNY:

"If it isn't the Queen of the Nile." The boys lowered Isadora to the ground. I noticed she'd also waxed her legs.

I don't mean like got rid of the hair, I mean, they shone like fine furniture.

ISADORA:

No, girlfriend, I am now the Queen of the Love Shack. I got me a new gig. I play tonight. I've been reborn. Guess who.

ALAN:

"Donna Summer!" I blurted out.

ISADORA:

I wasn't talkin' about that kind of reborn. Banish that name. No respectable drag queen would do her. She betrayed us.

ALAN:

You're too svelte to be that woman anyway. And she was—this affair with the young hot-blooded boy was definitely doing Isadora good. She had presence: here was a man over sixty looking like a woman under forty. About then, our illustrious chief of police showed up with a smile on his face. He was waving to everybody along the way, like he was running for office or something. His bushy gray eyebrows stood up at attention when he got sight of Isadora. He pointed at her.

BULL:

"Hey, you're Diana Ross. My wife, she's Betsy Ross. Betsy and Diana Ross. No relation though, I guess?"

FRANNY:

"Mystery solved."

BULL:

"My wife, she's gonna be all dressed up in a white wig and sitting on a chair sewing the flag. You gonna sing?"

ISADORA:

"Maybe...if my audience demands it. But I perform tonight. Come on by, I'll be at the Love Shack." I pointed at Ricardo's posterior.

BULL:

"You know I feel so good about this parade. I'm so happy. Suddenly I realized I should just enjoy this wonderful sunny day. I don't know what happened but something told me...take it easy; you know?"

TERRY:

We knew.

BULL:

"Why have a heart attack? It's just so beautiful, makes me love my town; makes me love my country. Well, so, I come to ask a favor.... We just have a small problem. The veterans, they started the party a little early, shall I say? So they can't carry the flags.... Would you lead the parade, Franny? Do you think any of your men, or women, you know, your people could carry the flags?"

FRANNY:

"Of course." I clapped my hands and the boys came running. "The chief just asked us to lead the parade—let's go!"

ERIK:

"Wow...It's like Santa asking Rudolph to guide the sleigh."

ADAM:

"I never thought about it before, but Rudolph was the gay reindeer!"

The Parade
The Fourth of July

TERRY:

Mickey and I pulled the cars into formation. Then Jimmy and I helped Franny up on top of the Miata's trunk. I made sure her crown was straight, and then we attached and unfurled her train. It was gorgeous. It extended a good fifty feet back. It was so wide, Jimmy couldn't hold it fully open at arm's length.

FRANNY:

Mark arrived with a bunch of guys and gals from the AIDS Support Project. When I told him the story, Mark wanted to run off and get the Mary-Janes delivered properly. I got him to send somebody else out with them. I had plans for him. I had plans for him and Jimmy. "Jimmy!" I gestured him to come up and be introduced. "Mark, this is Jimmy. Would you help him carry my train?" They shook hands, and Jimmy gave me a look.

MARK:

"It would be my pleasure. Am I dressed okay?" Franny appraised me and called for Stevie.

STEVIE:

A good drag queen always carries extra accessories in her pocketbook. I mean, you never know when you might be invited on the spot to a swanky dinner or something. I searched in my bag, and the best I could come up with were a long pearl necklace suitable for a flapper and red elbow-length gloves. I had Mark take off his jean vest and go bare-chested. Those rings going through his nipples were so obvious. I adorned him with the pearls and gloves. I stood Jimmy in his top hat and tails beside him. "It's just not right. They don't quite coordinate!" Then I had the inspiration. "Jimmy, give Mark your hat." And that did it. They looked paired.

ALAN:

Stevie took the rumble seat up on the Cadillac's trunk. I must say she looked stunning. I hid my normal outfit—a flannel shirt and jeans—under a red velvet cape. I rode in the backseat with Nightstar. She dressed in a traditional Native American outfit. She is descended from a Connecticut tribe. She wore feathers and would occasionally beat her drum. She also put a box of tools up on the front floorboard in case the old Caddy broke down.

I held up a fishbowl of the multicolored condoms as we drove down the street. We had those coin-shaped type. We got them in red and blue and gold—they didn't come in white. Stevie would grab a handful, fling them to the crowd and then hold her hand above her head like a showgirl to acknowledge the applause. They loved her!

ADAM:

Franny told me to carry the American flag and Erik to carry the Massachusetts state flag. We marched about ten feet in front of the Miata. I'd look back, and Franny would be waving and blowing kisses. Right after we got started, I got the idea. "Let's all do the royal wave," I told Erik. We passed back the word.

ERIK:

We'd start it and everyone else would follow. It's the Queen Elizabeth wave—right arm out stiffly in front of you, with your forearm pointed up at a ninety-degree angle. Then you rotate your open hand one quarter-turn, back and forth back and forth, you know, very stiff, very bothered, very British.

TERRY:

The lineup of the parade went like this: We led, then came the high school marching band, then came the town's old 1950s fire trucks with kids riding on top throwing candy. Behind the truck the Senior Squares do-si-doed and swung their partners. When the band wasn't playing, we'd hear the country music punctuated by yahoos and laughter, lots of laughter. The horses followed, and then the cowboy-hatted pooper scoopers—two little boys carrying a shovel and a broom ran along in front of a red wagon pulled by a little girl. Bull's wife, as Betsy Ross, rode on a flatbed delivery truck with a huge flag across her lap. Then came the 4-H'ers in green and white and the Italian-American club in a rusty old black Buick convertible and the bank's float with a dancing teller machine and the town ambulance with a warbling siren and some Shriners in little go-carts who raced in zigzags between themselves letting off firecrackers and that was about the size of it.

MATTHEW:

I carried the sign for Franny's house, with help from Billy. We were both in wheelchairs. We planned to wheel ourselves through the parade. But two young guys from the project volunteered to push us, so we let them. Good thing actually, because holding that long banner was a tiring chore. We had the one that said: FRANNY'S HOSPICE AND THE AIDS PROJECT CELEBRATE INDEPENDENCE DAY.

BILLY:

Two women from the AIDS Project carried the other sign: NEIGHBORS HELPING NEIGHBORS TO LEAD INDEPENDENT LIVES. They're a couple, Michelle and Lydia. They have the cutest little boy, Curtis. He's four. He had an American-flag–motif shirt on. He ran back and forth from his two moms to the crowd and handed people condoms. Everybody on the sidelines was trying to get their picture taken with him—that's how cute he was. He suddenly got tired halfway through the parade and curled up on Franny's lap in the convertible.

MATTHEW:

I have a confession to make. I had never done drag before. In fact, I used to be a little embarrassed by drag. I used to be a carpenter—a typical nail-driver. I worked with men, straight men mostly, and I never understood why a guy needed to dress up like a gal.

BILLY:

I, on the other hand, used to be a florist—a typical flower-fluffer. When Franny asked me to carry the banner with Matthew, I immediately consulted with Stevie. We knew we couldn't get him into a dress, so we decided on bonnets—big bonnets. Stevie dug two huge floppy-brimmed straw hats out of his closet. I added dried red roses and long streamers of ribbon—all the gay colors of the rainbow.

MATTHEW:

You only live once. I felt resigned to the embarrassment. I put it on when Billy handed me the hat. And suddenly I felt different. Soon as I put on that crazy bonnet, I felt freer than I had ever felt before. I felt defiant.

ALAN:

Soon after the parade pushed off, I looked forward. The wind had lifted up Franny's train. It arched up into the blue sky ahead and formed the shape of a natural rainbow. That's when I understood why the rainbow flag really did represent our liberation. Because when we find the end of that rainbow, there will be a pot of gold.

ADELE:

Rose and I followed behind them. I looked great as FDR. I gritted that cigahrette holdah between my teeth and I'd lean my head back and shake it when people clapped. And Rose, you looked supah! That puhrse hanging from your arm and those little white church gloves and that shah-t gray-haih-ed wig with a little hat on top—nobody'd recognize ya."

ROSE:

I am just not as big as Eleanor, but I tried to look stern. Adele held a sign that said: REMEMBER FDR? Then on the side of the wheelchair we attached signs that said: IT'S TIME FOR A NEW DEAL. PEOPLE BEFORE PROFITS. REFORM HEALTHCARE NOW!

JIMMY:

People cheered us as we headed down Commercial Street. Mickey beeped the horn and the band started up behind us. Mark and I walked in perfect step. The rainbow train rippled in the breeze—our own version of the mile-long rainbow flag our brothers and sisters had carried in the march on the United Nations just the weekend before in New York.

MARK:

And then they started throwing money onto the train. Fistfuls of silver coins and crumpled greenbacks sailed over our heads and onto the colorful fabric.

JIMMY:

We never imagined anybody was going to start tossing money.

ISADORA:

A stage performer knows that if the crowd starts sending money your way, you turn up the volume. You encourage that behavior! I decided to sing in front of Town Hall. "Boys, let me down," I said. "It's time for us to go to work."

RICARDO:

I gave Terry a tape and asked him to play it in the Cadillac's tape player. Better yet, he had a boom box in the car and he put on the tape. Then Isadora—he belted out—what else? "Somewhere Over the Rainbow!" We improvised dancing to back her up. Man, can he sing! Gave me goose pimples! And when Isadora finished, us guys ran up and lifted her over our heads. She, I mean he—I believed he was Diana Ross—he was waving and waving. Then the money starting flying. It was like it was fallin' from heaven. That's how good she was!

MICKEY:

We started the parade back moving again. But when I looked in the rearview mirror, I saw that the fire trucks behind the band weren't going anywhere.

TERRY:

The lead fire truck's engine had sputtered and died. They couldn't get it started, and six of the firemen came out in front, lifted the hood up, cursing. Lesbian mechanic to the rescue…. Nightstar jumped out, left her drum with us, and grabbed her tools. Everybody knows she's the best mechanic in town, so the firemen just stood back and handed her what she called for. She's small, though, and it kind of looked like a kid had crawled right into the engine compartment of that big truck and disappeared. You just saw this feathered headdress sticking up under the hood.

ROSE:

The Senior Squares took over the entertainment responsibility this time. They were in fine form. I'll tell you, later on they'll be wondering just what happened and how they got all that new energy. Nightstar had the truck purring in no time, though, and we were back under way.

ERIK:

It didn't take long for us to reach the west end of town, and we were just about to pass in front of our house. We could see a big crowd up on the porch and on the lawn and sidewalk waiting for us. We started waving the flags when we got up there, and Mickey and Terry honked the car horns. Franny screamed out the names of people in the crowd, shouting "Hi!" I know they were all shocked to see us leading the parade.

ADAM:

Then came the surprise. Erik and I planned it with Stevie. We had to let Mickey and Terry in on it so they'd stop the cars and help out. We ran back to be in position to the side of the pink whale. Terry helped Stevie down from the trunk of the Caddy and then set up the boom box for music.

MICKEY:

Franny looked back when the boys left with the flags to go stand by the Cadillac.

FRANNY:

"What's wrong? Is there something wrong with Stevie?"

MICKEY:

"Nothing's wrong, just wait and see."

ADAM:

Stevie walked out in front of Erik and me. We were standing with the flags at attention. The hospice had become a grandstand, and the street in front of us was the stage.

TERRY:

I hit the play button and the boom box filled the street with the voice of none other than Bob Barker, singing "Miss America." And as he started to sing, "There she is, Miss America," Stevie raised her right gloved hand to her mouth, bit down on the middle finger, and pulled the clinging white glove down her forearm and off her hand gracefully. Then she did the same with the left glove. She strode a few steps back and forth throwing her mane of hair back at each turn, then motioned for Erik to come forward. He handed his flag to Adam, walked to her, and unzipped her gown. Already wild applause and whistles came from the grand-

stand. Bob Barker crooned, "There she is, Miss America…,"
in a reprise, and she let it fall. The gown slipped away
from her body like the skin of a snake. She stepped out of
the coil of sequins at her feet and posed in her red satin
stiletto heels and a shimmering, strapless red swimsuit.
Erik rushed forward again and lifted a sash over her shoulder which read: MISS AMERICA. And then he nestled a
tiara into her hair.

ALAN:

The crowd went wild for her: Stevie—a man of fifty, a
man dwindling in strength and size from a disease that
was eating him from the inside out, a man with gump-
tion, a man with the balls to do a striptease for the talent
competition and crown himself Miss America! That is the
man I helped ever so properly back into the pink Cadillac.
I spread out my cape on the trunk to cushion him as he
arranged himself—now in a swimsuit with a victory sash
across his chest—in a seated position. I waited upon him
for the remainder of the parade in awe. I subserviently
handed him—our Miss America!—condoms to fling with
nonchalance and grace to the adoring throng who loved
him not even a fraction so much as I.

FRANNY:

When we got to the end of the parade and turned away
from Commercial Street where it meets the sea, I cried. I
cried because I felt so much love for everybody and so
much love from everybody. Adam ran up to me, saying:

ADAM:

"What's the matter, Franny? What's wrong?"

FRANNY:

"Nothin's wrong. I'm just too darn happy. How are
you. How do you feel?"

ADAM:

"I'm proud."

FRANNY:

"I just love hearing you say that. I can't tell you how
much. Tell me again what you think of all us queens."

ADAM:

"I'm proud of us...all of us!"

Rub-A-Dub-Dub, Queens in the Tub
Late afternoon, Monday, the Fourth of July

ISADORA:

The girls decided to take a quick soak in Franny's hot tub before we went to the fireworks. My joints were sore from lyin' on that litter, Franny's behind was sore from sittin' on the convertible, Rose's feet were sore from her pumps, Alan's arm was sore from holding up that bowl of condoms, and Stevie's whole body was sore because she'd overexerted herself. Alan was the last to get in and that did it, sent the water spillin' over the side.

ALAN:

"Who'd have ever thought I'd get so fat? Remember when I was just hunky? Pass me the joint, Isadora—I haven't had any yet."

STEVIE:

"As they say, 'Get fat, don't die.' If only it were so easily done as said."

ROSE:

"Did you notice that Matthew and Billy bonded over their bonnets?"

ISADORA:

"Oh, yeah, they're like inseparable now. Don't get that reefer all wet now, Alan."

ALAN:

"And Jimmy seems to be getting on with Mark, too. He told me Mark wants to photograph him."

STEVIE:

"In the nude, no doubt. Do you believe those rings in his nipples hurt?"

ISADORA:

"It depends on how hard ya twist 'em."

FRANNY:

"I've been hearing on the news the events that made history twenty-five years ago. Most important to us, of course, was the Stonewall rebellion. And second, that Judy Garland died, which some say put the queens in a bad enough mood to revolt. Which I can't totally disagree with. All the friends we've had dying puts me in the mood for some kind of revolution. Then the first man walked on the moon."

ROSE:

"One small step for man, one giant leap for mankind. I'll take that, Alan."

ALAN:

"And there was the summer of love at Woodstock."

ISADORA:

"We tryin' to play connect the dots here or somethin'? How 'bout playing pass the joint back this way?"

ALAN:

"There is a connection. I think we had a lot of hope for the future back then. We thought we homosexuals were suddenly going to be equal rather than abnormal. We thought love might save the world and that science might feed the hungry and cure all disease."

FRANNY:

"And these days, I had a lot of hope that this President Clinton—who we queens elected—was gonna really create a Manhattan Project to find a cure for AIDS. We thought he really was going to lift that ban on gays in the military by executive order. I cried when he said he was going to lift that ban. He coulda made history with the sweep of a pen. And I'm antiwar all the way—don't you get me wrong. But the military is the biggest employer probably in the whole world. And all those gay kids who join—or get drafted— before they even know who they are, got a right to self-respect. If he'd have done it, he'd have sent the message: gays are equal. But he betrayed us. And then he betrayed us again on AIDS."

STEVIE:

"If America could send men to the moon in a matter of years, America could find a cure for AIDS."

ROSE:

"I had a nephew. He was gay as a goose. I knew it since he was five years old. I was already living in Boston when he was drafted for the Vietnam War right as he came out of high school. I told him to check the box, tell them you're homosexual. Not only did I not want him to go and possibly get killed, I was afraid for him because he was nelly. He was the kind of boy that got teased for it in school. But he believed it was his duty to serve. And he did, decorated for valor, he came back from the war and then decided to stay on in the service because that was all he knew how to do. And then the bastards did it. The military pegged him, followed him, and threatened to discharge him if he didn't resign. He shot himself with the military's own gun before they could do it."

FRANNY:

"Wasn't his fault. Their hate got inside of him."

ALAN:

"Exactly. And that's why Clinton represents capitulation. He has conceded his promises and surrendered the playing field to the so-called Christian right. His 'don't ask, don't tell' policy for gays in the military is simply saying: Back in the closet. Worse, it is telling them—us—to self-censor. It is telling us to internalize their uneasiness with us. He wants us to do their dirty work for them. It is a form of imposed self-hate."

ISADORA:

"Tell it, brother!"

ROSE:

"I think we made history today in our own way, in the parade."

ISADORA:

"Oh, we gave 'em somethin' to talk about. But you know, think about it. This is small-town America, and they threw money our way!"

FRANNY:

"The straights was supportin' us. No doubt about it. Maybe we're just a start…but we are proof. We belong. We are as American as apple pie."

ISADORA:

"As marijuana muffins!"

ALAN:

"There's one more tidbit of Americana left for us to experience this evening. I speak of the fireworks, of course. What's the plan?"

STEVIE:

"What shall we wear?"

FRANNY:

"I say we go as ourselves."

ISADORA:

"What does that mean? Like how we look in the mirror when we get up in the mornin'?"

FRANNY:

"Take it however you want. But it's not like dress up for a parade. We should go as red-blooded American queens—we the people!"

Fireworks
Night, Monday, the Fourth of July

TERRY:

We all met back at Franny's just before nightfall so we could walk over to The Boatslip together. Mickey and I came directly from our trip to the beach. The fireworks were being set off from Fisherman's Wharf. The wharf extends a good distance into the bay so the deck of The Boatslip was an ideal viewing spot. As usual, pandemonium reigned, and Stevie still wasn't ready.

MICKEY:

Franny was tapping her foot waiting for everybody to arrive. He wasn't wearing a wig for the first time since I met him and he had on very little makeup. His hair had streaks of gray running through it and was cut short around his ears. He was wearing a white sweatshirt that had a drawing of little kittens chasing a ball of yarn on the front. He wore white slacks and white sandals. After what I'd gotten used to, he looked plain. But what I said was, "You look nice."

FRANNY:

"Thanks, hon. Could you do me a favor and help me turn Joseph before we leave? Like now?"

MICKEY:

We went in to Joseph's bedroom, and he was watching TV. He seemed to smile when he looked at me.

JOSEPH:

"Well, Franny, I don't know where you're finding all these muscular young men to come and tend me, but keep it up."

FRANNY:

"His name's Mickey." We also had to change the sheets. One promise I will always keep: everybody in my house always has clean sheets.

MICKEY:

To switch the bottom sheet, we had to roll Joseph over twice. His face winced in pain every time we moved him. But then he'd open his eyes and smile at me.

FRANNY:

We tried to turn Joseph gentle as can be, but it hurt him, especially his feet. He has neuropathy, which causes great pain and sensitivity in the feet.

JOSEPH:

"Have fun at the fireworks. I think they're romantic. We won't be able to see them from here. But, Mickey, when I hear the booming, I'll think of you." I winked. Flirtation is about all that's left of my sexuality.

FRANNY:

We came out of Joseph's room and the living room had filled up. Erik and Adam were there. They had on matching pink T-shirts and white walking shorts. Jimmy and Mark arrived both wearing black sweatshirts and jeans, that artist look. Nightstar was there in jeans and a T-shirt. Lydia and Michelle and Curtis wore matching Provincetown sweat-shirts. Rose sat in an armchair, her Laura Ashley flowered skirt spread across her lap. Alan leaned in the doorway wearing suspenders over a checked shirt. And Billy and Matthew were ready, too, and still had on them bonnets. Of all of them, Adele looked unusual. She wore a black leather jacket, the biker type. "What's with you and leather, all of a sudden?" I asked her.

ADELE:

"I heah-d I was supposed to come as myself, so I thought I'd show ya all that I am one of the boys."

FRANNY:

All we lacked was Isadora and her crew, and Stevie. "Stevie!" I yelled. "Let's go, Stevie!" But she didn't answer so I went upstairs. I found her sitting at her makeup table with her back to me. She'd found a theatrical costume to wear. Red, white, and blue ostrich feathers stuck up from a hairpiece, and she wore a white satin gown. "You got your face on? We need to go." And then it started, his little padded shoulders shaking, and his head falling down into his hands. He was sobbin'. "What's wrong?" I asked as I knelt beside him.

STEVIE:

"I can't go, Franny. Here I've gone to all this trouble, and I can't even stand. I don't have the strength to get up."

FRANNY:

"Are you sick?"

STEVIE:

"Of course I'm sick. Have you forgotten? I have AIDS! Oh. Franny, I'm sorry. I don't mean to yell at you...of all people, not you. I just tried so hard. I felt myself getting tired, and I told myself I'd get energized once I got dressed. Mind over body."

FRANNY:

"We can stay home together. It's not important…some silly fireworks."

STEVIE:

"No, give me two minutes to fix my mascara. I've been dreading it…that the time might come—get the wheelchair."

ERIK:

Adam and I helped Stevie into the wheelchair and then carried her downstairs. There was a lot of tension in the livingroom when we came down. Isadora stood at the foot of the stairs in a sleek red gown with a slit up the front which exposed her legs. Ricardo stood beside her holding a full-length jacket of fake leopard fur. He wore nothing but a loincloth of matching fur and big black combat boots. Everybody was staring at Stevie.

STEVIE:

"Well, how do I look?"

ISADORA:

"Fabulous!" I said it first. And then everybody else chimed in like mockingbirds: fabulous, fabulous, fabulous, fabulous, fabulous.

STEVIE:

"Then let's roll!"

TERRY:

Even though the crowd was mostly drunk and a little rowdy at The Boatslip, they were real cooperative with us. They cleared a path and let us get the wheelchairs right up to the deck's railing so Stevie, Matthew, and Billy could see the fireworks once they got started. Mark offered to buy a round of drinks and took Erik and Adam along to help carry them back.

FRANNY:

Lots of people told Stevie he looked great in those ostrich feathers as we went through the mob. It sort of perked him up. But I was keeping a close eye on him just in case he needed to leave.

TERRY:

The guys came back and passed out the drinks. I grabbed ahold of Mickey and said, "I have an impulse to feel the sand under my feet. Want to go down on the beach?" He said yeah. Erik, Adam, Jimmy and Mark thought it was a great idea and joined us. We slipped under the railing and jumped down about five feet to the sand. "Anybody want a hand down?" I called back up to our group.

ROSE:

"Some of us are in heels and prefer firmer ground."

FRANNY:

About then somebody started singing "The Star-Spangled Banner," and the whole bunch sang it way off key. Isadora looked around at our group and asked:

ISADORA:

"Y'all remember 'America the Beautiful'? Were gonna sing it."

ALAN:

And then she belted it out. We sang along, but she was high, high above all of us. Everybody stood back, like she needed room to breathe.

ISADORA:

O beautiful for spacious skies,
For amber waves of grain,
For purple mountains' majesty,
Above the fruited plains,
America, America, God spread her grace on thee,
And crown thy good in brother- and sisterhood,
From sea to shining sea!

FRANNY:

"You did us proud, Isadora," I told her after the applause had quieted down. "When a bunch of queens sings 'America the Beautiful,' it makes me feel like this country really is ours."

ALAN:

"It's true. Even when we sang the national anthem, I

thought that the American flag belongs as much to us as to the Republicans and their family-values, bible-thumping, fundamentalist backers. And the Constitution and the songs are ours. We can't just let them lay claim to American history and its symbols."

ROSE:

"And on this Fourth of July, we led the parade."

MATTHEW:

"We made history."

STEVIE:

"History is fine, but I want fireworks! When are they going to start?"

FRANNY:

"Well, look down there, folks." I pointed out to my boys—Erik and Adam, Terry and Mickey, Jimmy and Mark. All three couples were down at the edge of the bay, kissing.

ISADORA:

"Done look like the fireworks already started."

FRANNY:

And it was like on cue. The sky just lit up in fountains and streaking comets and starbursts in all the colors of the rainbow!

The Living Room

JOHN:

Can you move the ashtray closer? What do you think? It was a happy ending. Yes, sort of like in Shakespeare. All this coupling. Is it too much like heterosexual marriage? I don't know, Will, do you really think they are expressing commitment and responsibility while not excluding other sorts of relationships? I will agree, V. K., that it does convey hope and continuity. Yes, the main message is that queers must stake their claim to America. And, you're right, Franny has to believe in happy endings, in hope. How else could she run an AIDS hospice?

I'm thirsty. Could you hold my water closer, turn the straw toward me? I feel so weak. I was up all night with my brother Marvin. We covered a lot of things we have needed to talk about. I really don't want to sleep. V. K., what are you thinking? What are you looking at? The cactus in the window is a Christmas cactus. No, I can't see it. Did it really bloom since you've been here? It doesn't have its seasons right. Oh, I have no energy. No. I don't want to eat.

Do you want to go out of the room, V. K., while they turn me? Every two hours, and I'm still getting bedsores. You met the visiting nurse, right? Cindy. I just don't know if I'll have enough time. There is still so much to do. Will, could you use your impressive upper-body strength to help Cindy turn me? It hurts so much. Okay. I like it better on my left side. I can hold my drink at least with my right hand. It's easier to smoke. Will, bring your chairs over to this side. Tell V. K. to come back in. Can you believe it? A female nurse handling the catheter on my penis. Diapers on my butt? Come and sit where I can see you. Will, how is your life? You're withholding from me, I can feel it. Of course you can hold my hand.

Agnes came over with the mail early this morning and read me a long letter from a boy who has read my erotic fiction. He wants to come to Portland. He wants to meet me. He wants to have sex with me. I feel so weak. No, Tom, it's more than needing sleep. I feel it going out of me—life going out of me. I don't want to sleep, V. K. Believe me, there will be plenty of time for that.

Did you get off those letters I dictated? Did you send out that copy of my book review to the bragging list? Is my protégé, Michael, coming Tuesday? You know, I told him that if he doesn't hurry up he may lose his chance to sleep with me. Someday he'll regret it. My mother and sister are coming Wednesday, and I'm getting interviewed tomorrow—is that right? Cindy told me I'll have time to finish what I need to complete. We also decided to up my morphine again. At some level it will put me out for good.

It's just a matter of time. I feel it. I am dying. Yes, I was up all night, so maybe I do need to sleep. I hate to sleep.

V. K., I know you need to catch your plane. Get your hands off my lilies. Now I can see that you have forced them all. Yes, they smell wonderful in full bloom. I guess it is a good time for you to leave. You've been a great help. We have gotten a tremendous amount done. My darling, thank you. Don't forget the notebooks. Tom, you're going to take her to the airport? You all go on now, Will can stay with me. I am going to finish my cigarette, and then I'd like to commune with Will in silence.

HOT TALK

Stan Leventhal

Standing alone at a bar, Friday night, I didn't expect much to happen because ordinarily very little does. A typical gay establishment with loud music, a pool table, lots of guys hanging around, not much happening. But I noticed a guy with an attitude, watched him strut and swagger like the macho men at a construction site. Bearded and mustached, in tight jeans, scruffy work boots, a skimpy T-shirt, his body looked as solid as a bronze statue. I assumed he was just another queen in butch drag. But my eyes lingered long enough for him to catch my stare, and he began to look me up and down. Without any further encouragement from me, he walked over to where I leaned at the bar and began to rub his rough hands up and down my arms. I wore jeans, moccasins, a tank top, and enjoyed the warm sensation of his calloused palms on my cool skin. He leaned into my ear and whispered, told me I have the skinniest arms of any man he's ever met. No argument, I admit I do have skinny arms, but I could not think of a response to this remark. Then he leaned in again and said that he wants to beat me up. Believing I hadn't heard him correctly, I said, What? And he repeated his words, I want to beat you up. At this point I must have taken a sip of bourbon, taking the time to think of a clever rejoinder, and it occurred to me that this guy is not the tough macho man he pretends to be and that we were playing a game. I love role-playing, so it's very easy for me to slip into a different attitude mode pretty quickly. I responded to his words, displaying a challenging bravado I was in no position to back up. What makes you think a pussy like you could beat up a stud like me?

As soon as I'd uttered the words, I realized how ridiculous I must have sounded. But by the look of aghast surprise on his face, I guessed that I'd come off sounding more credible than I believed. Expecting him to laugh, it became my turn to be surprised when he responded with seriousness, leaning into me again, saying, You really think you can take me, pretty boy?

Realizing I'd have as much of a chance at defeating him as Bambi would Godzilla, I maintained my pose and declared that I might look like a cream puff, but could take care of myself handily if the situation demanded it. He looked me up and down, measuring me, actually assessing his chance if we fought.

The slack rod in my underwear became a stiff pole as we stood there, near the bar, the challenge between us like a tall weed that could be uprooted and tossed away. Usually quite timid, always the first to turn the other cheek, the feeling of raw sexual desire heating up my body emboldened me and I responded to him as though I believed what I said. Not only could I take you, I replied, but when I'm done, you'd be begging for more.

More? he echoed.

I'd beat you so good you'd pass through the pain into pleasure, and you'd become more than just a willing slave.

Shit! he said. But I could tell the possibility intrigued him. And my words had been convincing. He now looked at me as thought I might have some special knowledge or talent for martial arts, boxing, wrestling.

At least I'm not a cocksucker, he said.

Already aroused by the friction of this encounter, my body went into overdrive at these words, taking us out of the realm of fantasy and into the real world. His words stung me like a scorpion's tail, one of the most loathsome things in the world being the many hypocritical gay men with whom I occasionally collide.

Why am I a cocksucker and you not?

Because I never suck cock. And I never take it up the ass. I'm always a total man.

And what makes you think that I'm not a total man?

You suck dick?

With relish.

You take it up the ass?

At every available opportunity.

Then you're a faggot. Am I right?

Presumably, you put your dick into men's mouths, I said.

Absolutely.

And you fuck men in the butt?

With pleasure.

And you think these sex acts with men are somehow not homosexual?

That's right.

Look, I said, angrier now, frustrated as well, when two guys do it, both of them are being gay regardless of the role they play; whether they're married or not, in the closet or not, loud and proud. You may not think you're gay or want to be gay, but it if walks like a duck, talks like a duck... My voice left the words hanging in the air between us like a dare.

Says you, he responded with a humph. At this point I expected him to walk away or say something insulting.

But he leaned into my ear and asked, What are you drinking? Then he fetched me a fresh one, and a beer for himself. I like you, he said, handing me a shot glass of bourbon. Then whispered, And I still want to beat you up.

Right now?

Later. For now let's talk. I like the things you say.

Is your dick hard? I asked. Mine is. I must like the way you talk. Too.

He actually blushed, tried to glance at his crotch furtively, but I saw his eye motion despite the dimness of the bar light. Looking down, I could tell by the way his crotch bulged that he was just as turned on as I was.

Now what was it we were talking about? he asked.

You seem to think you're not queer. But baby, when I meet a three-dollar bill I don't mistake it for anything else.

He glared at me, and I thought surely now this encounter had ended. But what I perceived initially as closure was simply a temporary pause, like the silence between two symphonic movements. After all, the tension can be stretched only so far before it will break. Relaxing it for a while can result in renewed energy, further details.

He said he had to go and pee. I felt that same pressure in my groin, too, but chose to keep it that way, enjoying the warm pressure in my gut, waiting for him to return. As soon as he did, like a rerun, we started all over again. He rubbed my skinny arms and told me he wanted to beat me up. I told him he wouldn't stand a chance. Then he surprised me completely. Without preamble or warning, he leaned over and stuck his beer-soaked tongue in my mouth, pulling me into a bear hug. Though the hardness of my dick hadn't slackened, I suddenly became harder and hotter, returning the kiss, first sucking his tongue, then pushing mine into his mouth. The sensation grew intoxicating, and I fell into a swoon as our burning tongues thrust and retreated, rolling over each other, wrapping around, sliding in and out of our throats.

I had to pull back to catch my breath, heart pounding, forehead sweating by this time; and when I did, he cupped my crotch, rubbed my hard rod, squeezed my balls, pressed the buttons of my jeans into my groin. It felt grand, so I grabbed his crotch and my temperature rose even further when I felt the wetness there. Had he peed in his pants? Missed the urinal? Or had he come, a zipless fuck, so turned on he couldn't restrain himself? Or was that his plan? To come in his pants with a stranger in a bar? These questions flew by my consciousness but the answers did not need to be found out. My mind felt fully occupied with all of the dazzling synaptic responses of pleasure, enough to keep me in ecstasy.

He pinched my right nipple through the cloth of my tank top; I responded by stooping slightly to get his right nipple between my teeth. I bit it gently, sucked it a little through his T-shirt, and after he moaned several times, pulled back and looked at him. A circle of wetness tented on his shirt over the hard nub of his tit. Raising my face to his, a smile of joy and high-intensity light beams from his eyes told me that I'd managed to discover a very sensitive part of his body, one that I'd manipulated properly. Seeing his beatific expression increased my ardor as I stood there staring at him, wondering what might happen next.

For a moment I came out of the spell and realized where I was. The loud pounding music, the adorable boys gathered around the pool table, the shirtless waiter with his tray of drinks, the video games and porn screen in the corner had all disappeared as I became more entangled with my hypocritical gay man. And I successfully tuned it all out again as we began the final movement of the symphony we'd begun unintentionally.

Do you want to go home with me? he asked.

I had to think about it. Couldn't respond immediately. I wanted us to preserve and extend what we'd already started. To stop now, leave, travel, arrive, and try to recap-

ture the moment might not be possible. By not responding right away, I hoped to prolong the mood. I started
kissing him again, and as our tongues lolled and locked, I
decided that I didn't want to go home with him, wanted
to sustain the present feeling, thought that just maybe
somewhere in private he might be as rough and tough as
he'd claimed, that perhaps he really did want to beat me
up and all of his hot talk should not be taken lightly. And
besides, something told me that whatever magic we'd
conjured had probably run its course. Not knowing when
to stop might destroy the moment, lead to a diminishing
of the contented feeling, end with despair instead of
happiness.

Although I'd decided not to leave with him, I had to
figure out how to sever the bond, make my escape without hurting him or creating an ugly scene. Because I'd
spent some time and he'd spent some money, maybe he
thought he had some claim on my time and energy. I
feared telling him something he might not want to hear,
but knew that I must as the enchantment faded, and he
became more insistent that we retire to his lair.

I decided to feign drunkenness, pretend that I'd had
too much to drink and would not be very good company.
Yet I didn't have to pretend or try very hard to convince
him since both of us had actually consumed quite a fair
amount of alcohol by then. When I told him I was too
high, he thought about it for a second or two and said
that he felt kind of out of it as well. We stared at each
other through bloodshot eyes. Suddenly it occurred to me
that maybe he had been thinking the same things as I,
that maybe this rendezvous had ended, anything subse-
quent might be a letdown. Perhaps I would make good
my boast and beat the shit out of him. In any case, after
I'd declared my drunken state, he became less insistent
about us leaving together to go someplace—the only
thing remaining, to figure out a graceful way of parting.
Not interested in having his phone number or giving him

mine, the traditional method of ending a bar encounter would not suffice.

Well, I said finally, as we stood there awkwardly, not knowing what I would say next, hoping that the words would come.

Well, he said.

I guess I should be going home. It's late, and I've had too much to drink, and I've got a big day tomorrow, I lied.

I should probably be going, too. Let's go.

Although I'd determined long before that I would not leave with him, we wound up departing together, and it occurred to me that there had been a rather large audience to witness our public display, who would assume that we would be spending the night in the same bed. Out in the street, the fresh air felt good. As I shook his hand and wished him a good night, I hoped that I hadn't blown it as far as wanting to see this guy again. But since he hadn't pressed me for my phone number, I figured he'd arrived at the same conclusion as I: that we did not stand much of a chance of a future together. If I keep insisting that he's queer, and he denies it continually, there would be little basis for love and affection. Probably a lot of arguing and resentments. That is, if we don't get violent and do each other harm.

I didn't go directly home, as I'd said, but stopped off at another bar on the way after leaving him standing on the sidewalk. But when I finally did end the night and get into bed, I started fantasizing about him, couldn't sleep, and finally got up to get some lube. I jerked myself furiously for hours, concocting wild scenes involving me and my new dream figure. When I felt completely spent and satisfied, finally I slept; my last thought before losing consciousness was that I'd done the right thing in not going home with the tough-talking guy. I probably would have been so nervous, wondering if I'd be maimed, perhaps I wouldn't have been able to get hard. Of course, maybe it was simply wish fulfillment or rationalization, but I honestly believed that the solo orgasms achieved by myself in my lonely room were far more intense and exciting than anything that might have happened had I decided to travel the night companioned.

THE YELLOW

Michael Lassell

For John Preston,
who said, "Write about what you know,"
and meant it…
and then published it.
The only gesture of gratitude left me is words.

It begins, of course, with desire—or, rather, *in* desire—
this time on a Passover Saturday night in New York City,
the night before Easter, too. Where the desire begins is
anybody's guess, perhaps in fever. This time it began in
the sky, in a cloud cover so low—the way it gets in
spring—you feel…immersed, caught in the act, drown-
ing. And the Empire State Building is lit up a kind of
yellow that doesn't exist in nature, not in healthy
nature, but you can't see the top of the building,
anyway, because of the clouds: a translucent mist
rendered opaque by mass, volume, density—the whole

thing looking like special F/X for hell or some urban apocalypse movie.

You know the sort of film. They were popular in the '70s: It's the year 2000-something and the island of Manhattan is a penal colony, blah-blah-blah...young men encased in tight muscles and leather vests, headbands. Hollywood shit. But not ineffective. The kind of thing that gets under your skin no matter how you resist: hard rival males, little more than schoolyard Caesars, battling for supremacy and the nubile charms of this year's pouting starlet, a fight to the death that establishes the right of the fittest for supremacy (fitness being measured not only by strength but by cunning and moral rectitude, movies being fiction, after all, and not the glandular dance of the cobra and the mongoose).

Yes, it's on nights like these that the city seems most Darwinian, nights that conjure the Tortugas, amphibians crawling out of the ooze, nights of survival, jazz, and ejaculation.

Soaking into the fog like amyl into cotton, the light looks like an incandescent blotch on heaven—God's urine in stained glass on an awesome scale, a hotly contested work of art, perhaps, by a painter/photographer of Latin American extraction, or a cathedral, say, in Rome, the flaked and scaling plaster mapped by brackish water and mildew, a cathedral where the Polish pope is no doubt droning Easter mass right now, it being later there than here, so probably tomorrow already. And it's spreading, the yellow fog, like sweat on sheets or hatred. That's what the light of Easter through the unseasonably raw Saturday reminds me of. And of London, Jack the Ripper, fish and chips in yesterday's *Evening Standard,* of unheated bathrooms, longing, and brandy hangovers in an Earl's Court bed-sitter.

I'm watching this sky from the bed of a fourth-floor flat on Ninth Avenue where a somewhat-overweight but extremely intense young blond is finger-fucking me while sucking my dick. No condom. It's still sort of safe now, or it isn't, or it sort of is, or some people think it is, or people are so sick of everybody still being dead they figure, *Who gives a shit?* Resurrections, like the Japanese yen, being in greater demand than supply these days, we pilgrims settle for a naked hard-on incubated for an hour or so in mucous tissue at 98.6 degrees Fahrenheit.

The hair's a dye job, of course, and actually *streaked*…or *tipped*—a subtle distinction, to be sure—but it started out reasonably fair and it's long, the way I like it, and smells sweet—like papaya. There's some kind of scented candle thing going on, too, but they all smell like wax to me. But sweet. All burning things smell sweet. The day after the old ghetto burned, the whole neighborhood smelled like marshmallows, but that was long ago and far away—well, about sixty miles on the I-95. It smelled like roast fowl, too, but that's because the Mesopotamian next door kept a flock of guard ducks that never got out of their pen.

You just dial, you see, seven little easy-to-remember digits. *Punch in,* is, of course, more accurate, since you need a Touchtone phone to proceed. Listen to the "menu," then poke the six to listen to the "*actual voices* of New York's *hottest professionals.* 'Hi, I'm Jim. I'm five-foot-ten, weigh one-fifty. I give a hot-oil full-body Swedish massage with a sensual release, and more.'" Oooh*, baby!*

Take notes. Choose. Call the number. Leave yours on the machine. Wait. Dial again. Leave your number. And again. Wait. Wonder if any of them will call back. It is, after all, a holiday Saturday night. Desperation rises from the smoldering coals of desire: You will agree to see whoever calls first, no matter how much he charges, no matter where in the city he lives, even if it's the Upper East Side. Desire—sprung from the ether like crocus through the unsuspecting snow.

His name is Chip. Right. He's six-two, one-eighty, -ninety, twenty-four, from Massachusetts. Shaved balls for some reason. An angel puppy with a hot mouth—and I've got the bite marks on my unshaved ass to prove it. I did his lover yesterday, who is better looking but less enthusiastic. Neither of them knows. It's my little secret (and, by the way, I'd like to have them both together).

A hundred bucks. It doesn't seem like much until after you come. Well, holidays and all...and one from each side of the family tree. Special occasion, that sort of thing. He's Caucasian, not my usual choice. They look better dressed, as a rule. Maybe it's the northern light. Too much unrelenting pallor for passion, perhaps, or for honesty, as far as that goes. There's something about white that lies on its face. If you pass white light through a prism, it breaks down into its component colors: puritan purple, repression red, entitlement green, conformity yellow.

This white boy is an exception, I think, as I watch the Empire State Building through what looks like the steam that water turns into when hosed onto an inferno. Back in the early '80s there was a bathhouse in San Francisco that had a steam-room maze. I sucked weenie until I practically passed out from dehydration. I learned about chemistry in bathhouses—not from the red tin box of chemicals I got from my parents the birthday I asked for drums, or from the minister of our church, who did little lab experiments on compulsory Wednesday-night services during Lent, turning some clear liquid red, which was supposed to remind us of Our Lord and Savior Jesus Christ's first miracle (turning the water to wedding wine at Cana). I don't imagine that indemnity carriers allow toy companies to market chemistry sets anymore, although it was all pretty benign. Nothing at home ever turned colors. Just into a sludge, like powdered chocolate that stubbornly refused to dissolve into milk.

In bathhouses, in the pitch dark, you can touch a dozen men and feel nothing but flesh—the same feeling you might get rubbing up against an old woman on the uptown local. And then you touch another man, his arm or chest or waist, and your dick leaps to attention like it's on a spring and you are engulfed by him. That's chemistry, when the elements overcome the prejudices the mind has insulated the senses in.

This Empire State Building yellow is the same yellow they lit it that Friday night after St. Patrick's Day, as I recall, the first time the poor oppressed Irish Catholics who run the city of New York refused to let any queers march in their boozy parade (I keep track of holidays by how much pain they cause—ask me about Fourth of July of '76, or Halloween, 1970). There was, of course, the year the Empire State Building was illuminated especially for the troops in the Persian Gulf. Before it was a footnote—Desert Storm? The war in which American GI's were poisoned by chemical weapons invented here and supplied to the enemy by us. It's almost as ironic as the fact that Irish faggots march routinely in St. Pat's parades in, for example, Dublin and Belfast. It's only Fifth Avenue that's too narrow for fairies.

Of course, even piss yellow was better than the red, white, and trite fucking blue they were shoving down our throats before the war was over. Patriotism. Sounds lethal. Like botulism. And it is. You'd think they'd go for something less cadaverous, chromatically speaking, for so prominent and phallic a landmark—a nice white-inspired yellow, like wheat or a Yalie's argyles, suburban kitchens of the 1950s, or sunlight on the arm hairs of a Norwegian sailor, a sapling swabbie on leave abroad and not sure where to berth his buoy, not some revolting color that looks like what's been sitting in a stopped-up toilet at the Eros All-Male Cinema on Eighth Avenue for a week or two underneath that scrawny nude kid who'll take anybody or anything into his mouth or up his ass or all over his body. You've never seen hunger until you've said "I don't think so" and looked into those eyes while you let loose your stream into a nearby urinal while that scabby desperado nearly weeps to see you waste it. It's nice to be so sure of what you want. I envy that. It's the obsession that frightens me, for obvious reasons.

Here's what makes me puke: that washed-out bow-ribbon yellow florists were doling out to tie around trees in working-class Republican neighborhoods in Brooklyn and Queens during the Desert Storm fiasco, the satin ribbon they paste gold paper letters on to spell out CONGRATULATIONS and BELOVED UNCLE GUIDO and so forth. Of course, even that isn't as bad as the yellow they aim at the Empire State Building at no doubt enormous cost, a yellow that has some Gaelic emerald in it left over from the No-Pansies Drunken Mick Pig Parade—or else some khaki in it to remind us how cool America is for having the biggest army in the whole wide Western world.

How long has it been? A year or two, and it's so over it's like it never happened. Except for the dismembered orphans and the troops of veterans who are rotting slowly from the inside, thanks to the American army. All those dead people, and nothing to show for it but an oil slick the size of Nebraska. And don't get me started on Vietnam, where a hundred thousand American boys are buried in rice weed. It's a tourist destination now, and I'd go if I could. Just to be near the place where Ralph died—in the days when boys still died one at a time and not in droves like the firstborn of Egypt. The angel of death doesn't pass over very many anymore, ram's blood or no. Maybe blood just isn't as repellent as it used to be now that the national immune system is…compromised.

So the roiling midtown sky is blazing like it's National Water Sports Week instead of Easter. And Passover. Like the skyline is an Andres Serrano "Architectural Icon Suspended in Urine" lithograph. And the country's finances, like those of its citizens, are in the toilet. It was Kenny's humiliation that he could no longer get himself onto a toilet seat that finally did him in. The will just cracks, like the Liberty Bell, like Easter eggs boiled too fast on a gas stove, or a vial of poppers. Twenty years ago, when I was young and Ralph was already dead, on the night of a lonely birthday, I got smashed on beers at a bar uptown and this blazer homo named Wayne took me to his luxury doorman tower to piss in his mouth, which, as I remember it through an amber haze of guilt, memory, and a dozen bottles of brew, kept turning him yellower as I let loose—pulling hard on his scab-crusted nipples all the while—yellower than hepatitis eventually turned my eyeballs: mustard-gas yellow, the spewing sulfurous billow above a chemical plant in Baghdad hit by a U.S. SCUD, the pus color a kid's legs get when they've been blown off at the knees and there aren't any antibiotics left in the country so the kid will die real slow of infections, of peritonitis, just like Bette Davis in merciful black-and-white, without brain fever and hallucinations in Arabic. Maybe we didn't really kill tens of thousands of Iraqi civilians, as impartial international observers insist. But, knowing us, we probably did, killing being the thing we do best. I'm so proud to be an American I could just shit shamrocks.

So what do you think, it's a coincidence that the same day Irish queers march for the first time in the St. Paddycake Parade (unauthorized, of course, by the Ancient Order of the Ku Klux Hibernians), two undercover vice goons bust a naked dancer at the Gaiety Burlesk for solicitation? So now there are no more private shows because the Greek broads who run the place are paranoid city, and Joey Stefano says, laconic as August in Ecuador, "Pigs are pigs," and eats a cold McDonald's single burger by the pay phone in the Get Acquainted Lounge, which used to smell of grass, cash, and impending sex, but now smells only of ammonia, where a Lebanese kid mops up the room behind the stage so the dancers won't slip on the generic-brand baby oil they use to get their dicks hard before working the runway for their second of two numbers.

I've spent a lot of time on floors in my day. Wooden floors of back-room bars passed out on coats, linoleum floors of peep-show arcades working my jaws over any available hunk of sausage, tile floors of bathrooms in places like the Chelsea Hotel (coming to with dead Danny's dick up my ass), cement floors of various…institutions, let's say. And what I remember most is the smell of Pine Sol, industrial strength. It's an aphrodisiac to me now, like glue, however toxic when inhaled. Behind the screen at the Gaiety Burlesk, it used to smell like semen and the mellow illusion of possibility. Now it just smells like sweat. There'd be a lot less hypocrisy in the world, I always say, if human odors were indelible. Of course, there'd be a lot more flies, too.

I've spent a lot of time at the Gaiety Burlesk, too, and a lot of money in that sleazy little temple of Priapus where you tend to run into people like the clerk from the mailroom at work and David Hockney. It's a microcosm, you know, although too many of the dancers on any given night are likely to be white. Most of the clients are bigoted old queens who get up and leave the auditorium when the black dancers come on, or the brown ones. Well, one thing about fags: we have not got our race shit together. But there were lessons to be learned at the Gaiety Burlesk, and not all the boys were white.

There were Latin boys of such devastating beauty I could get off just touching their flawless skin. Hairy Italians who all wanted you to think they were tops, and, okay, some of them were. Asians who set off every nerve in my body with their fingertips. And a black man once, a model in need of some emergency cash, who didn't want me even for money because I was so fat at the time, but who got so turned on backstage when I went to work on his nipples that he came when I did.

And there were special cases, too, boys I'd fall in love with just at the moment I shot a load all over the floor behind the screen wishing I had drenched them in that special way I have of spewing a load so big even the professionals gasp (and I'm not just bragging), and I'd visit them time after time. Luis, or whatever his name was, a Puerto Rican from New Jersey who was working his way through landscape-design courses at Rutgers, I'll never forget. I'll never forget the curving angle of his enormous rock-hard dick as he kneeled over my head at the Paramount Hotel (before the chichi renovation), or watching him shower, or his smile, or seeing him again in L.A. and taking him to dinner, and wanting him so bad through my pants I could feel them dampen. If I still had his phone number I'd call him right now and dump a load anywhere he'd take it.

And there was Vladimir, of course, who got famous on late-night cable TV, Vladimir who was named after the vampire in a Dracula movie his mother saw once, who came home with me one night-before-Gay-Pride-Parade-Day and waved to his fans along Christopher Street (I was so proud), and then stripped in my bedroom and made leisurely, reasonable love with his bulked-up body for an hour or more. And Rocky, who got famous for a minute or two, too, when he teamed up with Madonna for a book and a video, but whose real name he told me when he came to clean my apartment—fully dressed—which was his legit day-job way of making money. Told me once in a hotel room he'd never been fucked (like that surprised me) or ever even fucked a man, which did take me aback—I mean, what with his muscles and dick and tattoos and dazzling smile and all, not to mention his profession, I'd have thought there'd be men around with enough cash to cajole him into it. And what was the most amazing thing to me was how he just seemed amazed that gay men could like it, not that he thought it was disgusting or anything, just outside his experience (which extended to war). There was, of course, Brazilian Julio (in Portuguese, you pronounce the "J," as in Juliet), who was, as I was, born in July, a real dancer, with career potential. "You are so big," he said to me that first night we met, the night of the hotel that overlooked Lincoln Center's Christmas tree, "you are so big you can do anything to me," he said. So I did. I fucked him—again and again. I fucked him in hotel rooms and I fucked him in my apartment when I finally moved to New York and I even fucked him behind the screen at the Gaiety Burlesk, which ran strictly counter to the dancers' code.

"You are crazy," Julio said once while I was fucking him off the floor by the emergency exit, alternating my dick and half a hand so I wouldn't come too soon.

"Do you really think so?" I asked, wondering if it was true.

"But it's okay," he smiled, "because I'm crazy, too—I love it."

And he did, this sweet and generous boy/man who was as beautiful as any man I've ever desired, even in Carmen Miranda drag, which he wore to the Gay Parade for years. He was beautiful beside me at the ballet, too. He was the tiniest man I ever had, and I wish I had him again now, to toss in the air and catch on my dick like a game of quoits.

Yes, those were the glory days, when sex was encouraged right smack on the premises, like a cut-rate brothel. But the Gaiety is not the scene it was before the Gulf War (not, strictly speaking, named for the oil company, but obviously fought on its behalf). So...what? You think the bust at the Gaiety was related to the war at all or just a coincidence? Or the parade where you have to be an RC het-breeder to be Irish? Or are the war and the parade somehow linked to this crackdown on grease-smeared asscracks just by the general, you know, ethos of the time, the odor of *fascismo* on the rise numbing its prey like a giant water beetle?

So, I told myself the first night I turned up at the Gaiety after the "No Sex, Please, We're Busted" message went out, "Well, you might as well tie a yellow ribbon around Rocky's cock since you're not gonna get your lips around it, not tonight." So I stuck my middle finger straight up for those shit-Mick douche bags who booed and spat on the Irish queens in the city's lousy St. Pat-my-ass Parade. I stuck it straight up the fuckhole of a new dancer named

Daniel in his room at the Milford Plaza, which cost me a whole lot more than backstage folderol but turned out to be worth it.

Daniel's American-born, but he's one of those border-town Lone Star Latins with hair longer than a girl's and crooked teeth in front. Couldn't be more appealing (as at least one big-deal photographer has discovered), though I could do without the safety-pin tattoos. His eyes are swimming in something he uses so his brain won't see things the way his eyes do. He calls me Daddy Bear and has the usual gigantic uncut dick, which is nearly blue it's so dark, but I don't care, even if it does remind me of Roberto, dead and alive. I just want something up his ass. I'd use a shillelagh if I had one. He'll take my dick if I'm willing to renegotiate, and there is nothing I'd like better than to sink myself up to the ruby pubes in those fleshy buns of his, but I'm not making the bucks I was, so we settle on fingers, which I give him 'til we both come, simultaneously, which I take as an enormous compliment, since even at his age he can't afford to come with every trick, so most of them don't ever. I've been lucky that way, since I don't find a lot of pleasure in it unless I'm turning on my partner in the process.

"It's a gusher," he drawls in his cutesy way when I geyser all over his too-fleshy middle. He eats a banana, chugs a politically responsible Bud Lite, belches real ladylike, and says, "I don't know, I think everybody's queer." It's a hustler's perspective, sure, but you gotta admit there's some truth in it. In the elevator there's a Chinese escort hostess in silver rhinestone shoes and fake leopard coat who clocks our number before we drop half a floor, and a little blonde girl with brand-new breasts who's here on a school trip from Virginia and who hasn't got a clue and never will, unless, of course, she winds up working this same hotel. It can happen. Even in Newport News. She looks like she's dressed for a junior prom sometime before the Beatles' TV debut. It'd be a fun group to get stuck on an elevator with, but of course we don't get stuck (that waits until I'm trapped with a hysterical sumo wrestler who hasn't bathed since Tito died).

We sashay out of the elevator, across the lobby, through the crisscrossed laser glares of the Jamaican security staff, their scrutiny thick as chemical warfare, but nobody says jack shit. That's what business is all about: that smell of printer's ink, of fine engraving and finesse. Which is why it's so funny not long after when this rich Italian entrepreneur gets busted at the Milford Plaza for bringing a far younger and far more African young woman to his room for immoral congress (U.S. legislature, take note). Only it turns out—big oops here—the young lady is not exactly working, she is exactly the Italian's *wife*. Red faces everywhere and banner headlines in the *Post*.

Speaking of which, I don't think it's all that much a coincidence that the *Post* does this giant cover story—right after the mayor of New York—the good one, not the one we have now—marches down Fifth Avenue with a clutch of lilting laddies and lasses of the Old Sod and Gomorrah persuasion—with this sensational big mother headline announcing that there are hustlers on Second Avenue at 53rd Street—a fact that every two- or four-legged sodomite has known since Cain set up shop on the northeast corner. Talk about your phenomenal scoop, right? Yeah, scoop of dog shit. Somehow it all comes down to Ireland. I used to like Ireland. Used to think the IRA was a righteous club, a kind of Black Panther Party with red hair and freckles.

In London, once upon a time, before Ralph was dead or I'd ever fucked a man to sleep, I met a drunk in Russell Square, a beggar: Irish, beard/moustache, fingers stained yellow from unfiltered cigarettes, Turkish when he could get them—and I bought him a whole pack near the poetry bookstore and the School of Economics. "Watch out for Ireland," he said, as broad in the blarney, I thought, as he was in the brogue. "Another Vietnam, my son, as sure as

I'm standing." And he was, still standing, breathing the most fetid breath I'd ever smelled, being young. I was "Up the Irish" for years after—Yeats, O'Casey, Behan. Now I'm sick of it. Sick of blowing up the English just because they shop in Harrods. Sick of the prig English, their stiff lips and limp dicks, but mostly sick of every Roman Catholic country on earth.

Fuckin' Ireland. The country's about as big as Staten Island and they can't even figure out how to have two religions without killing each other (a lot like Israel, but don't get me started). No doubt about it, religion has caused more evil in the world than all the hookers put together. Religion is the process by which God is eliminated from matters of the spirit and replaced by human will, the empirically fallible will of a self-protective priesthood. Simple as that. And isn't patriotism, like cannibalism, a form of religion, really?

So I just eat an overpriced ham sandwich at Jerry's on Prince and wonder if these really deep, shrewd news hounds at the *Post* know that black men sell dope in Washington Square or that there are rainbow-colored junkies in this city washing windshields for quarters to support minor children. I have a cousin who's missing an eye for refusing one of these overzealous spot-removers. An oft-wed black sheep (son of an oft-wed black sheep), he was once married to one of the Rockettes, who used to dress up like nuns for the Easter show at Radio City Music Hall and carry white lilies up to this stage-set altar to form a giant cross (for which spectacle we'd wait outside on 50th Street for hours, me mesmerized by the stark-naked Art Deco cement men above the entrance to Rockefeller Center, the first men I ever coveted in my heart, and still do).

And I wonder if the *Post* boys know how heroic old Manhattan pissed on the potato-eaters who built the bridges and subways and City Hall, those same County Corkers who lynched escaped slaves from lampposts in the Village during the Civil War riots. Talk about casting a

jaundiced eye. I guess that's why they call it "yellow" journalism. Because of the cowardice.

So I go to visit the folks on the Island, during the Gulf War,
which turns out to be the usual mistake, and of course,
masters of the mundane, they have a yellow ribbon tied
around the trunk of a tree I grew up with and got to know
fairly well. I even sat in that tree, and here it is hung with
this hate-thing. Oh, the next-door neighbors have a bigger
one, the Irish neighbors (no one's speaking to the Polish
neighbors because the old man, who used to sell Wise
Potato Chips, has gone completely dotty), and a flag in the
picture window that says THESE COLORS NEVER FADE.
Sweet, sweet as new corn. Catholics and politics. So this
friend of mine in California, not, to be sure, a bastion of
rigid news sourcing, tells me this rumor that's being investi-
gated in Europe that the pope, the Polish one, was in fact a
collaborator with the Nazis during World War II, that he
actually turned over the names of Jews to save his own
skinless kielbasa. I believe it. Popes have been helping Nazis
all along—take Pius XII, please! It is said, and by Roman
Catholics themselves, mind you, that Pope John Paul I,
whose pontificate was shorter than the Gulf War, that
Johnny Paul Uno was actually murdered right there in the
Vatican by an opposition claque of Machiavellian minions.
Chris (for Christian, not Christopher) says he doesn't
believe any of it, but then Chris goes to Georgetown, were
Jesuits teach Skepticism 101 no matter what the curriculum
is called. He admits, though, that the whole clergy is queer,
including New York's reigning necrophiliac, Cardinal
O'Connor (who likes his cock-swallowing acolytes dead,
you see), that "We're not in the business of saving lives, but
of saving souls" anticondom pro-lifer, that genocidal bog-
hopper with a piss shooter the size of a leprechaun's. "Why
didn't someone try to kill him?" I can remember asking
about Hitler, since he was so obviously evil. Same goes for
O'Connor. How come he's still alive?

So somebody pistol-whipped a priest in Queens or Brooklyn or someplace to feed a wicked jones with the parish lucre and everybody's all shocked and alarmed. Right. Fucking priests been pistol-whipping faggots for centuries. Kill 'em all. that's what I say. Like cockroaches.

So it's Easter, and Passover, but I don't miss chocolate bunnies under yellow and lilac cellophane. You know what I miss? Rubberless fucking, since fucking with a glove on is no fucking at all, as any man who has ever done both will tell you. Oh, it might be worth giving up "unprotected" sex to save a life, but what's a life that has only protected sex in it? Rhetorical question. It's like a bullfight where the sword stays in its sheath.

Bullfights. They make me weep, they're so inaccessibly beautiful. They are, of course, the ultimate *symbolic* entertainment: Either the matador will fuck the bull (with his sword), or *el toro* will fuck the toreador (goring him with one or more horns). It is, Carlos Fuentes assures us, the ritual of man's supremacy over nature. But it's really about fucking, which is to say about man's total abandonment to, and submissiveness in the face of, nature.

The bullfighter is dressed magnificently in second-skin topaz satin, his asscheeks clenched tighter than fetal fists, his bundle of genitalia casting harsh shadows on his hard thighs. The bull comes equipped with a prick the size of the man's arm, two horns, and a lolling tongue that looks like a dick and a tongue combined—one of those giant mollusks on display in Chinatown fish shops. Of course, the bull will die even if he manages to take down his tormentor in the process; immortality, like justice, is a fantasy.

Two men fucking is like a bullfight, too, a ritual of man's confrontation with the nature in himself. No illusions of sanctioned procreation to dilute the event, no easy retreat into the uncomprehending "otherness" of opposites, just man as he is, man doing to himself—and having done to himself—the thing the world has taught him will most surely damn him for all eternity. So the bull dies, fucker or fuckee. And blood glistens in the parched sand of the arena. A man fucking a woman is beautiful, too, in its way, I suppose. But there is no mortality in it. It is, if ritual at all, an enactment of the myth of life. Queer sex is nature in the service of itself in the present, not the future.

The greatest of all epics, the *Mahabharata* tells us, that every man must die, and yet each day lives his life as if he is immortal. In the face of such wisdom, such clarity, it hardly seems to matter if there is an eternity at all.

Once upon a time when Easter and Passover happened on the same day, I was sitting in the administration building of the college I went to by mistake, along with a third of the student body, in protest over fraternity exclusion of blacks and Jews. I remember a chevron of geese flying overhead and a balmy, spongy-earth day with daffodils blooming wild on green hills, and I remember hope. (That's why preserving the hope of the young is so important, so it can be remembered later in life.)

The upstate Maytime sky was clear and blue, like Chip's eyes as he veils his hair now over me and puts his tongue onto my tongue like the Host. The body and blood of Chip. As often as I do this...I remember all kinds of men. Most of them dead. Like the reed-thin corpses of the Holocaust (their exposed genitalia the first human penises I ever saw, enormous-looking, enticing even attached to dead men). Like the saints and disciples. Horrible deaths, most of them. Crucified, stoned, burned, quartered, fed to wild beasts—just the sort of thing the church has been doing to fairies forever.

Now Magic Johnson has AIDS, which is sad I guess, but I can't get all broken up about it. Arthur Ashe has been dropped as a crossword clue in the *New York Times,* so there's some real impact on my life there. "Isn't it awful about Arthur Ashe?" some twinkie in Lycra biker shorts gushed at the gym right after that news became public. To tell the truth, I didn't actually give a shit about Arthur

Ashe. Or any other heterosexual. They've had their millennia, and they've blown it (up). The world is better off without them. There are too many people anyway. Too many people who hate. So I guess the world would be better off without me, too, since I have learned to hate so purely. But then, the world won't have long to wait for that. I'll be going one of these days, one of the ways we're dying: bad blood, tainted blood, spilled blood.

We're all dying of the yellow anyway, of the Empire State Building piss yellow of religious holidays and patriotism, an oily yellow lost in a mist that looks like it should smell of subways, that bum-urine and burnt electric cordite smell of blue-white sparks on gleaming tracks. Instead it smells sweet. Like the licorice jelly beans my Polish Catholic godmother picked out of the Easter baskets she gave me before she died and went to burn in hell forever for marrying a Lutheran and loving her queer nephew unconditionally.

So it's late. The car alarm out front finally died after about six hours since the police don't have the authority to do anything but beat up faggots who have the temerity to hail a yellow cab outside the Stage Deli. My fingers still smell like Chip, like the scented massage lotion he rubbed on my body and I rubbed on his, of my own semen and his, of Obsession for Men, and large, luminous eyes, of views of the Empire State Building from the floor-level mattress of a part-time hustler who's moving south at the end of the month to pursue a career in music. It's Easter already by the digital Bulova on my desk. It's raining, which means the smeared diuretic dog shit is being washed from the sidewalk out front with the soot from chimneys a century old and more. The acid that turns copper green is washing out of the air onto the cobbled streets of lower Manhattan while a small rat forages under my sink for the poisoned oats an exterminator left there on Good Friday.

The rain falls onto the aluminum hood of the kitchen exhaust fan, reminding me of an intravenous drip and nickels. Some unkillable fungus grows under my toenails (I call it Cardinal O'Connor). But despite it all, despite the pot of coffee and a quart of diet Pepsi I just ingested in lieu of the blood of Christ, I'll sleep soundly tonight, while junkies curl up in doorways and shoot tepid smack into their veins, grateful not to go to sleep sick. After all, it's a holiday. I'll take an aspirin against the pains of holidays and age and I'll sleep with memories of Chip in my mouth, of Joey Stefano (higher than a kite, his asshole open to accept the loneliness of the male world). I'll think of lovers who smelled of formaldehyde even before they died and jerk off wondering if Ralph was ever happy. And I'll drift off on clouds of beer-swilling Texican Daniel. He was a rose, all right, a yellow rose that I am dreaming of, of Danny Boy from Dallas, of hate in Irish eyes, and vengeance.

WHIPMASTER

Cecilia Tan

Author's note: A few thoughts on why I wrote this story in tribute to John Preston.

John Preston and I met only once, briefly, less than a year before his death, and I gave him a copy of my book of self-published SM erotica, Telepaths Don't Need Safewords. *He probably would not have recognized my name, though maybe he would; I will never have the chance to know now. This does not matter. The things that matter are the things we had in common. Both "pornographers" (his word and mine) on a disenfranchised fringe, both writing fiction about dominance, both concerned with things like mentorship, discipline, and fantasy. In my most deep-seated archetypal fantasies, John Preston was the mentor that I, as a pornographer of this kind, never had. And in sitting down to write this tribute, I found I could not write an essay or reminiscence about him or his writing or his funeral. I could only express what he "meant" to me through this kind of fiction that we both shared.*

In the story, my sadomasochistic creativity is replaced by the symbols of my sadomasochistic libido—the pen becomes a whip, and my unfulfilled longing for a masculine, disciplined, experienced mentor becomes embodied in the character of the whipmaster. But a mere fantasy in which all is exactly as it should be is interesting to no one but the author, and the snarls and difficulties of real life compel me as strongly as any libidinous image. And so, in come the troubles, some shadowing real life, others not. This is a piece of fiction. Like any fiction, it is a creation of the hopes and desires and visions of the author. I don't know what John Preston would have thought of it. I can only hope that the values I think he espoused will be in some way embodied here, and that how sorely I miss him will, also.

I moved to New England just in time for the winter, just in time to get settled and start hibernating in a town where I knew no one and didn't relish slogging through the mixed precipitation to find them. There was one thing I hoped to find, now that I was single, and well away from the gossipy, backbiting, conformist queer culture I had known in Pennsylvania, unfettered by antisex feminists, leather-phobic lesbians, clingy, monogamous significant others...I was free and alone, and I started looking for a whipmaster. The personal ads did not seem promising—there was no section for "Sadists Wanted." So I put up a sign in the one bar I thought would attract the right clientele, and waited.

It was a long wait. I had a couple of calls from guys who sounded like they were calling from the pay phone in the bar, looking for a quick screw. Most of them hung up when they heard the answering machine pick up. I went to a couple of meetings for local social groups, but felt as if most everyone knew each other already and I didn't stick around long after the meetings broke up. Around February I was starting to kick myself and wonder if maybe I should give up on this fantasy when a phone message came to my machine. "This is a message for Roe. I have received word that you are in need of some instruction. If I find you a suitable student I may be willing to tutor you." His voice, so staid and reserved, encouraged me that maybe he was what I was looking for, and made me tremble at the thought that I might not measure up to his standards, one in particular. He left details of when and where I should meet him—the next evening, at the bar.

That night his voice entered my dreams as I slipped into fitful sleep. I woke up restless, jittery with anxiety. I slid a hand to my crotch hoping to tire myself out as I turned over visions of long black coils of leather striking out. The beauty of their dance, the precision of their discipline, the smell of the oiled leather between my fingers, these things I knew. But the vision could not go beyond that—I did not know what he looked like, and worse, if he would take me at all. The fantasy felt empty, false—I lacked the vision to see what would or could come next.

I spent the whole next day preparing to meet him, thinking on the coil of energy in my belly, and strutting back and forth in my apartment in torn jeans, an undershirt. I spent a long time looking at my arms in the mirror, my shoulders. I had been doing push-ups, chin-ups, curls, it was something to do on cold winter nights, and I was happy with how beefy my triceps had become. But my chest was still a problem and probably always would be. A leather jacket fastened at the bottom but not zipped made it look almost right. I coiled my best whip with care and attached it to my belt loop. On the left. Our rendezvous was still four hours away.

I decided it was best to be early and went to the bar at 8:00 P.M. instead of 9:00. Outside, two men were leaning against the wall, one lighting a cigarette and the other talking in a low voice, his breath fogging in the air. They both watched as I swung open the unmarked door to the place and went in. It wasn't the first time I'd been there, but I was not what you would call part of their regular clientele. No one gave me any particular looks as I made my way past the pool tables to the back room, and whether this was a good or bad sign I did not know. I passed the bulletin board where my "classified" note still stood. "Wanted: A Whip Master's Expertise. There is only so much one can learn from oneself. I crave to learn from a practiced expert. Let me prove myself worthy of your instruction. Roe."

The other details of that night do not matter—they blur into all the other nights I'd spent in dark smoky bars alone. What does matter are the memories I have like snapshots, sound bites, that play in my mind sometimes. How he took me by the hair and said, "You must be the boy I'm looking for." I struggled a bit—oddly, I felt as though the struggle was the sign he wanted that I was willing to play along. He forced me through the bar to the far side of the room. Men were looking at us; I heard the hush as we caught their attention. John's voice was loud. "Where did you get this?" With his free hand he pushed my leather jacket from my shoulders, pulling the sleeves until it slipped off my back to the floor. "My boys earn their leather. Do you understand?" It was not just a simple question. In it I heard the unspoken "Are you with me?"

"Yes, sir." The answer slipped out as easy and natural as could be.

He tore the undershirt from my back, then, and I suppressed the urge to cover my tits. I kept my head down, my eyes down, not wanting to see the looks of shock or disdain from the circle that was gathering. "Be proud, boy," he said in my ear. "Your skin is what I want." His hand turned me by my bare shoulder to face him. "So," he said. "You want to learn the secrets of the whip." He had two whips at his belt. "Tell me why."

"Yes, sir." But no easy answer came this time. A jumble of images came to my mind, of penitence, of gladiators, of an old movie childhood, of a fist, of power. "I want a slave of my own," I said. "I want to be able to deal the ultimate discipline, I want to master the tool...."

"Bullshit," he said, and took me by the hair at my neck again. "Tell me about that whip." He pointed with his chin to the one I had looped at my hip.

"I made it myself, from a book on whipmaking. I keep it through my belt loop, so it takes some time to draw."

He smiled, then, a rare, terrifying smile. "Very good. A whip is not a tool of random violence. Its use is deliberate, calculated, focused. To use it is itself a form of discipline. It is never to be used without thought and care, without weighing the costs of bringing it to life." His words were like a gospel I had waited all my life to hear.

"Now tell me what it feels like." He pulled me closer, and I felt his breath on my neck as he spoke.

I hesitated. "It—It feels like the wrath of God."

His eyes searched mine. "You've never felt it, have you?"

I mouthed the word "No," as it seemed all my energy and substance ran out at that moment, no voice, no will, no power...my knees were buckling. My body knew even before I did what was to come. He sat down on a stack of beer cases and pulled me down with him, my bare back like a blank slate in his lap. He ran his fingers over my shoulders, down to my hipbones. "I told you I wanted you for your skin."

"Yes, sir."

"If you are to learn the secrets of the lash, you must start here. Do you understand?"

"Yes, sir."

"If you say no, or if you tell me to stop, I will. But only once."

"Yes, sir."

"That rule is good now, and is good ever. If you ever call for a stop, it will be your only chance. Lose your nerve, break your spirit, whatever—if you ever beg me to stop, it will be the end. Do you understand?"

"Yes, sir."

He whistled, then—a sharp taxi-hailing whistle—and

another man came up to us. He was a classically beefy
blond, in black jeans and a heavy motorcycle jacket. John
positioned him so that I was pressed face against his back,
his leather cool against my cheek, and the man held my
hands in front of his stomach. His grip was strong. John
walked away from us with measured steps, the heavy tap
of his boot heels like a drum tolling, a countdown. Then a
long pause, and I knew he was uncoiling the long whip,
taking his time, deliberating, and I knew that this was the
moment I had been seeking, the moment of truth. The
skin on my back felt electric with anticipation, hungry and
eager as my heart pounded and one small part of my brain
questioned whether I could go through with this or not.

And then the blow came. I did not cry out. My scream
was paralyzed inside me as every cell in my body joined
the frantic scramble to process the pain, to absorb the line
of fire burning across my back, the lingering ache deep
inside me.

Then John was there. "How did that feel?"

I smiled. "Like the wrath of God."

He gave a little nod, then, as if he'd made a decision.
"Fair enough." He pulled me free of the muscle man and
pointed at the wall. My little classified note. He motioned
for us to stand back and several other men took steps back
for good measure. The whip whirred in the air as it flew
and then, with a quiet crack, shredded the paper into
oblivion.

He coiled the whip with slow circles and tucked it away
before he turned back to us. "Gary," he said to the man
who had held me, "meet my new boy." Gary gave a curt
nod to me and walked away.

I had passed the first test, but now, as my training began, I
realized that I had to pass my own test every time I picked
up a whip or stood under the lash. We settled into a
routine where I came to his house on the outskirts of
town every Saturday for instruction. I was eager to learn,

but reluctant to make a mistake or to show how poor my skill was. You would think that it would be easy, to have a master to force one through what one is shy of doing. But perhaps that was the strongest part of John's mastery. He never "forced" me to do anything. If I did not want to do something, I always had my choice—walk away and never come back. And so I persevered. It began with caring for his leathers, learning the difference between mink oil and neatsfoot and hard fat, between cow leather and deerskin, latigo and oak, and learning to cut leather strips as straight as a ruler and as long as a car. I braided and unbraided and rebraided a new whip until it was perfect enough for him, or until my fingers were too stiff to continue. He let me handle some of the short whips, no more than four feet long, with soft falls that would do no damage if they flew astray. And I bared my skin when he requested it and learned lessons of pain and ecstasy, fear and surrender.

On a sunny April day, he told me the time had come for me to earn my leather. "If you're ever going to use this," he said holding the coils of the newest whip we had made, a finely braided four-foot signal whip, "you'll need the armor."

"What do I have to do?"

The tiny curve of his lip twitched which I knew by now counted for a smile. "You've already done a lot, don't you think?"

It sounded like a trick question so I kept quiet.

"Tonight's a special night at the bar. There'll be…challenges." I could tell from the way he said it that he'd say no more about it. We hadn't been back to the bar since that first night we'd met.

When we arrived in the back room, he instructed me to strip to the waist and put on a kidney belt. Now my suspicions about what kind of "challenge" I would be facing were confirmed. I noticed a number of other boys there, prancing about shirtless, too. Not one was without a collar. My fingers brushed my throat. John must have seen me looking. "Do you want one?"

I hesitated. Unless the answer was an unconditional yes, I always had trouble speaking. Again he gave his little smile. "That's because a collar's not for you. You are not a slave. Do you understand?"

"Yes, sir."

He exchanged words out of earshot with some other men, Masters, Tops, and then whistled for attention. Even among Tops, he was in command. He issued a challenge then, to them, to pit their boys against me for ten lashes. There were immediately some takers, and I knew it had all been set up beforehand. John selected the first boy and beckoned for me.

They put us up against the back wall, hip to hip and the boy gave me a comradely smile. I sneaked a look back to see John going through his little ritual of uncoiling. Then came a single crack, the signal that it was about to begin. I drew a deep breath and tensed for the blow. The whip sliced through the air and I twitched expectantly— but the first blow fell on my companion, who howled out the pain. For that moment I felt weightless, like a ghost with no substance, as if the whip had passed through me to strike him, so strange it was not to have it connect. But then the second one came down on me and made me whole and real again. It was a hard blow, and I wished I had something to bite on as the pain raced up and down my back as if I did not have enough skin to contain it. The first one was still hurting when the next one came, landing just below the first, multiplying the agony. The third came just below that. Like notches in a tree, I realized. Both my companion and I lasted through all ten. Then he was replaced with another one. Again, a single crack in the air. And then the blows began to fall, creeping slowly down my back on one side. I stopped breathing when the whip would connect, then gasped for air in the respite. I can do this, I told myself, this is just as we've done it before, only this time everyone is watching. Just last week I had taken twenty five strokes on each side, and felt like I could take more. How many boys were there, five? That would be fifty? My math was disrupted by the next blow. I had lost count of how many I'd had. I told myself it couldn't be too many more, could it?

It was. Boy after boy was put into place beside me, and it dawned on me that John had only just started on the left side of me. I had those long-distance runner thoughts going through my head—just past halfway, that's good, keep breathing, breathe, if you've made it this far you can go this far again...trying to ignore the fact that each blow that fell seemed to multiply the pain of the others and I felt as if every pore in my skin was screaming just as I was screaming, not stopping between blows anymore...until the blows did stop.

It took a few moments for me to realize that someone else was being put into place next to me, but that something was happening behind us. I turned to see Gary and John with their heads together. Several others were murmuring behind them. Gary spoke up, then. "This test is bogus, old man! You're letting the bitch off too easy."

John's face was red with the effort of the whipping and with controlling his temper. "What do you mean?"

"If my boy's going up against her, I want to be the one to dish it out." There was some noise of assent from the background. "If you want her to prove her 'worth'"—at which point he snorted—"let someone else have a crack at her. It's only fair."

John was grinding his teeth. "And you think it should be you."

"My boy's the last in line. Why not me?" He was already brandishing the whip.

John looked into the faces of the others. "Very well."

I looked away. Gary was snaking the whip in front of him like a rodeo trickster. His boy would not meet my eye so I closed them and waited. I knew from the fire on my skin that there was no inch of it untouched on my back.

This time the salutatory crack came right across my shoulders in a long slash that sent me up against the wall. His boy merely flinched a little and grunted. The second came directly on top of the first—like Robin Hood splitting the fucking arrow, I thought. Dear God, let him hit me somewhere else.... The third snaked around my ribs to lash me in the tit, and I knew without looking that it would well up in a black bruise. I couldn't look; I couldn't do anything but scream. Gary's boy still hadn't done much more than say "uh." The bastard, I thought, is doing exactly what he accused John of doing, taking it easy on his own bottom...he lashed me across the buttocks and it felt like I wasn't even wearing jeans. My mind was idly wandering, wondering about the tensile strength of denim, of skin...he got me in the soft flesh under my arm, high on my shoulders near my neck. Too damn accurate...I remembered that first night in the bar when he'd held me for that very first blow. Had there been bitterness in his tone? Looking back on it now, it seemed that there was something passing between him and John that I hadn't been able to read...still couldn't. Then three blows in a row fell in the same spot across my shoulders, and suddenly I wondered about the students John had had before me, and why Gary wasn't still his student now. Some part of my brain was thinking this over while the rest was overloading on the pain. Hang on, I thought, this is ten coming up now! And the tenth blows fell, one on me, one on his boy, who cried out this time. I was about to take my arms down and move when I heard the whip crack. Gary roared, "Stay where you are!"

And the whip began to fall at twice the speed. The other boy was screaming now, but I was beyond scream-ing. I kept my eyes and my jaw clenched tightly and just prayed for it to be over. Now that the blows were coming faster, I stopped thinking about each one, and tried to sink down into the endorphin haze that had been built up over the evening. I doubted I had any skin left on my back. John will stop this if it goes on too long, I thought. Gary's blows were beginning to miss their marks. He caught me once on the spine, and once missed, so all I felt was the air of the lash in motion. The boy started sobbing. John had brought me to tears with the whip, too, on other nights. But now I was not crying. Now I was on fire, and with each deep breath I breathed fire, power welling up in me like a flaming torch. Gary was growling now as he threw the whip again and again, and his boy sounded like a wounded animal.

And suddenly the boy started crying out. "Please! Please! No more! Stop, oh, stop, enough!" He was still crying as he slumped to the floor. When no one moved to help him, I knelt down and cradled his head on my knees. That got Gary to move. He pushed me aside. "Are you all right?" His voice sounded small and ridiculous. The boy curled into a fetal position.

John leaned down to Gary. "I told you, you never did know when to stop." Gary tried to return a bitter look, but his eyes sidled away.

John took me by the arm then and walked me around the room. Each man we stopped in front of admired my back, and a couple of the boys shook my hand. Some said "welcome" and some said "congratulations." When we had gone all the way around, Gary and his boy were gone. John sat me on a bar stool to let my shaky legs recover and talked with some of the men. In my daze, I don't recall anything they said.

The next moment that was clear and real, we had just stepped out of the bar onto the sidewalk, into the street-light glow and noise of taxis, and Gary was there, leaning against a black-and-red motorcycle. The smile on his face was plastered with sarcasm. "So, John, we don't see much of you anymore. How've you been?" He came forward as if to put his arm around John's shoulders.

John took a step back. "You're a disgrace—"

Gary wasn't listening. "You know how we worry about your health."

"Get away from me!" John's slow boil was beginning to steam, his face reddening.

Gary actually laughed. "Old man, you gave up the right to give me orders when you cut me loose, remember? I was such a bad slave, too. Never obedient. Not like this one—"

"Be quiet," John was saying.

But now Gary had turned to me.

"He's going to leave you, you know. You don't have what he needs. He doesn't need your little tits, sister, and he's going to be gone soon—"

"Shut up!" John's hand flashed toward Gary's cheek, but Gary knocked it away.

"Uh-uh, you gave that up, too, didn't you, when you put me out?" The calculated coolness of his voice was beginning to crack. "And for what! For this little cu—" Thereafter his comments degenerated into mere profanity. John hailed a cab. Gary was still ranting on the sidewalk as we pulled away.

That night, as John rubbed some Chinese salve on my welts, he apologized for losing his temper. "As you can see, that boy can be mighty trying."

I said nothing.

"I know you're thinking about the things he said. You'd be a fool not to."

This time I nodded. I wanted to forget all the things Gary said and just feel John's fingers on my skin and remember each loving touch of the whip. For that's what they were, now I was sure, having felt the difference between his strokes and Gary's. Loving. I folded my arms across my breasts and said nothing.

John snorted, and lifted up my arm to slather some medicine on the welt that snaked under my arm and over my breast. "There are two things I love a boy for," he said. "Your skin, and your heart. And that is all. And Gary, well, is just a prick." He gave a little laugh. "Most of all is your heart. That is where obedience, loyalty, honesty, and self-worth reside. That is where all that I teach you goes. Not your arm or your eye." And he pulled me back to lean against him and said softly, "Do you understand?"

"Yes, sir."

"But I suppose I should explain some of what he said." He sat back and looked at my glistening skin. I did not turn around. "You've probably guessed that Gary was formerly a boy of mine. The exact details do not matter. He wanted me to teach him to throw a whip, and I kept telling him no. He wasn't mature enough for it. But then I did start to teach him. A mistake. He does not take criticism well and wouldn't listen. Eventually he became so unmanageable that I told him to get out."

I had guessed all that. But what else had Gary said? Something about John's health? My neck muscles froze as a thought occurred to me, and I kept myself from turning to look at him. My voice was gravelly as I asked, "What made you change your mind and start to teach him?"

The long silence before he answered confirmed my hunch before he said, "I learned a while ago that I have cancer."

"How long...?" I blurted out before I could stop myself.

"Don't know." He stood up. "You can sleep on the floor in the workshop if you like. Or I'll call you a cab."

When I didn't move or answer, he continued, "Pillows, sheets, in the linen closet." I went to retrieve them.

As I lay in my makeshift bed, waiting for sleep, my mind sifted over the evening's events again and again. An ugly thought reared up: There's nothing special or worthy about you—he's teaching you only because he's desperate to find someone before he dies, and anyone other than

Gary would do—even a girl like you. I tried to quash it. He had been genuinely proud of me, hadn't he? I remembered my earlier thought, about how John's whip had felt. Loving. Eventually I fell asleep and that stopped me from arguing with myself.

In the morning, my whole back and shoulders were stiff, not to mention Technicolor. John recommended a hot shower, and I took one. When I came out, clothes were laid out for me: my heavy boots, new jeans, a black undershirt, some deerskin gloves, and a leather jacket so new I could smell it from across the room. As I put it all on, I found a pair of safety goggles in the breast pocket. I fished them out. While I was wondering if I should put them on, I heard a noise like a cap gun firing in the backyard. John was out cracking, calling me to join him.

That day he started me on a six-foot bullwhip, showing me how the stiffness in the handle gave me just a few more inches' margin of error, and how the reach was actually longer than six feet including the cracker. He could hit individual leaves off of the linden tree in the yard with it. He also showed me a scar on his chin that was years old, now just a thin white line that looked as if he might have done it shaving. He assured me he hadn't.

By the end of that day I could hardly move my arm, but I could hit the pillow on the picnic table more than half the time.

I kept wondering when we were going to go to the bar again; but, as I found out, John didn't go there very much except for a few club meetings. "Bars are for drinking in," he told me. "Which is fine if drinking is what you want to do." So most weekends I would go directly to his house, and care for his whips, and learn to repair them, and practice with the pillow, and on Saturday nights he would whip me and let me sleep in the workshop that smelled of mink oil and dye and leather. He served up the whip as a main course that he garnished with a touch of flogging, rabbit fur, mist from a spray bottle.

One night we went to another master's house for a new boy's initiation into the group. John gave me a quirt to carry, just two and a half feet long even including the fall, with a slightly stiff handle, very easy to aim and use, and very hard to do any accidental damage with.

The master's name was Henry, and he insisted that we have some cheese and crackers while we waited for the others to arrive. A few men I recognized from the bar were there, already seated on a leather couch that creaked against their leather pants and jackets as they rocked forward to pick up a cracker or turn toward a conversation. One of them I recognized: Gary's boy, but Gary did not seem to be anywhere around. He smiled when we sat down in chairs across from him.

"I don't think we were formally introduced," he said, holding out a hand to me. "Andrew."

"Roe." It was my last name, but I liked it better than my first. We shook.

"John." They shook, too, and I saw John's eyes roving in appraisal, though I could not discern whether or not there was approval in them.

Two more men came to the door, Henry let them in, and then we were ready to begin. Henry led us all down into the basement. His boy was already blindfolded and adrift on the soft music while he waited on a soft padded whipping bench—a kind of sawhorse with attachment points for his wrist and ankle cuffs. We stood in a loose semicircle while Henry explained the rules. I saw the boy's ears perk up as he heard his fate being discussed.

"You each must introduce yourselves to Michael by name before you begin." He indicated the bound bottom with a sweep of his hand. "You can each deliver a maximum of ten strokes to his back or ass. He really likes it on the ass," he said with a mischievous lilt and we laughed a little. There were ten men in the circle and me. I wasn't clear yet whether I was going to participate or not and looked at John. But John was looking at Andrew at the moment. "The final rule," Henry said as he stepped away from the bottom, "is that I get last licks."

The assembled crew held paddles, riding crops, whips, heavy floggers—the two men who had come in last were rifling through their heavy toy bag evaluating what they had brought and vetoing each other's choices. One of them eventually stepped into line clutching a hairbrush, the other a plain leather belt with a chrome buckle. I watched him swing it and slap it into his own palm several times. He was short, and somewhat heavyset, and I watched the belt end land squarely in that palm a few times before I realized that something about those hands was attracting my eye.

She was a woman. Or, at least, biologically speaking she was—or had been recently. I felt as if a new spin had just been put on reality. Should I say hello? I wondered, I mean, a special hello—a double-X-chromosome hello? And why did I feel even more reluctant to talk to her/him? I decided to wait and see if we were introduced, cringing at the thought that Henry, the perfect host, might catch us by the hors-d'oeuvres spread and say, "You two have a lot in common! I bet you have lots to talk about!" Just be yourself, Roe, I told myself. I'd been a dyke for years before I figured out that I always felt creepy in "womanspace"— like some kind of secret invader, a sleeper agent. I didn't dislike being female, I didn't dislike women, either, but I always felt like their expectations of me were all wrong, especially dykes in all-women circles. It just rubbed me the wrong way. Not to mention the fact that the only people I'd ever met who tried to oppress me for my sexuality, my leather sexuality that is, were lesbians supposedly fighting for their rights to love as they wished. Get a grip, Roe, I thought. This person isn't one of them, or she wouldn't be at this party. The guys accept her; get used to it.

I was so preoccupied with this train of thought that I

didn't even pay attention to the first men or the boy's yelps and cries. But then John was stepping forward and uncoiling a four-foot whip (anything longer wouldn't have fit in Henry's basement) and I snapped back to attention. I'd never seen him use it on someone who was lying down, where the striking surface was horizontal rather than vertical. I watched as he swung his arm over his head and the whip moved slowly out through the air until—crack—the tip exploded right on Michael's near cheek. What was different? It seemed that something was, but only watching for ten strokes, five on each cheek, I couldn't quite discern what he did differently. The wrist?

And then the man with the hairbrush got up to take his turn, joking before he began that it was high time Michael got what he deserved after working so long in a hair salon. Michael laughed a little, even as he braced himself for the blows. The hairbrush looked so innocuous to me, I was surprised how loud it was and how loud Michael was in response. How much could it hurt compared to the whip? Of course, the hairbrush was being laid on top of the whip welts, so perhaps it hurt a good deal more than it would have otherwise.

Then came the woman. I heard her introduce herself to Michael as Uncle Bulldog. "Bull for short," she said and most people laughed. She was good with the belt, using more of it with each stroke until on the last couple she was holding it right by the buckle and laying it on with her full arm in motion. Michael said, "Ow!"

The only people left who hadn't delivered any blows were Andrew, myself, and Henry. Henry gestured at Andrew who took half a step back, shaking his hands. "Come on, Andy" Henry said. "Just this once." But Andrew declined.

Henry turned to me. "Roe?"

John was somehow behind me then. He must have been there for a while. "Go on," he said, giving me a small nudge. "That's why you have the quirt."

"Yes sir," I said, and stepped up to Michael. "Michael, my name's Roe."

"Hi, Roe," he said, sounding a little drunk on endorphins. "I'd shake hands but—"

And a little more wordplay came out of my mouth, as if some divine playwright was prompting me. "Don't worry, little puppy, I'll teach you to shake." And I snapped the quirt between my gloved hands so it was arrow straight. His head twitched at the sound it made. I was aware of the men at the periphery snapping to attention at the sound, too. "Ready, puppy?"

He clenched his buttocks which I took as a definite yes, and brought the quirt down across them. He howled, very doglike, which gave me such glee I gave an undignified hop to his other side to see if the fall of the quirt had wrapped around his hip. It hadn't. I hit him again, this time from the other side, and he howled again. I patted him on the head and he gave out some high-pitched dog whimpers. "Good puppy." I gave him a few more, and then patted him again. He nuzzled my gloved hand, then bit the edge of the glove and growled playfully, shaking it back and forth. I whacked him across the shoulders then, and he let go, yelping. I used up the last few strokes all in a row on his butt and stood by him waiting for his howling and yelping to die down. I patted him and scratched behind his ears. "Good puppy?" He panted happily, tongue lolling, and wagged his 'tail' vigorously. I gave him a last pat on the head and stepped back.

Henry was looking at me with a huge smile on his face. "Well, that certainly gives me some ideas!" he whispered as he went past me. Time for last licks; there was no one else in line.

After all those different implements, his choice showed a lot of class and intimacy. He used only his hands on Michael's ass, and he went way beyond ten smacks, taking Michael up to gasping shaking and thrashing in his bondage, and back down until Michael was just grunting limply under each blow. Henry then lay his body along

Michael's red ass and Michael sighed and the rest of us broke into spontaneous applause.

Once Michael felt up to walking again, Henry and John helped him upstairs, and some of the other men tried out the bench. I wondered if now I was going to be introduced to Uncle Bulldog and wondered if I could say that without laughing and still couldn't decide if he or she was more appropriate. But as we neared the top of the stairs, John faltered, stumbling the last step into the living room.

"Well, Henry," he said, shaking hands with our host, "I think I'd better call it a night."

"Thanks, John," Michael said, looking sleepy as he wrapped a blanket around himself. He kissed John on the cheek. "Thanks, Roe," he said to me, and held out a hand to shake, a gesture that we both appreciated.

John asked me to drive, holding out the keys while he rubbed his eyes with the other hand. He sat with his eyes covered for a few miles and said nothing. When we were nearing his house he said, "No, no, your place," and then lapsed back into silence. I did as he asked. If he didn't want me sleeping in his workroom, I certainly wasn't going to insist. I thought about asking him if I should leave him off at his place and take a cab, but I turned the car toward the center of town and didn't question him.

As I was getting out of the car and he came around to take the driver's seat, he stopped in front of me and looked me in the eye. "You did a good job tonight."

"Thank you."

"Be on time next weekend. And don't forget to practice."

"I won't."

He gave me an affectionate cuff on the top of the head and smiled just a bit. Then he got into the car and drove away.

I did practice. The next couple of months I spent a lot of time in the basement of my apartment building, as the bullwhip was too big to swing in my apartment. As I got better, I discovered to my delight that I was able to pick off large cockroaches as they scuttled across the floor. I wondered what John was going to say when I told him I'd been able to blast roaches and wasn't sure whether he'd be more proud of my skill or disgusted at my choice of target. Somehow it felt slightly sacrilegious. You can be sure I cleaned the cracker very well after that. I was practicing so much it was going to be time to replace that one soon anyway. Maybe this weekend, I thought.

Saturday morning came, and I took my usual public-transit route out to his place. It was a crisp fall morning, probably one of the last warm days we'd see before the chill of November really set in. I expected he would be out on the lawn already, shredding brightly colored leaves off the trees. But when I went up the walk the house was quiet, and the leaves hadn't been raked. I rang the bell and waited.

When there was no answer after several minutes, I rang it again, listening to be sure it actually sounded inside the house. Then I tried the door. It was open.

I didn't stop to wonder if this was some game he was playing with me. I ran straight up to his bedroom and looked in.

He was asleep on the bed, face down as if he had fallen there and not moved all night. But I could see his chest rising and falling under the thin blanket. I backed away, trying to decide if I should wake him up.

I decided not to. I started a pot of coffee brewing in the kitchen and went down to the workroom to change that cracker. When that was done, I looked in on him again. He was still sleeping, but now he had rolled to his side and was snoring. I went into the backyard.

The maple tree was afire with crimson leaves and dropped spinning seeds into the air with each gust of late

October wind. I started stretching out my arm, my back, loosening up muscles grown tight with the close work of changing the cracker. This one had no fray in the end and sliced through the air like a shark fin through water, quick and leaving no trace. Soon I was cracking that thing, feeling like I could cut the thin sunlight with it. I wondered if I could pick the leaves off the trees now, the way I had seen him do so many months ago, wondered if I dared try it.

I discovered that not only could I hit the leaves I wanted, I could often use the same one several times as I sheared it away bit by bit, as long as the wind wasn't blowing. When a gust did come up, sending leaves and spinners into the air, I found I could keep my eye on one leaf and nail it as it floated toward the ground. Soon I was waiting for the next gust to try it again, keeping the whip moving in even circles over my head.

I heard the bang of a windowsill being thrust open. "Not bad," he said, his voice a little hoarse and just loud enough for me to hear. Then he ducked back in, and the window closed.

I drew the whip in and tried not to hurry in to the house.

I found him sitting in the kitchen with a cup of cold coffee and an old gray bathrobe wrapped around him. I had never noticed before just how thin he was. He stood up slowly when he saw me and moved into the living room, where he settled himself into a big chair. I sat on the couch.

"You've made excellent progress, Roe."

"Thank you." The sound of my name goosed me a little. He'd never used it before.

"I think you are ready to think about trying that on a person." His eyes flickered toward the whip still coiled in my hand.

Are you sure? I wanted to ask, but I knew better than to interrupt.

"I was planning to test you today. But you've shown you would have passed it."

But I want to be tested, I thought. This seemed like letting me off too easy, and I was uncomfortable with that.

"So you might want to keep your eyes open for someone to put at the other end. Don't try anything just yet, though," he added, wrinkling his chin. "There's still some things about people you could learn." He had to pause to cough, then covered his eyes with his hands in what was becoming a familiar gesture. "There's so much more you can learn—" And again he was coughing. This time it took him longer to stop. "Too much." And I saw a dark emotion in his eyes, something like sadness and regret.

After all this time my first thought still was that I had failed him in some way; but as I came to understand later, he was most sorry for the fact that a lifetime's wisdom and knowledge is not passed on in anything short of another lifetime. That afternoon we sat and talked in his living room for hours. I fetched us water and sandwiches when he asked, although he ate only a bite or two, and he told me things about his life.

For a while he was silent, his eyes steely on the back of his hand. "You've been the best student I've ever had," he said. "I wanted to tell you that while you were under the lash. But I'm too groggy to swing a whip right now, and I am not fool enough to put off saying some of these things." He was not looking at me as he spoke, but now focusing on the air in front of him. "When people die, they always leave things unfinished, but that doesn't stop us from trying like mad to finish them."

It seemed like my best chance to ask what I had always wanted to know. "Why did you decide to teach me?"

His lip moved a bit before he began to speak. "Gary was a failure—you know that. So, I needed someone I didn't want sex from, or who would want it from me. I wanted someone loyal, diligent, mature, and undistracted. I wanted, myself, to be undistracted. Also, knowing that

I"—he paused for a sip of water—"might leave things
unfinished, I did not want to leave behind a blubbering
dependent slave. And considering that I might have to
rush, I had to choose someone who"—he paused again, as
if testing the words like pebbles in his mouth, rolled back
and forth—"had an admirable sense of self-restraint and
wisdom to begin with. You seemed to fit the bill. Does
that answer your question?"

I nodded, feeling oddly exposed in the truth of his
answer, now that my buffer layer of doubts and delusions
was stripped away.

"There's a contest tonight at the bar. I think you ought
to go."

"What kind of contest?" I was picturing one of those
leatherman beauty pageants.

"A skill competition. They do it every year. I don't
think I'll be going. You go on. I think you'll do well."

That night, after dinner, he felt good enough to put the
floodlights on in the yard and show me a few tricks.
"These are going to take you some time to master, but in a
couple of months or years you probably can." I was particularly impressed with the way he could toss the whip out
and make it crack, then wrap tightly around a pole, or my
outstretched arm. But soon he was tired and went inside
to lie down. I helped him out of his boots.

"You know," he said as he lifted one bent leg into the
bed, "there were some things very handy about having a
slave."

"If you need a hand, I could come around more."

He started to say no, but I stopped him. "Not to be your
servant, John, to be your friend."

He held out an arm to me and I let him pull me into a
bony hug. "You go on, now," he said. "The contest starts
at nine o'clock. I suppose I could stand to have you come
around a couple times a week to help sort out the workroom."

"All right."

So it was settled that I started visiting on Tuesday and Thursday evenings, and spending Friday through Sunday with him. That night I went down to the bar and walked away with fifty bucks for being able to hit a cigarette out of Andrew's mouth without touching him. Afterward he and I talked a little. I told him about the cockroaches and answered his curiosity about crackers and different types of whips and things. I got his number and decided to invite him to have dinner with me and John some time very soon, and discuss the state of his skin.

GANGED

Carol A. Queen

*We join our protagonist Miranda, a bisexual cross-dressing
femme switch with a taste for leather daddies, not long after
her meeting with Jack Prosper—the only gay man she's ever
picked up who didn't throw her out when he figured out she
was really a woman—even after she changed into femme
drag.*

Jack and I had been running together for several weeks.
He knew which bar I hung out in; a couple of times he
had sauntered in and found me there. He didn't stay to
meet my friends; he'd haul me out and back to his place.
We usually only got as far as the alley before his dick was
out.

He had been to my apartment only once. It was more
comfortable at his place; he didn't have any housemates,
whereas I could never predict when mine, Ariel, would
come home, half the time dragging a john. So mostly our

relationship developed within the charmed and secret space of his rooms.

The one time he was at my place, though, I found him nosing around my room when I came in from the kitchen where I'd gone to get us something to drink. At the bedside table he picked up a book—a very battered copy of *Mr. Benson*. He grinned, and slung himself on my bed as though he habitually lounged there to read. He held the book in his left hand and of course it fell right open—to the part where Mr. Benson takes his new boy to meet all his friends.

"Stroke book, eh?" Jack was, I could tell, amused.

I just said, "You've read it, I suppose."

"Read it? Honey, I'm sure you were still in junior high. For a while there, this character was everybody's role model—or dream daddy." Jack was fingering the teeth marks where one time I had bitten the book during an especially big come.

I blushed. "Well, that historical moment may be over for you, but the dykes have gotten hold of him now."

"I'm not even sure I can picture that," Jack said. He stroked his moustache absently. "You know, I have a few buddies of my own. But God knows, Randy, you'd embarrass me. You look like *baby* chicken when you're in drag."

I'd all but forgotten about that when I got a call from Jack on my voicemail. "Okay, Randy, I want you over here tonight at eight o'clock. Punctually. Butched up as much as your fey little ass can get. You won't need your girl drag, but bring your makeup."

I showed up at five minutes till eight and sat on the steps till it was time to ring the bell. I had on my engineer's boots and Levi's, and in a jockstrap I was packing a small one. My breasts were bound down and I had a worn a black T-shirt under my leather jacket.

Jack answered the door. "Randy, for Christ's sake, you look like a dyke."

"Jack, there's hardly any difference in this town!"

"Oh, yes there is. Get in here, kid. You need a little more work."

Jack put me into a black leather-bar vest that just fit me. He didn't tell me where it came from, but it was much too small for him. He asked me for my makeup. With the dark pencils and mascara brushes he found in the kit he darkened my eyebrows a little and stroked the fuzz on my upper lip with color until I had a moustache. "This stuff better be waterproof," he muttered. Finally he stood back and looked at me. "Where in God's name do you get boots that tiny? If only you were a few inches shorter. I could just tell them you're a dwarf."

"Jack, you're a total bitch. Who's 'them'?"

"Never mind, son. You'll see soon enough. Now drop to your knees, boy."

Happy to be back on familiar ground, I knelt with my cheek resting on Jack's thigh, filling with whatever the emotion was that his daddyness brought up in me. An instant later I felt a chill coil of chain wrapping my throat and I started; Jack had never collared me before. At the click of the lock, my cunt spasmed as if he'd flicked his tongue over my clit.

"You're *my* boy tonight, got it? You're going to keep your mouth shut and your jockstrap on. I'm upping the ante on our little social experiment, boy, and you're in it till it's over. No safewords, no femme drag, nothing but what I tell you. I'm taking you to a little party. You *might* just be the guest of honor." His eyes narrowed—I could see he was dead serious. "But if you don't keep up your end, you'll never be invited back—and I probably won't either. Don't fuck it up."

I stared up at him, welling up with the weirdest mixture of pride and stricken fear. I had only about a shred of an idea where we were going, but it was pretty clear Jack wanted me to pass on whoever we met. I had no idea how I was going to pull that off. I don't think I'd ever passed on anyone for more than about a half an hour in my life.

He put a blindfold on me before he handed me a helmet and straddled his Harley. I was left to grope my way on, and I held him tightly as the bike's acceleration threatened to knock me off balance. I tried, blind as I was, to follow the turns he took, but I was lost within a couple of blocks, and all I knew was that soon we were speeding up even more, crossing a bridge—I guessed the Bay Bridge, for in the middle the sound changed as we whipped through a tunnel. I clasped him, feeling the dildo I wore nudge his buttcheeks while his big bike throbbed under us like a very butch sex toy.

He didn't take the blindfold off until we'd entered a house, which might have been in the Berkeley Hills, or Oakland, or who knows where. It was a large house, obviously, and Jack had let himself in without ringing. We left our helmets on a shelf in the foyer. We weren't the only ones here, I noted: some helmets were there already, a briefcase or two, and a profusion of coats. Most, but not all, were leather. Jack instructed me to hang my own jacket on a hook—he always said it was too fucking ratty to be seen in—and kept his on. He led me down a long hall.

The room we entered at the end made me gasp. It was clearly a dungeon, though it was not the low-end made-over-basement I was used to from the city. Somebody well-to-do lived here, and he had obviously put all the care into constructing his playroom that some other gay man might spend collecting art or learning to be a four-star chef just to impress his friends.

At one end it didn't look like a dungeon, but a really classy den, a library without the bookshelves. It had several wingback chairs arranged around a low table and facing a fireplace, where a small blaze flickered and cast shadows. A sideboard held a silver coffee service—a nice antique one, I noted—and several plates with sandwiches and other easy-to-eat food. A bottle of champagne lay icing in a silver bucket, but the cork hadn't been popped —no one seemed to be drinking. Three of the chairs were occupied by men in leathers, men who would look just as sexy and appropriate wearing very fine suits as they did in this gentleman's club atmosphere.

The other end of the room was, like the part that looked like a den, wood-paneled. It might have been in a restored Victorian, except the rest of the house looked newer. Setting off the dark wood was wrought iron fashioned into cages and suspension bars. A wooden St. Andrew's cross, leather-upholstered horses, and other dungeon implements furnished the place. I had been inside a few dungeons before, but they'd all looked tacked together compared to this.

As Jack stepped into the room, one of the seated men got up and extended his hand. Jack clasped it. "Sir Sebastian," he said, with affection as well as great respect in his voice, "how good to see you again. Thank you, as always, for your hospitality." Sir Sebastian, like Jack, had an impeccably trimmed beard, but it was mostly white, and he had white at his temples, too. I put him at fifty, perhaps. He was distinguished, calm, had seen everything. His gray eyes shone with warmth at the moment, but I could imagine them glittering menacingly; power was all over him. If Jack was my daddy, Sir Sebastian could be his.

"Jack, my darling man. You're welcome here at any time." He had looked me over once the moment we entered the room, and now he continued, "And what have you brought for us tonight? It's fortunate this isn't a public place, my dear. No wonder I haven't seen you in the bars with this lad."

Jack only smiled. "Sir Sebastian, his name is Randy. In my experience the name suits him very well, and he is not entirely new to all this. Tonight, of course, will be a test for him." As Jack said my name, I sank to my knees and bowed my head. He hadn't told me what the rules were, except "don't fuck up"; I figured at the minimum I ought to put on good dungeon manners and hope I didn't miss any cues.

Jack continued, "Randy is forbidden to speak tonight, and I do hope none of you gentlemen will take offense when he does not answer you. Also, his cock belongs to me, and neither he nor anyone else may touch it." I had a wild image of popping the little Realistic out of my jock-strap and handing it over to Jack for safekeeping. "He is bandaged from a cutting, a rather extensive one, so I'd like you to leave his shirt on. Beyond that, however, he will be at your disposal."

At that my heart jumped wildly. Somehow I'd expected Jack to test my passing skills in a dark leather bar, not in a playroom full of masters. Why couldn't he have just snuck me into Blow Buddies? More was at stake tonight than whether I could keep the dildo on straight. I'm not a heavy-sensation bottom, and while this place was beautiful, it could've hosted meetings of the Inquisition. I prayed I wouldn't break.

Jack ruffled my hair for the tiniest instant, then left me kneeling and turned to the other men. I stole glances up at them as best I could. One man was enormous and muscular, his head shaved, his tits pierced. I couldn't tell his age—somewhere around Jack's, perhaps. Jack called him Stone when he greeted him. He addressed another man, a lithe young blond with icy blue eyes, as Marc. Marc seemed a good deal younger than the others, maybe even younger than me. But he wore authority like so many men in the bars wore leathers with the squeak and smell of Mr. S. still on them.

Two more men came in. One was substantially older than the others, his hair quite white, and when he spoke I heard the tones of well-bred Oxford English. Unlike the other men, he did not wear leather; he was dressed in a suit that doubtless came from Savile Row. Jesus, Jack ran with some power daddies! "Ah, St. James, sir," Jack said when he saw the man, reaching to grasp his hand and, I noticed, inclining his head respectfully.

St. James's companion stepped forward to greet Jack, and at the sight of him I almost forgot to keep my head bowed. Tall, black, with sculptured muscles, he was one of the most beautiful men I'd ever seen. He had a similarly galvanizing effect on Jack. "Demetrius! How long have *you* been back?" he cried, and to my surprise threw his arms around the man. Demetrius laughed and hugged Jack. Even when the embrace was over they stood close, with their hands on each others' arms. I realized I was looking at someone who meant a lot to Jack—a lover, probably—and from my post on the floor, I studied him as carefully as I could. He wore a white silk shirt that draped over his muscular arms and tucked into black leather pants almost as tight as his own skin. His boots were fine leather, unadorned, and polished to a high black gloss. His voice was deep and smooth.

Sir Sebastian had stepped to the sideboard and rung a small bell. A very pretty young man entered the room. He was dressed like a formal waiter, except he didn't have on any pants—only a leather jockstrap. His sandy hair curled around his face—he'd do flawless drag, I thought, then reminded myself that I probably wouldn't be let loose to play Barbie with Sir Sebastian's staff. Maybe Jack could get the loan of him sometime and we could play lesbians. He couldn't possibly have his obvious need to cross-dress indulged hanging around with these leathermen.

The waiter-boy bore a tray with several champagne glasses. He set it on the sideboard and opened the champagne, not getting at all ostentatious with the cork, I noticed approvingly. It exited the bottle silently. He filled the glasses, presented one first to Sir Sebastian, then to St. James, and then to everyone else. He looked at me kneeling, poured a glass for me, and left it on the sideboard. "Anything further, Sir Sebastian?" he asked and left silently when the man shook his head.

"Well, this is quite a lot to celebrate," Sir Sebastian said smoothly. "Jack has brought his new boy to meet us. And Demetrius has come back from his wanderings. Shall we toast them?"

Jack picked up the glass from the sideboard and sat it on the floor in front of me, returning to lift his own glass. "New acquaintances and old friends," said St. James, and as the men all toasted I bent down and lapped from my glass like a rich old lady's overindulged puppy. So far this party was a piece of cake, but that couldn't last. I repeated Sir Sebastian's statement "Jack has brought *his* new boy"—in my head. Well, that was worth several hours of conversation about commitment and relationship status, eh? Jack's collar lay heavy on my neck, comforting as the touch of his palm on my nape. I stole another glance up through my lashes—he had his hand on Demetrius' strong, silk-clad shoulder, but I noted that he was reiterating to him and St. James the rules regarding my conduct. No speech—thank goodness; no removing my shirt, no touching my dick. Jack had done everything he could to set it up so I could pass.

Minutes later Jack was at my side, giving a lift to my collar. I scrambled to my feet and, at his gestured instruction, placed my hands behind my back at waist level. He beckoned and I followed—to the cage.

Inside the cage a set of leather cuffs dangled from chains. Jack adjusted them to my height, then held one open. Meekly I lay my wrist onto the fleece padding, and he buckled first that wrist in and then the other. The cage was tall enough for a full-sized man, but fairly narrow. Even with my wrists restrained, I could move right up to the bars on all four sides.

Jack took my chin, lifted my face up so I could gaze into his eyes. He was not quite expressionless—I thought I saw a hint of a smile. I figured that if we really pulled this off, Jack would feel like the cat that got the canary, and I—well, let's just say like the cat that ate the cream.

Then he released my chin and unbuckled my Levi's—
the jeans fell down around my ankles. Jack slapped my ass
once and grinned, then the cage door clanged shut; the
lock snapped into place. He crossed the room and
rejoined his friends.

"The devil never does get enough cock," Jack was
saying. "He's a little pig, really. I think I've satiated the
little bastard, and ten minutes later, he's pulling on my
balls again. He's tiresome! I finally decided the only thing
to do was bring him here." The assembled daddies
murmured sympathetically.

"I'm sure we can help," Demetrius said.

"Oh, I know *you* can," Jack rejoined. "A cock like yours
is really the only possible answer."

I listened to Jack with amazement. He was going to get
me ganged! I rubbed my dick against the cage bars, felt
my cunt simmer.

Sure enough, he returned accompanied by Marc. Each
was unzipping his leather pants.

"Now, boy, I know I don't need to tell you to be good to
my friends. You're here for our use. Take this."

Jack thrust his cock near enough to the cage bars that I
could just get to the pisshole with my tongue. I looked at
him imploringly, the look that would have been accompanied by a "Please, Daddy!" if I'd been able to speak. Jack
laughed and stepped closer, grasped the bars so he could
press his pelvis right up against the cage, and his big cock
came in for me to work on. I couldn't get hold of it with
my hands—the restraints gave me some movement, but
not enough—and so the only part of me that touched
him was my mouth. I tongued him all over, the taste of
him getting my saliva running, till his cock was wet and I
could slurp him in. Marc stood just to one side of Jack,
stroking his own cock—it had a downward curve, it would
slide right down my throat.

"Look at this fucking cocksucker, Jack—where'd you
find him? Look at this fucking kid." I knew how Jack liked

it by now—he made a low little noise each time his cock-head slipped past my throat muscles, and when he pulled it out I laved my tongue all around the corona. Once in a while I let it slip out of my mouth so I could scramble for his balls—this part was harder with no hands, but Jack stayed close, his cock bobbing up to slap his belly with a soft *thwack* whenever its head escaped my lips. I could get only one of his nuts in my mouth at a time, here without the use of my hands—when my hands were free, I knew, if I opened really wide, I could just get both of them in, and then I could suckle them. Now, though, I returned to his cock after a little attention to his balls, sucked him rhythmically, my tongue alert as it stroked along his shaft for the first pulsing signs of his load coming.

He didn't give it to me this time, though—gasping and swearing, he pulled out before I could finish him. Marc was in his place almost before I knew there was no cock in my mouth. His dick was a little longer than Jack's, maybe not quite as thick, but substantial, and with that down-turn. "Little sucker," Marc growled, "you can have my load, punk, if you can work it out of me." I went for him.

Demetrius and Stone stood a few feet back now, watching, too. As I breathed deeply, opened my throat, and started wiggling Marc's long curved one down as far as I could get it, Demetrius moved behind Jack and grasped his still-high cock in his big hand. Jack moaned, thrust into the fist like it was my cunt, and started working it. When Marc's cock was all the way down my throat, I started a fast gulping kind of suck. It flirted with my gag reflex, but I didn't care—that cock fit so perfectly in my throat, I didn't want to pull off it at all.

I was just about to drool from the saliva I wasn't bothering to stop and swallow when Marc started thrusting faster. This added movement pulled the long cock up and out, slid it back down and in, fast, hard, repeatedly, as the blond man built up quickly toward his come. Jack was right on the edge of it too, but he wasn't missing a thing.

"C'mon," he growled, "use that pig! Fill him up! Spray it right down his throat, man. That's what he's for!"

Marc bucked, knuckles white on the bars of my cage, and at the next thrust I felt the first hot pulse of his jizz hit the back of my throat. Jack's dirty talk had the same effect on me it always did—added to the sensation of come spurting into me, filling my mouth up with bitter, creamy spunk, waves of come took *me* over, too. I could just reach the bars and I held on so I could keep on Marc's cock even as my come threatened to tumble me off my feet.

Stone had inched closer to the cage. Now the huge man snapped the codpiece off his chaps as he stepped up to take the place Marc vacated. Not only his head was smooth—Stone's cock and balls were shaved too, and a sizable Prince Albert matched the rings that stretched out his nipples.

"Lick it up, little boy. Get it hard." Sucking in Stone's soft cock with the metal ring felt wild, and I suckled on it the way I liked to suckle Jack's balls. As it started to fill up, he took it out of my mouth and, holding it, nuzzled it around my face, sometimes past my lips, sometimes under my chin. My whole face got slick from the sliding cock, and I hoped the fucking makeup on my upper lip was *more* than waterproof—I didn't think they behaved anything like this in the Max Factor test labs.

"Jack, I'm gonna fuck your kid, okay?" Stone slapped his almost-fully-engorged cock against my cheek. "Sure, just get a rubber," said Jack.

Not an instant later the beautiful waiter-boy was at Stone's side, bearing a tray. Now where the fuck had he come from? I remembered that I'd heard Sir Sebastian's bell ringing a few minutes before. The boy must have come in then.

I could see his long pretty-boy meat outlined hard in his leather jock. I wondered if the help got to get laid around here, or what.

Stone picked a rubber off the tray, pulled it out of its wrapper, and worked it over his dick. The ring through his cockhead made the rubber fit a little funny, but I figured it'd probably work. Then he took a second one and repeated the process. While he suited up, Demetrius reached over Jack's shoulder and took a condom, too.

I heard the sound of a zipper. Whose was that? Stone and Jack already had their cocks out. Then I heard Demetrius say, "Peaches, my pants, please," and the waiter knelt in front of him to help work the leather pants over his shiny boots. Peaches folded the pants carefully while Demetrius shucked the white silk shirt, then took them away. Over at the other end of the room, disguised by the woodwork, I saw a door swing open, and Demetrius' clothes went inside.

Stone, clad in rubber now, moved to the back of the cage. "Get your ass up here," he rasped. He reached through the bars to position me—there was just enough room for me to press my ass against the back bars and still be able to reach a cock fed to me at the front. Peaches reappeared silently, lube on his tray. Stone slathered up his cock, worked a finger into my ass. I shook with wanting this pierced-dicked giant to shove it in.

He didn't shove it, he worked it, and it felt so fucking good I could have screamed. I just grunted, low as I could pitch, and wiggled up onto him. "Jack, you're right, he's a fucking little pig," said Stone, "and I'm gonna fuck him just like one—ready, you little fuck? ready to get it jammed up your fucking pig butt?"

He had only arched into two or three hard thrusts when I felt my mouth opening again for cock—Jack's. I could have died of happiness. I sucked him down, *You want pig, Daddy, I'll show you what a pig you have*—and it was a minute before I noticed that Jack had shed his pants, too. Peaches stood near, still holding the tray that held the lube.

Then Demetrius, rubber on, started working his cock

into Jack's asshole. Jack responded with a long groan, and I remembered that he'd been right up under an orgasm ever since I sucked him the first time. I backed off a little to give him time to get used to all the stimulation.

Pretty soon all four of us turned into a fucking machine, Stone and Demetrius pumping into Jack's and my butts simultaneously, me swallowing Jack's cock each time they did. We were all growling and all three of them were muttering, "Yeah. *Fuck! Fuck* your fuckin' ass, *fuck!*"

Thank God Jack's cock was too far down my throat when he started shooting to allow me any air to scream with—I was feeling like squealing, like the pig that I was—but his spasming cock kept me quiet. The minute he slid out of my mouth, all comed out, he bent forward and sucked his jism out of my mouth. The kiss shut me up again when I was about to howl. The minute his mouth left me, there was Demetrius' cock, out of Jack's ass, rubber shed, at my lips.

His dick must have been as big around as my wrist—at least. It had the most prominent head on it I'd ever seen—though of course I couldn't *see* it right that minute. As it popped past the muscle at the top of my throat, it burned, and I tried to shake my head, afraid I'd choke, afraid I couldn't. Stone, behind me and still riding me hard, saw. "*Take* that cock!" he bellowed, giving my ass a stinging slap. "Take it, you fucking little punk!" I took it, seeing stars, stretching wider than I ever thought I could, oh fuck, I thought, I'm playing with the big boys *now*.

Jack was back in commission. He was kneeling next to the cage, his face right next to mine, watching me growl and stretch to accommodate the thick meat. "Good boy," Jack murmured, "you're making me so proud, *little* man. Sucking that big hunk of cock. You can suck him, boy, you can get fucked by him, I know you want that, baby, don't you? can't get enough meat, hot little man."

That was it, wasn't it? I was where I'd always wanted to be, and I turned into a little demon, throwing my ass back on Stone's hard-pounding cock, suddenly finding room in my throat I didn't know I had. My hands clutched the bars for support and I worked both men for all I was worth.

"*Chew on it!*" Jack was still right at my ear. "Chew that dick, boy. Don't worry about biting him, he likes it." I growled like a junkyard dog around Demetrius' substantial cock, chewing it like Jack told me to. Freed from cocksucking's one overriding rule—*don't bite!*—I lost myself completely in the sensation of being filled up as full as I'd ever been. Thank God all the head I'd given already had filled my throat with that thick cocksucking slime—it lubricated even Demetrius' thickness. Stone pounded away behind me, and I had a feeling I knew how he'd earned his name.

But at last even Stone, who had been fucking my ass rhythmically for what seemed like an hour, started fucking even harder and faster. "Take it, you pig!" he grunted, really close to shooting, I could tell by his voice, and I felt Demetrius speed up, too, both of them about to hose me, mouth and asshole, full of hot cream. "Comin'!" Demetrius cried. "Comin' right now!" And naturally I was shooting up the ramp right along with them—I'd be a fine pig if I couldn't come right along with my tops, *right, Daddy?* I opened my eyes to look at Jack, wanting to know he was seeing this, pumped full of his friends' jizz. I couldn't suck any more—my mouth was open as far as the muscles would stretch it, in a silent orgasmic scream—but that was okay, because the big black man in front of me was fucking my face now with pounding thrusts.

I remember the first half of the orgasm, but not the second.

I blacked out. I lost it, don't know exactly how it happened but it must have had something to do with my engorgable throat-flesh forming a seal with Demetrius' expanding, coming cock. I couldn't get enough air, I guess.

When I came to I had no idea where I was.

I felt damp clothes, chill air, and motion, saw nothing but darkness, smelled the reek of not-quite-fresh piss. Where the fuck was I? A vehicle—a *trunk?* I felt around me in the utter black and yes, I was lying in a capacious car trunk, not bound, my leather jacket thrown over me, some kind of scratchy car blanket under my head, what felt like trash bags underneath my body. If I hadn't had such an extraordinary night, I'd have been terrified—but I was pretty sure this was part of Jack's buddies' idea of a good time.

The vehicle slowed, turned, turned again, and after a short distance stopped. I heard almost immediately the familiar sound of Jack's bike. Next, a car door slamming, then another. Two people? Then the trunk lid lifted.

It took a second for my eyes to adjust even to the dim alley light. We were outside Jack's place, back in the city. Jack and Demetrius stood there with a man I didn't know. He had on a driver's uniform, so I guessed that Sir Stephen had lent the use of his car to get me out of there. What would a distinguished man like him do with a pissy piece of fucked-out chicken? After all. But had I pissed myself? It wouldn't have surprised me.

Demetrius reached into the trunk and lifted me as if I were an unwieldy but not-very-heavy teddy bear. Jack had his keys out. The driver stood by silently. Sir Stephen's help weren't a very talkative lot, were they? But at last, as Jack stepped up to the door, the driver said, "Shall I wait, Sir?"

"Yes, do," said Demetrius, and he had me up the stairs and into the foyer.

"Here, let's clean the pig up," said Jack, gesturing Demetrius through his room and into his bath. By the time we got there, he had the water running in the shower. Demetrius supported me while Jack stripped off my jacket, the bar vest, which I noted with chagrin was pissy, too, and my boots and pants. He was about to thrust me under the hot spray with my shirt and jockstrap still on when Demetrius spoke up. "Go ahead, strip the girl down."

Jack and I both looked at him, eyes wide. I was stricken. I had been so exultant about passing! What gave me away?

Demetrius started to laugh, a low swell of a laugh that turned into a roar when he looked at me and saw my face. "Randy, girl, you did good. I don't know what the fuck that was all about, but you pulled it off. No one else noticed a thing. I'm the one who carried you into the car, darling, and I took the liberty of feeling you up. Yes, I know your Daddy made a rule, but I've broken plenty of his rules before." At this Jack started laughing, too. "Well, it's not like my meat hadn't just been all the way down your little throat. I felt further familiarities wouldn't be inappropriate. And your sweet little dick just seemed to come off in my hand. I tucked it back in, of course."

Jack was howling.

"I trust you have a bigger one than that, since you appear to be keeping Jack interested. I liked ganging Jack with you very much, dear, and I'd be glad to do that again anytime you two want to give me a call. Jack, I'm back at my former number. *Do* phone me when you get time. I see we have more catching up to do than I thought. Randy—it's been a pleasure." With that, he extended his hand gravely, and as I took it, I started laughing, too.

Jack still laughed as Demetrius engulfed him in a bear hug—God, he was larger than Jack by almost as much as Jack outsized me—and I went ahead and shed the damp T-shirt and jockstrap and unwound the binding. As I stepped into the shower, Demetrius took a look at me and said, "Sure enough, she's a girl, all right. Jack, you sick fuck! If St. James ever gets wind of this, he'll have his traditionalist boys come and turn your dick inside out. You and Little Bit here can go down to City Hall and register as domestic partners, and then you can spend your afternoons drinking coffee at the Whiptail Lizard Womyn's Lounge. You fucking wild man!"

Jack kissed Demetrius good night as I scrubbed off the piss. He ducked his head in the shower and kissed me, too. And then he was gone.

Still grinning, Jack dried me off, capturing me for a minute in the big white fluffy towel. "Want some ice cream?" he asked. "Good boys get ice cream."

"God, yes, I'm starving, Jack. I passed out before Peaches could come by with the sandwich tray."

Jack installed me in the flannel-sheeted bed, disappeared down the hall, and came back with two bowls. Before he started on his, he stripped down, took a fast shower, and then joined me in bed. "Kid, you're more fun than a barrel of novices. You were terrific. I'm very proud."

I glowed as much from this as from the still-very-memorable fuck I still hadn't come all the way down from. The cold ice cream felt so intense on my throat that I almost squeaked. It was pretty sore from all that action. "Jack, I got piss on your bar vest. I'm so sorry. I don't know how it happened."

"No, *I* got piss on your bar vest. Leathers have to be broken in, child. We all doused you after you went out."

"*What?*"

"Sometimes it wakes people up," Jack said innocently. "By the way, don't worry about going out. I think the first time I got down on that man's cock I passed out, too. I was younger then, of course."

Then he told me what happened after I blacked out. I'd have fallen over, but the men's cocks kept me suspended— Jack saw it as soon as it happened, though he let the guys finish coming. As first Stone and then Demetrius pulled their softening meat out of me, Jack reached into the cage to hold me up. Before he could even call for him, Peaches was there with the key, unlocking the cage door so Jack could undo my restraints.

"Jack, who were all those guys? Why didn't Sir Sebastian and St. James play? Didn't they like me?"

♦

"Don't worry, honey. St. James loves this group of men, but he almost never plays. He's an old-timer. A traditionalist. He doesn't approve of the free-form way so many of us play now. I think he has a group of men he plays with back in London. He wouldn't be caught dead playing in a room with people who switch. Talk to him if you ever get a chance. Not many like him anymore. Sir Sebastian would have joined us if St. James hadn't been there, but he's too flawless a host to let a guest sit unentertained. As to who they are, I'll tell you the whole story of how I fell in with them, but how about over breakfast?"

Jack snuggled me under his arm, the scent of which almost got me going again—but I was just too exhausted. I started to nod off to the sound of his murmurings, mostly of the "good little cocksucking pig" variety.

Right before I slipped under, I whispered, "Thank you, Daddy"—and then, "Daddy, can we borrow Peaches?"

SUCCESSION OF HONOR
Laura Antoniou

It had been a long time since I'd seen the old man. I figured, hell, it had to be at least ten years since I moved west, maybe more. Although we still kept in touch now and again, my travels hadn't taken me back home for ages. I was real busy, yessir. What with a house, my work, my community service, my own kids, and a former slave turned spousal equivalent, I had every spare moment parceled out.

But I can't complain. Shit, I should boast. In the time I had lived out here, I had amassed everything I ever wanted in life. Sure, I wasn't the young, arrogant piss-and-vinegar youth who used to look back at me in the mirror. And the scars have all but faded from everywhere on my body, except for that one special place. But, with all due kicking and screaming, I had become a mature human being. I try to set an example to those who serve me; I try to be fair and honest, to see them through the tough spots and guide them to their own maturity with a firm, loving hand.

After all, I've been taught by the best.

Even though my own western family had never met him, I taught them to revere my old man, to think of him as highly as I do. And when I took my first sash, under those bright lights, my body glistening with oil and sweat, I thanked him before the audience, wishing that he was there to see his boy triumph. I knew that he would have come, even though he hated the damn things, just to see me compete. He always said that I didn't need any studded cowskins to prove to him that I was okay. But I wanted them for me; external validation that other people could recognize.

Well, I kept winning. And each stop on my way to the top meant that my old man got another public thank you from me. It was the least—the very least that I could do....

I remember the first time I played with the old man. We were out at his place, after the longest courtship I had ever planned and executed with a top. I couldn't tell you what attracted me to him. It sure as hell wasn't his leather; the man didn't even have a vest. And it wasn't that someone pointed him out to me at some contest or bar, either; in fact, we met at a restaurant. But something about him, his classical manners, the little sparkle in his hard eyes, the way he looked at you when he was listening to what you were saying, all these cues told me that he was worth pursuing. I found out early that he was into SM. Not leather, he reminded me. SM. Sadomasochism. He liked to deal out pain, to train eager bottoms. And he wanted his bottoms to like that.

I liked it a lot. And let me tell you, that night, when he first stood back and had me strip down for him, when he pulled his worn belt through the loops of his jeans and pushed me easily over the edge of a table, I flashed on every other scene I'd ever done with a top. Every basement dungeon decorated in early Naugahyde, every spare bedroom with extra-strong bolts sunk into the studs, every rigged bed frame and every stroke of a paddle, belt, whip or rod. I remembered them all, in seconds of intensity that made my eyeballs hurt, and then watched as they burst into flames and crisped into ashes. All those memories were wiped away by the simple, powerful beating this old man gave me, and by the way he held me afterward and told me that I would have to take it much better than that if I wanted to be his boy.

Naturally, I thought he meant I had to be stronger, so the next time, I gritted my teeth, and grunted when I couldn't take it anymore. Then, suddenly, he stopped and pulled up right behind me. He laid the whip he was using across my lower back and asked me how I felt about what was happening. No other top had asked a question like that of me while they were beating me.

"I feel...good, sir," I answered. And there was a silence so heavy I swore I could hear myself sweat. Suddenly I realized that I should have probably said something like "Well beaten," or maybe "Eager to please you," or something like that. In an instant, I thought of about a hundred things I could have said that might have sounded better than "I feel good." What was I, James Brown? I cringed and waited for him to tell me to get dressed and get the fuck out.

Instead, he said, "Then why aren't I hearing how good it feels?"

I couldn't believe my ears. "What?" I even forgot the sir!

"I expect, when I put so much effort into using your body the way you like it, that you should express your happiness and gratitude on a regular basis," he continued. "Otherwise, I might think that you are not enjoying this, and therefore I'll switch to something else, and you will have missed out on a good thing."

"But...aren't you punishing me, sir?" I asked, my manners coming back even though the fog that was settling through my brain.

"What the hell could I be punishing you for?" He demanded. "I barely know you!"

That's when I learned that my old man never makes up stupid excuses to punish his bottoms. He likes to make 'em hurt, and so he does it. Over the years, through the various times that I actually was punished, he never once hit me with something I liked. Nossir, he would haul out the meanest, nastiest, most unpleasant things when I was rude, or sloppy, or when I forgot stuff. Or, he would simply send me away.

And you know that hurt the most.

On the plane east, I went through my itinerary, making sure I had enough time to see him for a nice long visit. I had three speaking engagements and about two other appearances, not counting the night of the contest. I also had a big surprise for him. I used the phone on the plane to call the almost-frantically eager young man who was picking me up at the airport. Sometimes it's nice to be a celebrity.

Of course, when I met my old man, I wasn't what you'd call a celebrity. Oh, I had done my time in the local clubs, wore some MC colors for a while. I was known enough in what passed for a scene, had a couple of brief relationships, and had done my share of workshops and committee meetings. But not more then most other folks. I admit that I was disappointed that the man I was chasing didn't seem interested in the leather scene; but I was arrogant enough to figure that when he took up with me, he'd become a part of it, come out to the clubs and bars, go to the shows and conferences. I guess he did, a little. It took me a couple of years to realize that almost every time he did come out, it was to please me. He would stand out in his shirt and tie and shoes, alone in enough black leather to make an entire herd of Angus. But he would come out for my sake.

I guess he was about one of the most generous tops you could get, really. I mean, he was tough with me, demanding in certain things and unwavering in his rules. But he was also patient and always interested in what I was doing. He never let me stay comfortable in one place, always pushing me to do better, to rise higher, to excel. "Your success honors me, he told me one night."

Well, it was time for me to do him some honor. By the time the plane landed and the neatly dressed young leatherman heaved my bags into his car and whisked me into the city, I was feeling pretty good about what I had in mind for my old man.

I remember the feel of his collar, the smooth leather that had no lock on it. "It needs none," he said. By that time, I knew what he meant. I swore, with all my strength, to come and to go, to do and leave undone, to speak and be silent according to his will and whim. He swore to protect me, to teach me, to improve me.

It took him about three years before he announced me improved.

They passed like dances after midnight.

I remember that I begged him to take me on again, swearing that there was still plenty of room for improvement. But at the same time, deep inside, I also knew that I was already starting to cruise the bottoms I socialized with, and that I hungered for my regular haunts and activities which my old man had never really denied me, but had encouraged me away from. I wanted to feel the power of a vest with colors on it, wear run pins and go to conferences and wild weekends. I wanted to show off my new manners and teach them to others. It took almost another year to pull myself away from my old man, and even then, I cried into his shoulder one night that I would always, always be his boy.

And he nodded. "Yes, you will," he said. "I don't see how I could hardly forget you, either."

It was only a few months later that I got the job offer out west.

I was smoothing out my chaps on the hotel bed when there came a knock on my door. I figured it was one of the organizers, so I opened it a crack and turned my back to continue what I was doing.

"Shouldn't do that," his familiar voice cracked. "Y'never known what kind of riffraff is skulking around these places."

My heart stopped, and the enthusiastic greeting I had planned for my old man got caught in my throat. Barely realizing what I was doing, I turned and sank down to my knees, and damn if I didn't blush the way I used to when I was with him so many years ago!

He took the gesture as honestly as I gave it, and then came over and brought me up into one of his great old bear hugs. It was just like him not to make a fuss over it, just to accept it and go on. And then we commenced to filling each other in on our lives. Or, rather, I filled him in. He seemed duly impressed by the photos of my kids and mate and grunted good-naturedly at my silver-encrusted sash. I asked him if he wanted to come to the contest, and he declined, which I expected. That was all right. The real surprise would come at the bar, afterward. We were able to have about two hours to ourselves before the calls started coming in, and I had to start getting ready for my appearances. My old man left, promising to come by the bar on contest night to see what I had for him.

I shouldn't have been surprised at the deep reaction seeing him gave me. And my visit with him made me realize that it had been longer than ten years. He seemed a lot older now, still the same old man but a little out of shape, a little slower. I loved him with a fierce intensity, and I knew that what I would do at the bar later on that weekend would be a peak moment for me. And for him.

All during the weekend, as I sat on panels and addressed groups, I kept flashing back to scenes from a previous life. Standing rigid against a wall, suffering in silence for an act of forgetfulness. Kneeling contentedly at his feet, keeping my need for further abasement in check because he wanted it that way, and feeling the pride of being able to control my emotions, allowing him to see them without making them into demands for his attention. Little tasks done at his command, each one thrilling because I was allowed to be useful.

I was so proud to have served him. He truly made me what I am today.

The contest was over before I hardly knew it. I made my speech to roaring applause and cheers, thanking my old man, and promising that he would be making an appearance after the show was over, over at the bar. I could see that many people were visibly touched by my declaration of love for him, and it made my heart seem close to exploding. This was my community, and my old man. At last, I was going to bring them together. And, the surprise that I had kept so well, was that my kids were gonna join me up on stage, both of them, and they were about to meet the man who made their own old man. They'd be on their knees, of course, and me, I'd uncover and give my old man a bow.

It was gonna be enough to make you cry.

We poured into taxis and private cars and shuttle buses, and marched into the bar in a raging sea of leather and chrome. We literally had to push our way through, and I asked at the bar if my old man had come by. None of the bartenders had been approached by any man answering his description. I should have seen it, right then; my old man was never late. But I was riding the wave of my own pleasure that night, my own fucking fantasy that everything would go as I planned. As time began to pass, I started to make rounds through the crowds, scanning, watching, trying to figure out where my old man could be.

When it came time for the short speeches, I began to panic. This was the time I wanted to gather my family on stage, and show how the lessons I learned are being passed down to my own, how our traditions continue through the years. Soon they had to start, and I waved the new winner onto the small stage and dived out the front door. But there was no sign of my old man on the street. I grabbed one of the bouncers and described him, shouting over the noise from inside the bar. The man seemed to understand what I was saying. But his own answer was partially drowned out, not by the ambient noise, but from a strange, heated roar that rose in my ears, accompanying the pounding of my heart.

"...shoes!" He was shouting back at me. Then "Not even [something] jacket!"

I stared at him, comprehension flooding me with chill throughout my leather-clad body. Figuring that I didn't understand, he pointed to the door, where the weathered sign hung. "Dress code!" he bellowed.

I almost walked away; I didn't know what to do. But no, my kids were still inside. I walked back in and, at the mike, the new sash queen grinned and waved me over. I was waved over to the stage with an enthusiastic move that made the sash glitter under the overhead spotlights. "And here's the one we all owe so much to," I heard. I looked back at the stage as if there were a lunatic shouting at me. My kids came up to me at once. They knew something was wrong. The older one, a man of the sash himself, took my arm—that's how bad I must have looked. I stumbled once as I made my way to the raised platform, and I looked out into the mass of my siblings in skin. I tried to say something, but the words couldn't come. I loved them, loved my place in this world.

My beautiful heavy sash fell with such a thud that it hit the mike and caused a single screech of feedback. I shrugged the vest off, heavy with pins and ribbons and bars, and it actually made clinking sounds as it fell. My cap sailed over inky puddles of similar covers, and the snaps on my chaps exploded open even as I made my way off the stage. And I turned away, stripping them from my legs, and started making my path back to the door as a new roar of confusion rose.

And my kids? Well, they made me proud. The little one

came and pushed the way ahead of me, making it easier for me to leave. And elder brother took his sash off, too, and left it in the damn bar, probably seeing his dream of wearing the bigger, fancier one go up in smoke. But they trusted me to act on what I did without questioning.

After all, I had trained them.

And I had been trained by the best.

I only hoped my old man would have the decency to send 'em out for ice cream while we had our little talk.

Dedicated, with respect, to those unrighteously turned away at the door.

CONTRIBUTORS

SASHA ALYSON's association with John Preston began with the publication of *Franny, the Queen of Provincetown*, by Alyson Publications in 1983. That same year, Alyson founded *Bay Windows*, a Boston-based gay newspaper to which Preston was a frequent contributor. In all, Alyson published thirteen of Preston's books, including *The Mission of Alex Kane* series and *I Once Had a Master* and its sequels. Sasha Alyson lives in Boston.

LAURA ANTONIOU is the editor of *Leatherwomen I* and *II*, *Some Women*, and other anthologies. Under the name Sara Adamson, she is the author of the *Marketplace* series of erotic novels.

THE REV. DR. E. M. BARRETT is an Episcopal priest and a historian specializing in medieval monastic history. She lives and works in New York City.

AGNES BARR BUSHELL is the author of the Wilson and Wilder mysteries, *Shadowdance* and *Death by Crystal,* and the political thrillers *Local Deities* and *Days of the Dead.* She has taught writing and literature in Portland, Maine, and at the San Francisco Art Institute and Golden Gate University. She is married and has two children.

PATRICK CARR is an escapee from New Jersey, and a graduate of Rutgers University. He was first published in John Preston's *Flesh and the Word 2,* and his work is scheduled to appear in the forthcoming *Flesh and the Word 3.* He lives in Brooklyn, in the House That David Built.

SAMUEL R. DELANY is a writer and professor of Comparative Literature at the University of Massachusetts at Amherst. He is the author of *The Mad Man, Silent Interviews,* and the Nevèrÿon series.

MICHAEL DENNENY, one of the founders of *Christopher Street* Magazine, is a senior editor at Crown and was general editor of St. Martin's Press's Stonewall Inn Editions. He is the author of *Lovers: The Story of Two Men* and *Decent Passions: Real Stories About Love.*

ANDREW HOLLERAN is the author of the novels *Dancer From the Dance* and *Nights in Aruba,* and a book of essays, *Ground Zero.*

OWEN KEEHNEN is a nationally syndicated interviewer and columnist for both *Forum* and *Man Style* magazine. His fiction has appeared in numerous periodicals, such as *Hyphen, modern words, Christopher Street,* the *Evergreen Chronicals,* and *Holy Titclamps.* He resides in Chicago.

MICHAEL LASSELL is the author of *Poems for Lost and Unlost Boys* (Amelia, 1985), *Decade Dance* (Alyson, 1990), and *The Hard Way* (Masquerade Books, 1995). His writing has appeared in several John Preston anthologies, including *Hometowns, Flesh and the Word,* and *Friends and Lovers.*

WILL LEBER's sex writing has appeared in *Flesh and the Word 2,* edited by John Preston. He is a native Californian and graduate of Stanford University. He worked for many years in the garment industry in New York, and now lives in San Francisco. He is currently at work on a collection of short stories set in San Francisco, and a novel about fashion models.

STAN LEVENTHAL, a former hustler and musician, is the author of several novels and short-story collections, including *Mountain Climbing in Sheridan Square, Candy Holidays* and *Skydiving on Christopher Street.* In addition, he is the editor-in-chief of MMG periodicals, and founder of the Pat Parker/Vito Russo Library at the Lesbian and Gay Community Services Center in New York City. He is the current editor of *Mandate,* a position which was first held by John Preston.

MICHAEL LOWENTHAL's first appearance in a book was thanks to John Preston, who selected his story "Better Safe" for *Flesh and the Word 2.* Lowenthal's writing also appears in the anthologies *Men on Men 5, Sister and Brother, Best American Erotica 1994* and *Wrestling With the Angel,* as well as in numerous periodicals. He edited a collection of gay men's pornography entitled *The Best of the Badboys* (Richard Kasak Books) and after Preston's death completed Preston's two final anthologies: *Friends and Lovers: Gay Men Write About the Families They Create,* and *Flesh and the Word 3.* He has also edited a collection of Preston's essays, *Winter's Light: Reflections of a Yankee Queer.*

WILLIAM J. MANN is publisher of *Metroline,* the queer newsmagazine for Connecticut and Massachusetts. He also writes for the *Boston Phoenix, Washington Blade, Philadelphia*

Gay News, Southern Voice, Windy City Times, and other gay publications. In addition, his work has appeared in the *Advocate, Gay Community News,* the Alyson anthology *Shadows of Love,* and *Sister and Brother,* the collection coedited by Joan Nestle and John Preston. He lives in Northampton and is working on a novel.

VICTORIA McCARTY is a New York City–based writer whose work has appeared in *Harper's Magazine, Penthouse,* and the *Flesh and the Word* series.

JESSE MONTEAGUDO is a regular contributor to a variety of lesbian/gay and mainstream publications. His work has appeared in several fiction and nonfiction anthologies, including *Hometowns.*

JOAN NESTLE coedited *Sister and Brother: Lesbians and Gay Men Write About Their Lives Together* with John Preston.

SCOTT O'HARA is editor of *Steam,* a quarterly review of sex and adventure for literate queers. He has also graced twenty-six porn flicks.

MARTIN PALMER lives in Anchorage, Alaska, where he practices medicine and teaches at the University of Alaska at Anchorage. His writing had appeared in *Men on Men 3, A Member of the Family, Hometowns,* and in the anthology jointly edited by John Preston and Joan Nestle, *Sister and Brother.* He misses John Preston profoundly.

FELICE PICANO is the author of six novels, a collection of poetry and of short stories, screenplays, plays, and the memoirs Ambi*dextrous* and *Men Who Loved Me.* He's the cofounder and publisher of SeaHorse Press and Gay Presses of New York, a longtime member of the Publishing Triangle, and coauthor with Charles Silverstein of *The New Joy of Gay Sex.* In 1994–1995, his work will appear in six anthologies, a gay novel will be published by Viking, and a gay SF novel will be published by Richard Kasak Books.

CAROL A. QUEEN is a San Francisco writer, activist, and sex educator. Her work appears frequently in sexzines and has been anthologized in *Leatherwomen, Dagger, The Erotic Impulse, Bi Any Other Name, Madonnarama,* and other collections of erotic writing and sex essays.

LAURENCE SENELICK is a professor of drama at Tufts, and has written widely on Russian and American theater and literature.

WICKIE STAMPS is a San Francisco–based writer who has contributed to numerous gay and lesbian publications, including the *Advocate, Gay Community News, OutWeek, On Our Backs, Girlfriends,* and the *SF Bay Times.* She also appears in *Sister and Brother, Dykescapes: Short Fiction by Lesbians, Leatherfolk,* and *Doing It for Daddy.* It was her great pleasure and honor to have met John Preston through writer Michael Bronski who, like John, remains central to her success as a writer.

BOB SUMMER lives in Nashville, Tennessee. He was a contributor to *Hometowns* and *A Member of the Family,* and will be in *Flesh and the Word 3.* He is a coauthor with Boyer Coe of *Getting Strong, Looking Strong; A Guide to Successful Body Building.* He is also a freelance magazine writer and book reviewer and a contributing editor to the *Lambda Book Report.*

CECILIA TAN is a writer, editor and sexuality activist who makes her current home in New England. She is the publisher and coeditor of Circlet Press; erotic science fiction and fantasy. Her erotic fiction and essays appear in *Penthouse, SandMutopia Guardian, Herotica 3, Taste of Latex* and in the forthcoming *By Her Subdued* (Masquerade

Books), *Herotica 4* (Plume), *Map of Desire: Asian American Erotica* (Anchor Books).

LARRY TOWNSEND, long recognized as a leading writer in the gay SM genre, is the author of *The Leatherman's Handbook*, in addition to more than two dozen novels. His articles and stories appear regularly in *Honcho* and *Bound and Gagged* magazine.